THE MADE-UP STATE

THE MADE-UP STATE

Technology, Trans Femininity, and Citizenship in Indonesia

Benjamin Hegarty

SOUTHEAST ASIA PROGRAM PUBLICATIONS

AN IMPRINT OF CORNELL UNIVERSITY PRESS ITHACA AND LONDON

Thanks to the generous funding of the McKenzie Fellowship at the University of Melbourne and the Australian Academy of the Humanities Publication Subsidy Scheme, the ebook editions of this book are available as open access volumes through the Cornell Open initiative.

Library of Congress Cataloging-in-Publication Data
Names: Hegarty, Benjamin, author.
Title: The made-up state : technology, trans femininity, and citizenship in
    Indonesia / Benjamin Hegarty.
Description: Ithaca : Southeast Asia Program Publications, an imprint of
    Cornell University Press, [2022] | Includes bibliographical references
    and index.
Identifiers: LCCN 2022026353 (print) | LCCN 2022026354 (ebook) |
    ISBN 9781501766640 (hardcover) | ISBN 9781501766657 (paperback) |
    ISBN 9781501766664 (pdf) | ISBN 9781501766671 (epub)
Subjects: LCSH: Transgender women—Indonesia. | Femininity—Indonesia. |
    Identity (Psychology)—Social aspects—Indonesia. | Technology—Social
    aspects—Indonesia.
Classification: LCC HQ77.95.I5 H34 2022 (print) | LCC HQ77.95.I5 (ebook) |
    DDC 306.76/8082—dc23/eng/20220609
LC record available at https://lccn.loc.gov/2022026353
LC ebook record available at https://lccn.loc.gov/2022026354

For waria, transpuan, *and those yet to come*

Contents

Illustrations

Acknowledgments

What is a book for? And whom is it for?

These are not trivial questions in a world where information is easily available and in which pressures to both consume and be consumed by knowledge are acute. I have come to think of the process of writing this book as crafting a document that is intended to hold together relations, and I hope that these relations will persist after I and those who are described in it are no longer here. There are the quotes from fieldwork, which can allow the reader to listen in to ephemeral conversations had in the everyday that would otherwise have been lost. There are references to theorists writing from and about other parts of the world, comparisons that help to orient material differently. Primary sources like newspapers provide a glimpse into fleeting accounts of events that happened decades ago, supporting shaky memories. Photographs serve as a record of memory, a trace that seems secure but that I found as fleeting as the instant of a glance given to the camera and captured in its frame. There is the author, who researches the material required and writes it up, giving a false impression that there is a singular and authoritative speaking subject. And there are the readers, individuals who come together to engage with the book in their own time and on terms that are meaningful to them. It is not an understatement to say that the period over which this book has taken shape has been challenging; just after I completed the main period of fieldwork for this book in 2015, a sustained series of attacks on LGBT people in Indonesian political life shook badly a hard-won sense of belonging among many of my waria interlocutors, who came to see their position in the nation as less secure than they had imagined it to be. The period of writing this book in 2020 coincided with the onset of the COVID-19 pandemic and the terrible and unequally felt impact on health and loss of life that it entailed, including in Indonesia. Fortunately, the process of writing this book has brought me into dialogue with so many people, with whom I have been able to work on so many intellectually sustaining, enjoyable, and valuable projects. I am so grateful to each of them; to me, then, this particular book is valuable insomuch that it reflects an archive of relations. In presenting it, I hope in my own way to contribute to bringing together a public that is capable of assessing the beauty and the complexity of trans history in Indonesia, not as something that is possessed and known on totalizing terms by any given individual or group of people, but rather as an open-ended promise that invites sustained forms of engagement, care and attention.

First and foremost, I offer my gratitude to the many Indonesians, and particularly the many warias, who have contributed to and continue to engage with this project; they shared their time, their memories, their hopes and dreams, and their personal records with me. I learned much from participating in the everyday life of waria communities in Yogyakarta and Jakarta, a remarkably talented group of people whose grace, humor, and intelligence is rarely acknowledged in any official documentation. This book is for them. In particular, I express my thanks to Mami Vinolia Wakijo, Mami Rully Mallay, Mbak Yuni Shara, Bunda Yetti, Ibu Shinta Ratri, Nancy Iskandar, Mami Maya Puspa, Ibu Lenny, Bunda Joyce, Chenny Han, and Meifei. Mami Vinolia's remarkable shelter for HIV-positive waria and other vulnerable people in Yogyakarta–Keluarga Besar Waria Yogyakarta (KEBAYA) and the Waria Crisis Center (WCC) have served as constant reminders of the importance of this book and as catalysts for action. Mak Tadi's lively narratives and photographs helped me to really understand waria friendship, and I am eternally grateful for her permission to include them in this book. I hope they serve as a testament to the vitality and beauty of waria life. Ibu Lenny and Bu Nancy provided me with guidance in the challenging context of fieldwork in Jakarta, and I learned much from their tireless efforts among communities of trans women through their work with the community organization Srikandi Sejati. Mas Toyo and his team at the LGBT advocacy organization Suara Kita provided me with a setting in which to present early versions of my work to a youthful and energetic audience in Jakarta. Many others who remain unnamed will see themselves in this book. As well as valuable advice, this audience provided me with inspiration and a sense of urgency to get it out there in the world.

Sandeep Nanwani was present in this project from very early on, and his energetic sense of social justice animated me to keep on writing and learning from every mistake. I am so proud of his remarkable achievements and can only hope to have absorbed some of his intellect. I also learned so much from the perspectives offered by intellectual interlocutors at Indonesian institutions, including Ignatius Praptoraharjo (Mas Gambit) and Amalia Puri Handayani at the Center for HIV AIDS Research at Atma Jaya Catholic University, Yanri Subronto at Gadjah Mada University, and Dédé Oetomo at Airlangga University, who are among those who have consistently reminded me in different ways that this project should above all benefit those whose lives it is about. I have been so fortunate to be able to keep working with them and many others on shared projects about HIV, an epidemic that this book does not directly address but that casts a shadow over it. I will not forget the many lessons that I have learned from working with urgency and passion in HIV activism in Indonesia, foremost among those mobilizing to advance greater access to health for waria and other transgender populations. Many other friends provided me with support, advice, and interest across the many different stages and enormous length of time that it has taken to move from research to publication. Special thanks go to Nova Ruth, Roy Thaniago, Ardi Kuhn, Beau Newman and the Queer Indonesia Archive, Malcolm Smith, Jimmy Ong, Mulyana, and Tamarra. I thank Samsul Maarif at Gadjah Mada University, my fieldwork sponsor for an extended period of research in Indonesia in 2014–2015, for his support and intellectual exchange. Perkumpulan Keluarga Berencana Indonesia (PKBI) Yogyakarta, the Family Planning Association of Indonesia, provided a source of inspiration and engagement, and I am especially grateful to Very and Pipin for their keen insights and persistence. The support of Ibu Yati Soenarto and Professor Soenarto at the Center for Bioethics and Medical Humanities at Gadjah Madah University provided me with an intellectual environment, among clinical practitioners, in which to begin to consider the theoretical implications of my research as an intern in 2015.

The School of Archaeology and Anthropology at the Australian National University was the ideal intellectual context in which the ideas for this project began to come together. I am grateful to all the staff and students who made my time in Canberra a period of growth, but a few deserve special mention. My supervisor, Christine Helliwell, offered much more than supervision, showing me ways of seeing and of living that resonate throughout this book and beyond it. Peter Jackson challenged me to consider the multiplicity of ways that gender and sexuality might be transformed in the context of modernity. Kenneth George's insights into Southeast Asian anthropology and his gentle and wise encouragement let me see the implications of my work in a way I would have not otherwise. Kirin Narayan helped me to consider why I write and to try to write better. Philip Taylor hosted a PhD writing group that accommodated an array of ethnographic perspectives and intellectual engagement that warmed with patience and grace. Margaret Jolly and Kathy Robinson offered a generative model for interpreting the breathtaking complexity of gender and sexuality in Asia and the Pacific and a model of how to approach scholarly life with grace and poise. Being in the right place at the right time meant a chance encounter with Don Kulick that set this project in motion. I am lucky to have benefited from friendship and conversations with Shiori Shakuto and Carly Schuster, which we formalized somewhat through our remarkable collaboration on the history of "doing feminist anthropology" in Australia at a challenging moment. I began the conceptualization of transforming my ethnographic material into a book in dialogue with Niko Besnier, whose sense of humor and incisive responses to my work were of a kind that I might only hope to emulate. Carla Jones, since the moment I read her deeply thoughtful engagement with my research about warias, opened my eyes to interpretations that would otherwise have remained concealed. A very special thanks goes to Tom Boellstorff, who pushed me to be ever more rigorous in my claims. I am grateful for his friendship.

This book has benefited from a great deal of institutional support, which has been vital for giving me the time and access to resources needed to bring it into the world. In particular, I gratefully acknowledge the support of the Australian government through its Research Training Program and the Prime Minister's Asia Australia Endeavour Award for providing the resources needed to complete the long-term fieldwork required for this book. I started this book while a Research Fellow in Gender and Sexuality Studies at Deakin University, a collegial and supportive environment. My position as a visiting scholar in the Department of Anthropology at the University of California, Irvine, funded by an Endeavour Postdoctoral Fellowship, provided both stimulation and a luxurious freedom to write a first substantial draft. My time there, with its concentration of interdisciplinary anthropologists and emphasis on science and technology studies, shaped in profound ways the direction that this book took. In addition to Tom Boellstorff, who was a consummate host, I am grateful to the dean of the School of Social Sciences, Bill Maurer, and the chair of the Department of Anthropology, Kim Fortun, for being so accommodating in making my stay possible and so welcoming. While a resident in the luxurious surrounds of Irvine, coffee, writing, and pondering with Nima Yolmo was a treasure, and my office mate Laura Kalba's eye for detail and advice came at the right moment. Good timing meant that Christoph Hansmann was also in residence during that fall, and our surfing and other sporting adventures enhanced my time in Irvine. I was also fortunate to spend treasured time in the good company of Jih-Fei Cheng, Dredge Byung'chu Käng Nguyen, and Hoang Tan Nguyen while in Southern California. I also thank Erin Martineau, my editor, for her remarkable eye for language and willingness to take on this project when it was only in formation.

In 2019, I received a McKenzie Fellowship in Anthropology and Development Studies within the School of Social and Political Sciences at the University of Melbourne. This support from the university and colleagues in the department was invaluable to the process of writing this book, offering a supportive environment and the time that I needed not only to finish this book but to make it the very best version of it that I could. Funding from my McKenzie Fellowship helped make it possible to produce an open access version of this book, which is important in making it accessible to audiences who would otherwise have been excluded. The institutional support for Indonesian studies at the University of Melbourne has been vital in sustaining this project intellectually. I am especially grateful to Associate Professor Kate McGregor, Dr. Edwin Jurriens, and Professor Vedi Hadiz for their custodianship of various precious schemes that have supported my research, including the Faculty of Arts Indonesia Initiative that allows Indonesian scholars to spend time in residence in Melbourne, which helped sustain me in the final stages of writing this book. I am grateful to all I have learned from my involvement in the Faculty of Arts Gender Studies program, and especially to Ana Dragojlovic and Kalissa Alexeyeff, for the opportunities that they provided to undertake forms of teaching and seminar participation that helped me to understand my work in new ways. I am especially grateful to two honors students whom I was fortunate to supervise while at the University of Melbourne, Dylan Strahan and Olly Southerton, who reminded me of the vitality of ethnographic insights in the field of queer and transgender studies and provided me with the energy to keep writing and thinking.

Early versions of some parts of this book have appeared in previous publications, and I am grateful to these journals for providing permission to reproduce them here. Chapter 2 appears as "Governing Nonconformity: Gender Presentation, Public Space, and the City in New Order Indonesia," *Journal of Asian Studies* 80 (4): 955–74. Portions of chapter 3 have appeared in "The Perfect Woman: Transgender Femininity and National Modernity in New Order Indonesia, 1968–1978," *Journal of the History of Sexuality* 28 (1): 44–65. Part of chapter 5 appeared in "Under the Lights, onto the Stage," *TSQ: Transgender Studies Quarterly* 5 (3): 355–77. Journal editors and special issue editors in these and other publications have generously provided time and advice that ultimately shaped the work that this book has become.

Many colleagues and friends left their mark on this book, more of them than I am able to list here, although I hope that they recognize who they are. I am fortunate to be in the company of a very formidable group of skillful Indonesianists in Melbourne, including Julian Millie and Sharyn Davies at Monash University; Annisa Beta, Ken Setiawan, Wulan Dirgantoro, Ariane Utomo, and Tim Mann at the University of Melbourne; and Monika Winarnita at Deakin University. For insights on portions of this book presented at so many different panels, public lectures, and as part of special issues, and for providing me with the opportunity to present it to an audience, I am also grateful to many colleagues. These include David Bissell, Matt Tomlinson, Sharyn Davies, Karen Strassler, Carla Jones, Michelle Ho, Jenny Hoang, Aren Aizura, Linda Bennett, Daniel Marshall, C. L. Quinan, Ariel Heryanto, Eben Kirskey, Sophie Chao, Shawna Tang, Ben Murtagh, Diego Garcia, and David Kloos. Although scattered in different parts of the world, Sylvia Tidey, Ferdiansyah Thajib, Paige Johnson, and Terje Toomitsu are all steadfast intellectual companions and friends, from whose work I continue to learn so much more about both warias and transgender life in Indonesia. I express my thanks to Hendri Wijaya Yulius, whose sharp intellect and witty advocacy for queer rights have been a light in dark moments. Natalya Lusty helped me to reflect on what academic work means and how to try to live your values, while trying to retain a sense of humor at the same time.

Annemarie Samuels at Leiden University and Helen Pausacker at the Melbourne Law School both read drafts of the final version of this book. Their input, commentary, and probing questions helped to improve the book and reminded me of just how lucky I am to be researching across the beautiful yet fragile and deeply flawed disciplines of anthropology, Indonesian studies, and transgender studies. My editor, Sarah Elizabeth Mary Grossman, has been a great support to this book, providing not only the administrative but intellectual sustenance needed for it to appear in the much-treasured Southeast Asia Program Publications series. Two anonymous reviewers generously offered a depth of engagement and guidance on where I might make improvements, which I have strived to accomplish. Editorial staff at Cornell University Press have done everything possible to smooth this book on its way to publication, including a trip to the library at Cornell University to scan an image when libraries in Australia were closed for many months as a result of the COVID-19 pandemic. Since an initial meeting with Jim Lance at the American Anthropological Association, the professionalism, courtesy, and guidance provided by the staff at Cornell University Press have impressed me, and I hope that this book does justice to their efforts to bring it to fruition.

If it were not for my family, who approach life every day with vitality, ethics, and love, I might never have departed for Indonesia or embarked on the process of learning and researching that has transformed into this book. I am grateful to them all for their interest and wise guidance since well before any of this was imagined to be possible. Jack Turley provides me with much to look forward to every day. Whatever the future holds, I present this book as a way to honor all of these and other relations. I am sure that the history of warias presented in these pages will be of use in the challenging moments ahead of us all.

Note on Spelling, Terms, and Pseudonyms

A central concern of this book is that language is shaped by bodily copresence, affectively charged political contestation, and processes of historical change. It is unsurprising, then, that the choice of terms—both in translation into English and across different periods of time—is challenging, to say the least. I am not trans and not Indonesian. For these reasons, I have not made decisions about terminology and language in isolation but in dialogue with my interlocutors and collaborators across what is now over a decade of research, out of a desire to aid further research on the complexity of the history of gender and sexuality inside and outside of Indonesia, and above all else to honor transgender histories in the archipelago, which continue to be such a vibrant and important component of public life from which we can learn so much.

To enable readers to understand the historical complexity of the way in which terms have changed and continue to change across time within their historical context, I have preserved the use of terms as they appeared in the archive or were recounted to me. For example, at different points, I use or refer to *banci* rather than *transpuan* or *waria*. Although *banci* as it is used today may appear to be inappropriate or even offensive (which, when used in some contexts, it certainly is), it was the very transformation from *banci* to *wadam* (later *waria*) across the 1950s and late 1960s through which my interlocutors interpreted and narrated a broader process of historical change. To remove it would be to miss this nuance entirely. As a result, I ask readers who may feel discomfort with my use of terms that may seem outdated or politically incorrect to reflect on what it is that about the term that provokes those feelings, and I invite them to try to sit with those feelings in order to sympathize with those who were present at the time as they engaged with forms of exclusion and sought to craft or create new terms. My hope in doing so is to more closely pay attention to who is left in or out of processes of crafting and using language, rather than searching for the correct term, the possibility of which I believe is itself necessary to question. I generally preserve the use of specific Indonesian terms in this way, referring to bancis, warias, and wadams in the plural form. I also tack to and from these Indonesian words and English-language phrases and terms that productively enable comparison with them where appropriate, most evident in my use of "trans women" and "transgender femininity." I use each of these terms in hope that it might be possible to

xviii   NOTE ON SPELLING, TERMS, AND PSEUDONYMS

keep alive the prospect of a more pluralistic and dynamic historiography of the meanings of gender and its relation to the self.

When spelling out Indonesian words, I have largely followed the new orthographic system adopted in 1972. In a number of cases, and particularly with the names of individuals and with proper nouns, following their usage in the archive, I use the old (that is, pre-1972) orthographic system. Where changing the orthography into the new system does not affect the meaning or connotation of the term, I undertake such a change for clarity and continuity of reading, while referring to the source using whichever orthographic system was used in the original. For example, I may use *banci* in the text, while the reference contained in the bibliography will use *bantji* in the old orthography. Unless otherwise stated, all of the translations from Indonesian are my own.

In this book I follow common anthropological conventions and attribute pseudonyms when introducing ethnographic data. Given that this book traverses the fields of history and anthropology, there are a number of exceptions. In particular, where the research draws heavily on oral histories, or the person is an important public figure, I provide the actual name of the person interviewed with their permission. This helps to make these histories as useful as possible and to offer a way to create a historical resource for a group of people sometimes considered to have no history of their own or who are understood as marginal within Indonesian national history.

MAKING PUBLIC GENDER

Maya Puspa steps out of her home and salon with confidence and grace, narrowly avoiding the puddles that have transformed her lane into a muddy track. She smiles, arching her thin, penciled-on eyebrows as she turns to a group of elderly men gathered over a chessboard. It is her evening walk and, cheerily greeting the men, Maya strides out of her lane and onto a city street.

Maya lives alone in one of the many poor, crowded neighborhoods in Jakarta, the enormous capital of Indonesia and a city in the center of a region populated by tens of millions of people. Enveloped by twilight, accompanied by the sounds of motorbikes and crackling evening calls to prayer from neighborhood mosques, Maya pushes on with athletic strength. She quickens her pace far more than her eighty-year-old frame would suggest is possible. Neighbors call out to her with the common greeting "Where are you going?" One middle-aged man on his way to the mosque—with a prayer rug slung over his shoulder and dressed in a sarong—grins as he spots Maya, greeting her with an honorific term of address reserved for senior members of the community. Her movement up the street is less a stroll and more a vigorous stop-start punctuated by warm greetings and playful cajoling from her neighbors. After powering up a steep rise, Mami Maya reaches a bridge that marks a halfway point to the community meeting that is our destination, before turning back to face the lights of the city. She surveils, with visible pleasure, the modern metropolis where she has made her home for over sixty years and where she plans to live out the rest of her days. This scene, unfolding in the middle of 2015, is a remarkable testament to Maya's neighbors' recognition of her as a respected member who belongs in their community on terms that are comfortable to her.

Born in 1938 in a town on the island of Sumatra in the last decade of the colonial Dutch East Indies, Maya migrated to Jakarta in 1950, not long after the revolution that followed World War II and Indonesia's declaration of independence on August 17, 1945. Since that time, Maya has been an active participant in the vibrant social life that the city offers to newcomers from all around the sprawling archipelago nation of Indonesia. More successful than most, Maya runs a salon from the first floor of her humble two-story shop-house. Her salon is overflowing with sparkling sequined dresses on dusty mannequins, rows of gold-embroidered blazers in dry-cleaning wrappers, and old salon equipment. She demonstrates her youthful beauty with framed portraits of her younger self in a glamorous and skillfully executed modern style of femininity. One framed photograph on the wall above her is an image of her wearing a carnival outfit replete with a gold crown and low-cut top. Although transformed by old age, she remains viewed by many of her neighbors as a person who in many respects demonstrates the values associated with a modern body, of which her polished femininity is a crucial attribute.

Maya described herself to me as a *waria*, an Indonesian word that combines the first syllable of one Indonesian word for woman (*wanita*) and the last syllable of one word for man (*pria*). A key aspect of narrative accounts of becoming waria lies in the shared narrative of having a *jiwa perempuan*, an interior sense of being a woman, which compels a person to transform their body through practices of *dandan*, or making up. Waria is a term that is in many respects indistinguishable from *wadam*, a neologism crafted in 1968 that combined the words for the figures Adam and Eve from the story of human creation, common to Islam and Christianity, but which fell out of use from the late 1970s onward.[1] In reports, minutes, and surveys, the Jakarta municipal government began to use the term *wadam* gradually from the late 1960s onward, after the city's governor Ali Sadikin—who roughly had the political position of a mayor—had endorsed the term as a modern and more presentable vehicle that enabled greater social participation. As warias moved between various locations in the city against the shifting terrain of mid-twentieth-century Indonesian politics and society, they articulated claims to recognition across disparate sites and domains of knowledge. The innovation of the historically specific terms *waria* and *wadam* lies in an elegant but simple combination based on the dualisms of male/female and mind/body that are central to modern formulations of binary gender. The term *waria*, and its emergence within and alongside the postcolonial state, reflects a modern conceptualization of gender in which a pair of dualisms can be held in combination within a single body. For this reason, warias cannot be separated out from longer histories of the unsettled relationship between technology and recognition in modern Indonesia. This book therefore addresses warias as inseparable from the history of "socio-technical imaginaries," that is, "collectively held, institutionally stabilized, and publicly performed visions of desirable futures animated by shared understandings of forms of social life and social order attainable and supportive of advances in science and technology" (Kim and Jasanoff 2015, 4). Gender plays a central role in naturalizing individual and collective visions of social life, in part through the techniques of self and body that "make up people" (Hacking 1999, 170). Take the weight granted to the public meanings of gender in its contemporary manifestation as a binary of male and female, organized according to stable social roles, as a specific alignment of an individual mind and body: in Euro-American societies, a perceived mismatch between body and mind has provoked significant anxieties, as reflected in the deployment of onerous medico-legal requirements and technologies designed to stabilize sex, gender, and sexuality (Stone 1992; Plemons 2017; Aizura 2018; Latham 2019). Rather than marginal to technological development, warias were entangled with the process through which public gender became central to the affective, material, and spatial meanings of citizenship in Indonesia. More than this, warias show how, rather than biological sex developing into a concept of social gender, the Indonesian state's definition of sex was in fact closer to gender all along. This book advances this argument by drawing on ethnographic and historical evidence of how warias were integrated into sociotechnical imaginaries of the postcolonial state.

The possibilities for Maya and those of her generation to name and to cultivate themselves with the modern clarity offered by the term *waria* followed a tumultuous period of transition in modern Indonesian history. The birth of the New Order regime in 1965 followed horrific violence during and after the imposition of military rule by General Suharto under the pretext of defending Indonesia from a communist takeover (Wieringa 2002). Suharto remained president for some three decades, until the abrupt end to his rule amid mass protests and economic turmoil in May 1998. During the New Order, gender was a foundation for naturalizing the narrow governmental concept of economic development (*pembangunan*) that served as the regime's guiding principle and justification for rule. Women's and men's participation in public life was mediated through the nuclear family and the gendered and sexual arrangements that it was predicated on (see Suryakusuma 1996). The history of warias reveals that gender during the New Order did not reflect "the technological put at the service of authority" (Siegel 1997, 5) but was a more unruly object of expertise. Situating warias within a sociotechnical history helps to understand binary gender as a system of knowledge that both reflects and draws together the meanings of a public as a collective experience of social life.

A key component of the desired future presented in New Order development lay in legal and social efforts to enforce upon men and women specific roles and responsibilities to family and society, but perhaps more crucially on advancing a concept of gender as a stable and innate attribute of the mind and body of a single biological individual. Warias were critical to this iteration of the modern state's project of normalizing and naturalizing male and female as a specific combination of attributes, organized into a specific configuration of personhood as a biological individual. The striking efforts to recruit warias into gendered modernity reveal the significant resources that the state employed to determine an essential basis for gender. The foremost object of state biopolitics in Indonesia was not primarily premised on the heterosexual/homosexual dichotomy, but rather on an effort to naturalize the meanings of binary gender at the level of the individual self. The efforts made by the Indonesian state to establish the meanings of gender as a product of the individual was reflected in strategies deployed to control the public appearance of warias. The history of warias reveals the highly contingent efforts of the postcolonial state to define gender as a broader condition understood in terms of an alignment between inner psychological state, outer appearances, and reproductive capacity within the individual self. As a result, interpreting gender in terms of an essential and ahistorical self, linked to an inner identity located in the mind, leads to several misunderstandings. These can be addressed by thinking more carefully about the relationship between waria and trans.

Waria and Trans

Scholars and activists have translated warias as trans—transgender and trans women—in both Indonesian and English-language media and research. In this book, I interpret the accounts of warias in relation to trans, a way to avoid placing warias on an essentialized grid of difference. The relationship between warias and the category transgender is complex in ways that frustrate attempts to locate and impose the most accurate or authentic term, and the limits of such efforts have been identified by scholars elsewhere (Alexeyeff and Besnier 2014; Boellstorff et al. 2014; Blackwood 2010; Boellstorff 2007). Inasmuch as *waria* is a term that emerged via processes of transformation at the interface of body and self, reflected in naming and being named, the history of warias shares some parallels with the emergence of the category of transgender in the United States. As David Valentine has argued in that context, transgender was not a neutral term for grouping preexisting forms of gender variant or nonconforming subjects, but reflected "quotidian forms of self-making and self education in which all modern subjects are imagined to engage" and which was "transformative because of its capacity to refine" (2007, 246). Moreover, warias and other Indonesians have long been active participants in shaping racialized Euro-American categories, including transvestite, transsexual, and more recently transgender.

Until the 2000s, warias were commonly described as transvestites in both Euro-American and Indonesian scholarship, policy, and journalistic accounts. The category *transvestite*, developed by German sexologist Magnus Hirschfeld in 1910 to refer to a wide array of gender-variant practices (Bauer 2017, 84), was adopted in fragmentary ways by Dutch colonial-era scholars and officials. The category was first used to refer to *banci*, a term referring to a wide array of gender ambiguity that dates from the nineteenth century and which was used well into the New Order (Boellstorff 2007, 85).[2] Starting in the 1930s, small numbers of European psychiatrists and anthropologists referred to banci as transvestites. Their use of *transvestite* rather than *homosexual* not only named but also shaped the historical development of the terms *banci*, *wadam*, and *waria* in the postcolonial state. Indeed, it was only after Indonesian independence that psychiatrists, doctors, and journalists more forcefully adopted transvestite as an object of translation and debate. Although certainly present in various guises, female and trans masculinity remained far less prominent in both the state's project of defining gender on individualized terms and in scholarship on the topic (see, e.g., Blackwood 2005a). The historical meanings of female and trans masculinity in colonial and postcolonial Indonesia—including the reasons for the visibility of trans femininity in the state's project to define gender as an individual property—remain an important area of inquiry. In the late 2010s, partially owing to the integration of warias within New Order governmentality, which assessed them as a public nuisance, Indonesian trans activists created a new term to speak of themselves: *transpuan*, a neologism that combines the first syllable of the global category *transgender* and the second syllable from one Indonesian word for woman (*perempuan*). A contested politics of sorting, affiliation, and disaffiliation based on the differences and similarities between waria and transgender is now widespread throughout Indonesia in ways that often overlook longer histories of connection between trans and various Indonesian terms since the colonial period.

I use *warias* in this book because those individuals I encountered at my field sites and in the archives presented themselves to me as warias, and because it was the term primarily used during the New Order; to replace *waria* with *transpuan* would be to deny the vitality of forms of self-expression and the various sexual, gendered, and economic lifeworlds and histories within which warias live. There is a complex temporal, cross-cultural, and class overlay to the use of each of these terms; *trans* and *transgender* are, however, suitable insomuch as they encourage a dynamic engagement with the historical and cultural position of terms such as waria in networks of global exchange. At the same time, it also would not be accurate to call all warias trans women, although some warias may also describe themselves on those terms. Transpuan and queer activists in Indonesia sometimes actively distance themselves from the term *waria* and warn against its use, because of its relationship to transactional and public sexuality. The fact remains that warias are often poor and are subject to economic marginalization, state violence, and health disparities, which have resulted in increased exposure to HIV.[3] This was the case for many of the warias whom I lived and worked alongside during the research and writing of this book. The use of *waria* or *transgender* then is largely contextual, but many of those who refer to themselves as either trans women and transpuan often have access to economic and social capital within the vibrant networks of trans and queer activism that have formed in the democratic space that has emerged since the fall of Suharto.

I also use *waria* because the history of the term offers rich theoretical insights that problematize the relationship between recognition and gender at the level of the individual. *Waria* emerged at the precise moment when the state more clearly sought to define citizenship in terms of a pair of male and female individuals. That *waria* appeared as a specific response to efforts to impose a male/female binary in postcolonial Indonesia was not coincidental. As Marilyn Strathern observed, efforts to assert essentialist categories tend to generate hybrids, objects of knowledge that condense within "a single item diverse elements from technology, science and society, enumerated together as an invention and available for ownership as a property" (Strathern 1996, 525; see also Haraway 1991). Given that the body and its relations exceed attempts to impose purity, gender in some way will always open possibility for gaps between what a given cosmology holds as natural and the processes that facilitate that naturalization (Butler 1990). This is not, however, to claim that the hybridity of warias made *waria* a fluid concept or reflects the liberatory potential of gender in Indonesia, a view that represents the projection of Euro-American theoretical preoccupations more than it does the production, reproduction, and organization of the body and person under specific historical and social conditions (Towle and Morgan 2002; Weston 1993).[4] Indeed, warias have at times been incorporated into transgender rights in a manner that appears similar to Kath Weston's observation of "the uncanny resonance between the anthropological 'discovery' of multiple genders and the nineteenth-century categorization of homosexuals as members of a third sex, midway between women and men" (1993, 354). Early in the twenty-first century, *waria* and other terms have been rediscovered within a rubric of transgender rights based on a concept of gender identity as a universal attribute of the individual mind. In one account published by the large international human rights organization Human Rights Watch that outlines the "quest [of transgender and nonbinary people] to obtain official documents that reflect their identities by using a non-binary 'X' marker in lieu of the typical 'F' or 'M,'" warias are described in the following way:

> After all, gender variant people have existed throughout the world and across time, celebrated in some cultures, denigrated in others. Some societies recognized people who embodied a gender identity beyond the binary, for example, hijra communities in South Asia, two-spirit people among some Native American cultures, waria in Southeast Asia and Fa'afafine in Pacific Islander communities. While the blunt classificatory instruments of colonial rule imposed new bureaucracies of gender assignment, these communities persist and continue to provide alternate ways of thinking about gender that evade binary classification. (Ghoshal 2020)

Rather than approaching trans as a way to plot one universal variation of psychologized gender identity beyond the binary, this book shows how warias emerged within the sociotechnical relations facilitated by the postcolonial Indonesian state. I hold particular concern for the identification of waria as a nonbinary or fluid gender used to justify a universal project of transgender rights, given that it tends to evacuate warias' claims of their political urgency within a specific political economic context, as well as simplifies the complex impact of colonialism and capitalism on indigenous cosmologies. Rather than being liberatory, *waria* reflects something of a parallel story to the enactment of essentialist cosmologies of sex and gender as part of the modern self that were invoked to justify Euro-American legal frameworks of medical transsexuality (see Stone 1992). Attending more closely to gender as a technology that emerges within specific historical and ethnographic contexts reveals a more complex story as to how warias have contended with the modern state's efforts to naturalize binary gender as a means to claim a monopoly on recognizing the limits of human difference.

Gender and Technology

Since the late nineteenth century, when the Dutch colonial state consolidated its rule over the Indonesian archipelago, technology has played a defining role in shaping the meanings of development as a symbol for aspirational, global modernity. The New Order state elevated development to a far-reaching governmental style through which it sought to impose territorial uniformity over the nation's archipelagic form. In postcolonial Indonesia, development was a "focus of authority and legitimacy" (Heryanto 1988, 11), symbolized in the establishment and display of sophisticated and expensive technological projects (Amir 2013). The Suharto regime sought to manage the changes wrought by rapid development by advancing a rarefied form of tradition, combining high technology with aestheticized ritual (Keeler 1988; Pemberton 1994). Authoritarian rule proceeded not only through violent terror and coercion, therefore, but also through efforts to instill in citizens a sense of responsibility for the progress of themselves as individuals and families, measured via economic goals. The perceived inability to use (or apathy directed toward) technology by the lower classes, expressed through the euphemism *belum* (not yet), was a primary rationale through which the elites justified their authority to rule over the large proportion of the population excluded from economic prosperity (Leeuwen 2011; Lindquist 2009). Although the moral force of development in Indonesian society has been the focus of extensive historical and ethnographic study (Barker 2015, 2005; Moon 2015, 2007), precisely how gender shaped the sociotechnical imaginary of the postcolonial nation has received scant scholarly attention.

This lack of attention to the emergence of gender through technology is surprising, considering that modern binary gender was critical to the sociotechnical imaginary used to sustain the legitimacy of the Suharto regime. In particular, femininity was an embodied guise that reached into the most intimate aspects of the lives of citizens, and Indonesian women were expected to take up and implement a vast array of medical, aesthetic, and domestic technologies in their legally defined role as mothers and wives (Suryakusuma 1996; Dwyer 2002; Jones 2010). Notably, Julia Suryakusuma (1996, 101) identified "State Ibuism" (motherhood) as a powerful ideological apparatus for naturalizing women's social role within the domestic sphere and limiting their political agency relative to men. Yet the growth of the mass media and access to consumer capitalism during this historical period meant that images of femininity were not singular but signified a range of contradictory meanings, as femininity could as easily be a symbol of national development or of moral decay (Brenner 1999). Although these feminist framings of New Order development highlight the centrality of gender to defining participation in the public sphere, in them technology is largely relegated to a tool for the implementation of state ideology. One result of the lack of attention to more hybrid formulations of gender is that male and female bodies are assumed to naturally correspond with the personhood of the individual self, rather than being addressed as one of its effects.[5] A corollary of this view is that male and female have been addressed as always already identifiable attributes of modern selfhood, understood as an alignment of appearances, inner psychological state, and genital morphology. Refusing to separate out the femininity of warias theoretically from that of women serves as one conceptual move through which I have found the ways that warias played a critical role in mediating the relationship between gender and the self.

In postcolonial Indonesia, as elsewhere, binary gender was a key cultural symbol through which political struggles over development and technology took place. Sherry Ortner, in her landmark 1972 essay, attributed gender relations to a universal nature/culture binary, through the application of a "notion of human consciousness (i.e. systems of thought and technology), by means of which humanity attempts to rise above and assert control . . . over nature" (Ortner 1972, 10). Rather than a nature/culture binary, however, political and cultural contestations over citizenship in Indonesia emerged primarily through efforts to separate the *asli* (authentic) from the *palsu* (false) (Siegel 1998, 54). This binary, one that recalls the colonial project to control contact between indigenous and European subjects, reveals the state's fragile grasp as the ultimate arbiter of authenticity. The relationship between the asli and the palsu was gendered in paradoxical ways, as the desire to train one's self "rested on an ironic tension between conceiving femininity as a natural expression of an inner self versus as a result of tutelage, a tension that perpetually threatened to expose the artifice of expertise" (Jones 2010, 271). Warias provide a distinct vantage point on the role of gender in the modern history of Indonesian citizenship. Rather than seeing the gendered self as always already asli, Indonesian, and therefore prior to technological intervention, everyday narratives among warias reveal that they see their gendering as the unfinished product of effort, one that requires human action and relations with others to fully realize. Warias' accomplishment of femininity does not reflect the assertion of an essential or authentic self but reflects the unpredictable, transformative power of gender to confer recognition.

A sociotechnical approach to the history of waria also helps in considering the utility of *cisgender* as a universally applicable term when applied at the level of the individual.[6] Cisgender, often presented on binary terms with transgender, has achieved near hegemonic status in Euro-American theory and politics as a concept that normatively refers to "individuals who possess, from birth and into adulthood, the male or female reproductive organs (sex) typical of the social category of man or woman (gender) to which that individual was assigned at birth" (Aultman 2014, 61). Yet any insistence on separating out individuals according to an essential difference between cisgender and transgender at the level of the individual comes with significant risks, given the set of Euro-American assumptions about personhood on which this understanding rests (Strathern 1988; Helliwell 2000). When interpreted via a concept of personhood based on the bounded self, the cisgender/transgender binary appears to smuggle an essentialist model of biological sex into a definition of psychological gender. The view that an alignment of sex and gender is possible reads onto the body one Euro-American model of personhood in which the individual can be separated out from society (Strathern 1993). Far from facilitating a radical critique of gender, the mapping of individuals onto a binary grid of cisgender/transgender in this way reflects an ethnocentric redeployment of the nature/culture binary. Sandy Stone (1992, 166) long ago critiqued the limits of theoretical perspectives premised on ontologized gender in her critical interrogation of dominant accounts of transsexuality in terms of the "wrong body," pinpointing their tendency to "foreclose the possibility of analyzing desire and motivational complexity." Gender—and the cisgender/transgender binary that it increasingly requires for legibility—is not the ground onto which individuals emerge, but a technology of classification.

Rather than replacing one nature/culture binary for another, sex/gender for cisgender/transgender, this book pushes against the inevitability of technological determinism by illuminating how warias appropriated the modern cosmologies of male/female and mind/body to forge dynamic claims to recognition. This helps in contending with the continuities between colonial logics governing racialized status and postcolonial binary gender, as well as illuminates the limitations of the cisgender/transgender binary in Euro-American theory. This opens an understanding of warias that moves beyond a narrow preoccupation with gender or sexuality at the level of the individual, helping to contextualize trans as inseparable from colonial histories of race and citizenship. In the Dutch colonial state of the early twentieth century, the adoption of various modern technologies by Indonesians prompted profound anxiety about how to evaluate the authenticity of racial appearances (Siegel 1997). Indonesians drew on modern technologies related to appearances, such as eyeglasses, modern clothing, and photography, to exceed their racialized status and lay claims to the status and public recognition that had previously been restricted to Europeans (van der Meer 2020; Mrázek 2002). Initially among elites, but increasingly among those of various social classes, individuals also seized on the new term *Indonesia* to lay claim to public recognition at around the same time (Ingleson 1975). At the moment that Indonesians asserted claims to recognition by their ability to change appearances and language in the early twentieth century, however, an emergent theory of race adopted by the Dutch colonial state stressed that individual psychological state was the basis for racial difference (Stoler 1995; Pols 2007). The history of waria helps to clarify how the postcolonial state advanced a logic of separating out and refining bodies, drawing on a colonial logic of racial categorization redeployed through an effort to separate male and female as naturally occurring and innate forms of human difference.

Together, the forms of recognition that warias accomplished were a result of their capacity to seize technological means and use them to undertake self-cultivation for a public audience. Despite the exhortations of state experts who claimed that the gender binary was essential and natural, the public meanings of trans femininity and the claims to self-knowledge consistently voiced by trans women undermined the state's monopoly on recognition. In this respect, a focus on gender and the body helps balance theoretical approaches to citizenship largely developed through a focus on an "imagined community" based on a shared language and print capitalism (Anderson 1996). For all the efforts of warias to accomplish acceptance, advanced through efforts to shift the use of terminology through the adoption of modern terms like *wadam* and *waria*, they found, like transgender women elsewhere, that the "aspirational aim of recognition is confronted with the body's material limits" (Plemons 2017, 154). The exceptional ability of warias to accomplish femininity placed them in an ambiguous position relative to technologies used to impose binary gender and the legal and social privilege granted by accomplishing it. Rather than displacing binary gender, the solution put forward by warias was to capture the dualisms of male/female, mind/body, and asli/palsu within an individual person as a means to achieve power through unification.

Although separated out in the chapters of this book, in everyday life technologies for enacting gender and having that gender recognized by a seeing public are experienced as inseparable from one another. Some of the warias whose expression of gender drew on a technologized framework of medical transsexuality deployed by the state in the 1970s, for example, were also captured in the raids undertaken by municipal police on public spaces, raids that targeted gendered appearances in ways that drew upon colonial-era sumptuary laws governing appearances based on race. Many warias have encountered technologies of feminization through their work in or as customers of beauty salons and have used visual technologies like photography to capture and represent themselves to a wider audience. As warias participate in technological modes of mediating gender, they articulate themselves—and are articulated—as a part of publics who receive them differently depending on the context. In contrast to a totalizing gaze founded in an essentialized form of difference at the level of the individual, warias' engagement with global technologies for interpreting and imagining gender offered a means to expand the meanings of what "the public" might mean and how it might be possible to claim recognition as a part of it.

The City

This book is based on fifteen months of fieldwork conducted in 2014 and 2015, when I lived continuously in the city of Yogyakarta with extended stays in Jakarta, and ongoing engagement with warias since that time. The archival and oral history research that I undertook for the book is therefore embedded within a broader ethnographic project, an approach based on a rich Indonesianist literature that creatively addresses the interplay between history and the present (Mrázek 2010; Strassler 2010; Steedly 1993). During fieldwork, I gathered stories about the past during everyday conversations, through oral history interviews, and in personal archives of material objects, including a rich collection of photographs taken during the 1980s. To supplement this material, I drew on newspapers, magazines, and municipal records from the period to better situate the histories recounted to me by warias. Tacking to and from ethnographic and historical approaches in this setting offered a rich set of methods that were both attentive to dynamic processes of change and refused the decontextualizing tendency of Euro-American theories of gender and sexuality that seemed to delimit their analytical focus in advance in ways that could not account for the rich complexity of waria life as lived. Refusing easy answers and heeding Mary Steedly's call to craft "our stories less to the plausible demands of the ready-made grid and the fully elaborated code and more to the everyday cadences of the perpetually open-end" (1993, 238), I strained my ears to listen to warias' narratives, pasts, and imagined futures as I encountered them within their ethnographic context.

My two main field sites, Jakarta and Yogyakarta, were not only centers of social life for warias but large cities and special administrative regions in their own right, located on the densely populated island of Java (figure 1). Participating in both cities in the daily lives of warias revealed the centrality to them of the scale of the city for conferring and limiting recognition. In Yogyakarta, I witnessed warias contest their exclusion from public space in response to a 2014 law on busking and begging, which revealed the ways that gender nonconformity had been addressed as a disruption of public space and a specific problem to be solved at the scale of the city (Hegarty 2016). This experience led me to investigate the longer histories of regulating warias as a disruption of public space and a specific problem to be solved at the scale of the city, rather than as individualized pathology. Rather than framing a study of two distinct cities, then, this book is a historical ethnography that addresses the scale of the Indonesian city, a scale that offers a distinctive view of the regulatory, technological, and social forms that enable inhabitants to imagine and practice citizenship in ways that are distinct from those of the nation.

My ethnographic orientation helped me to understand that much of the official discussion of warias did not take place at the national level but largely as city regulations governing public order (*ketertiban umum*) and public morality (*kesusilaan umum*). Indeed, the first form of official recognition granted to warias was by Ali Sadikin, the governor of Jakarta from 1966 to 1977, who strove to integrate them into the mechanisms of city governance with the aim

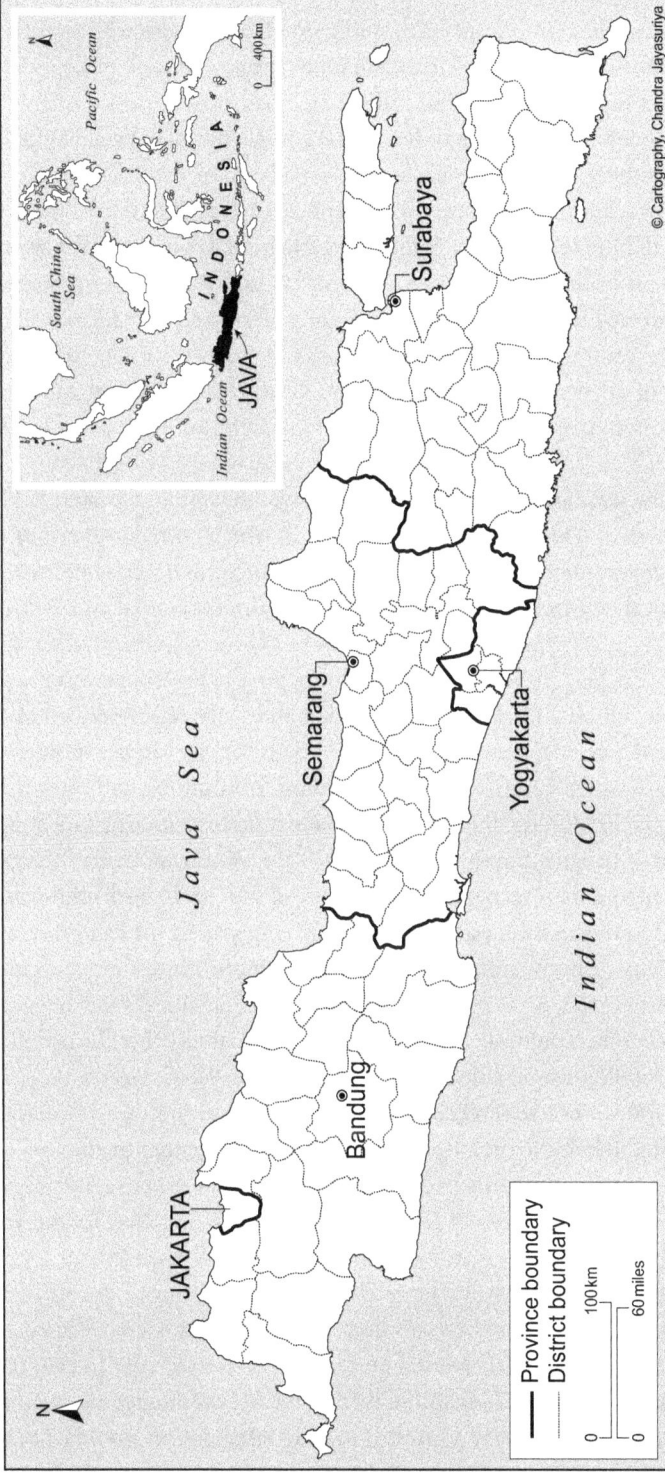

FIGURE 1. The island of Java, showing the boundaries of all districts, cities, and the special regions of Jakarta and Yogyakarta, ca. 1989.

Base map: Courtesy National Library of Australia

© Cartography, Chandra Jayasuriya

of transforming them into respectable and presentable citizens who formed part of modern Indonesian society. That these innovations first took place in Jakarta reflect the fact that, as the capital of Indonesia, it has served as a site where many of the techniques and meanings of municipal governance have been worked out. Jakarta holds the status of a province and is made up of five smaller cities that serve a largely administrative function (Kusno 2014; Nas and Grijns 2000). As is the case for all Indonesian municipalities, Jakarta is made up of smaller administrative areas including urban districts, subdistricts, quarters, and neighborhoods, which exist to facilitate various kinds of administration and bureaucratic administration. The centrality of the city in the narratives of warias also reflected the central role of Jakarta as one important site for essential forms of community building, economic opportunity, and claims to recognition since at least the late 1960s (figure 2).

A key characteristic of the administrative form of the Indonesian state has been a "two-tier system" (Malo and Nas 1991, 175), in which both autonomous local and central government bodies carry out various functions in the same area. This is reflected in the historical tension between centralized national and decentralized municipal governance (see also Legge 1961).[7] The development of the urban municipality has long played a crucial role in shaping Indonesian economics and politics at the national level. As Manesse Malo and Peter Nas described in their history of urban management in Indonesia, "just as the city can be considered an urban arena in which various individuals, groups, institutions, and categories of people struggle to promote their interests, many different meanings are attached to this organ of urban administration" (1991, 185). Warias were one such group who struggled to pursue recognition at the scale of the city. In both ethnographic research and in the archive, warias consistently emphasized the centrality of the scale of the city in both conferring and limiting opportunities for recognition. Hildred Geertz (1963, 34–35) observed that Indonesian cities were "integrating centers of economic, political, and intellectual life," that together formed no less than a "metropolitan superculture" of the nation (see also C. Geertz 1976, 378). This book locates waria squarely in the context of transformations at the scale of the city. Doing so helps to understand the role of public gender in efforts to confer the state's authority over the recognition of citizens in the postcolonial state.

The significance of events in Jakarta at the dawn of the New Order, which witnessed the birth of the term *waria* based on a novel engagement with the gender binary and an idiosyncratic relationship with the city's governor, cannot be overstated. The form of recognition provided through a loose integration with municipal governance bestowed on trans women a capacity to claim hitherto unthinkable forms of recognition. Yet to interpret the emergence of modern warias in Indonesia as entirely a product of state intervention would be both to

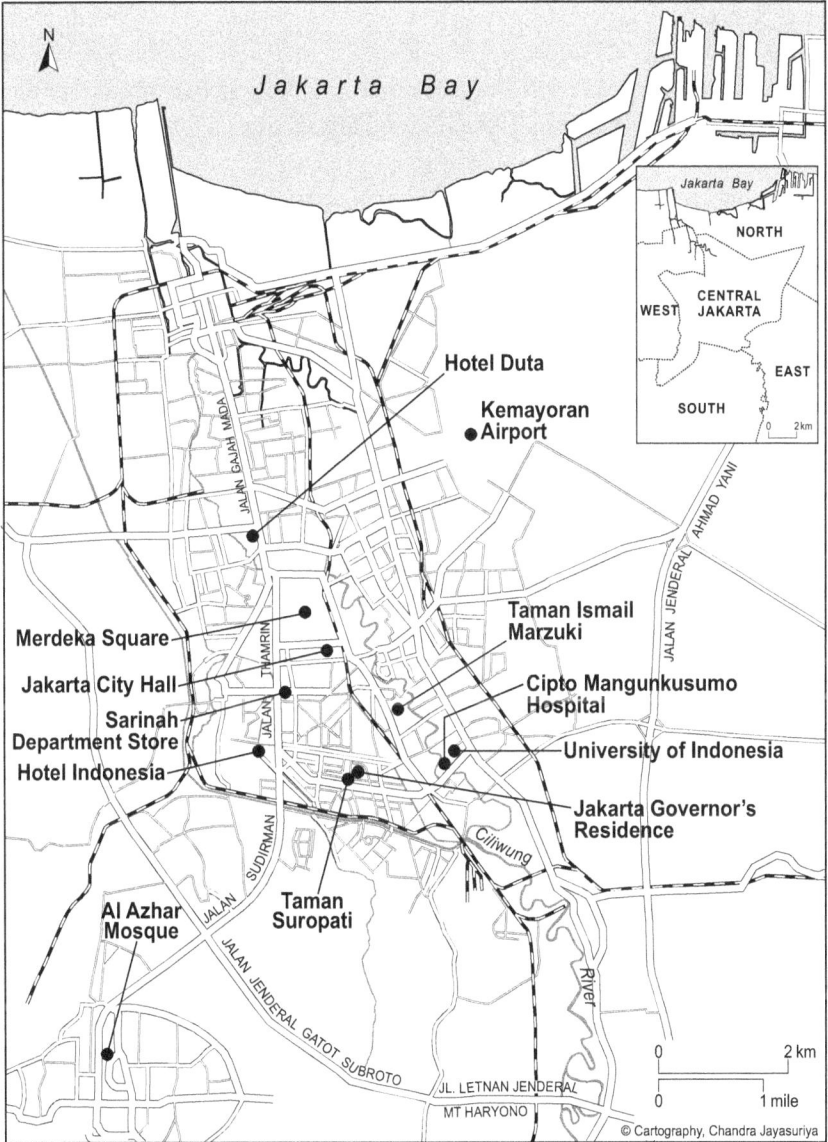

Base map: Courtesy National Library of Australia

FIGURE 2. Key locations in the city of Jakarta, ca. 1968.

succumb to technological determinism and to overlook the shared genealogy that governing appearances through gender in postcolonial Indonesia shares with governing race in the colonial period. Chapter 1 describes how colonial histories of regulating public space based on racialized appearances shaped the conditions for the emergence of warias. In the nineteenth and early twentieth centuries, European dress and comportment constituted part of a technology of race that was crucial both to the colonial state's imposition of racist hierarchies and Indonesians' efforts to contest them. As Arnout van der Meer outlined, rather than advancing an essentialist or biological view of racial difference, "the Dutch used clothing to maintain and visually express their distinction from and superiority to their indigenous subjects" (2020, 116). By contextualizing shifting assessments of the public performance of gender within the history of governing race in the Dutch East Indies, I show how warias were heirs to a "sartorial revolution" (van der Meer 2020, 121) that had been started by Indonesians who were excluded from participating in a modern public under colonial rule. The everyday refusal of warias to limit their performance of modern femininity through the public adoption of dress and makeup challenged the postcolonial state's monopoly on the recognition of citizens, seizing the semiotic logic of gender classification for themselves to command a position in public life.

This important connection to colonial histories of governing race through appearances notwithstanding, the predominant focus of this book is the New Order. This focus emerged from the narratives offered by many warias, recounted to me during fieldwork, that stressed the importance of this period. Despite the distinctive heteronormative framework of development pursued by the New Order, warias overwhelmingly described their recognition by the governor and integration into municipal governance as marking the dawn of a "golden age." This account, which was repeated so many times to me that it amounted to a shared narrative, led to a more sustained engagement with historical processes of transformation in the meanings of trans femininity than I had initially imagined. In settings around the world, including in Southeast Asia, historical processes of modernization have corresponded with a concern to extend the state's definition of citizenship in terms of gender that is both innate and limited to a binary of male and female (Peletz 2009; Blackwood 2005a). Although this certainly appears to have been the case in Indonesia, no waria I met in the course of fieldwork spoke of their experiences in terms of a narrative of decline. If anything, warias evaluated the state's efforts to impose two clearly demarcated genders and that pursuit's integration within processes of technological development as a positive move. After all, a creative engagement with a model of binary gender that demanded greater differentiation between male and female is what allowed warias to attain a certain status in public life that had been previously unthinkable.

The role that technology played in shaping warias' participation in public life is illustrated by events that took place in Jakarta in 1968. A group of warias presented themselves to the Jakarta city government, describing the horrific forms of abuse and exclusion they faced at the hands of other residents of the city, particularly when they appeared during the day and to a wide viewing public. The municipal police, in a practice that stretched back to the colonial era, pursued and temporarily detained warias in police raids on the public places where they gathered. In August of that year, the governor of Jakarta Ali Sadikin sought a solution by bestowing on warias new terms that would render them a more presentable part of modern Indonesian society. This intervention was laudable but not necessarily premised on a desire to expand the visibility of warias. Rather, his interest originated from reports in the popular press that warias' growing visibility on city streets was a disruption of public order.

Chapter 2 situates the events that established the unprecedented recognition of warias in 1968, contextualizing often contradictory demands and desires for improved presentability of this group in light of efforts to regulate public morality and order at the scale of the municipality. Central to this story of recognition was Sadikin, an innovative and charismatic urban reformer who sought to modernize the city and strove to integrate trans women through a combination of functionalist and aesthetic logics (Hegarty 2021). By calling on warias to make themselves more presentable in public, Sadikin approached public gender in ways similar to how other problem bodies were addressed in cities in New Order Indonesia, what Suzanne Moon called a form of "citizenship in legal and technological terms" that hinged on the degree to which they were "integrated into the day-to-day functioning of cities" (Moon 2015, 192). By contextualizing often contradictory demands and desires for improved presentability in light of urban efforts to regulate public morality and order, I show how this form of recognition was limited, and therefore embedded within anxieties over who could enter public space and on what basis. Nevertheless, it was through these legal innovations at the scale of the city that warias could demand the right to pass through city streets unimpeded wearing women's clothing and makeup, including in the middle of the day, should they so desire. In turn, the demand for recognition made by warias rested on the assertion that their gender presentation was not only a performance or play but an authentic component of their inner self, and thus a critical aspect of their claims to belonging in the city and the nation.

Expanded recognition achieved by warias through city-level innovations did not go uncontested. Anxieties about the appearance of increasing numbers of warias in public space, coupled with the state's technological ambitions, corresponded with a rather abrupt engagement with medical models of transsexuality by Indonesian experts in the 1970s. Chapter 3 charts the influence of an array of technological interventions that emerged under the guise of medical transsexuality and its relationship to the modern self, which had increasing global reach at that time. The meanings of the terms *wadam* and *waria* were shaped through a process of partial medicalization and through the discipline of psychiatry in particular (Hegarty 2019). This traffic in meanings between warias and medical transsexuality contributed to the greater visibility of a wider array of trans femininity than warias alone in the Indonesian media during the 1970s and 1980s. Through a process of sorting and disaffiliation that these technologies made possible, largely in the field of medicine, psychiatrists and doctors conferred the status of natural gender on the basis of an alignment between mind, appearances, and reproductive capacity.

This process relied in crucial ways on experimentation and discussion of wadam and waria, and eventually the imposition of a clearer boundary with those terms and the category "woman." Attempts to impose legal and social clarity over human difference, along with the distinction between public recognition and state recognition, nevertheless confounded the simplistic clarity of the state's efforts to make up cisgender normativity as the natural basis for citizenship. Although this was not inherently political, and indeed marked a use of technology to evacuate the powerful political claims advanced by warias, this engagement by Indonesian experts with modern technologies of medical transsexuality at various points called into question the naturalization of gender as an essential component of individual personhood. Warias' encounters with modern technologies of identifying and correcting gender along a mind/body axis at the level of the individual self influenced broader configurations of state citizenship, visually signifying the emergence of a newfound clarity in the moral meanings of public gender as a symbol of development.

Appearances and Authenticity

In 1968, the year that warias were recognized as a legal but nonconforming category on the grounds that they disrupted municipal public order, a major beauty pageant was held at the Duta Hotel in central Jakarta. Under the banner of "Miss Imitation Girls," a group of glamorous warias wore the latest women's clothing and styled their hair and makeup in ways that asserted a polished feminine figure. Contestants were evaluated and ranked by judges, to be awarded a prize sponsored by the Anda Mulya Beauty Salon. Sonny Sudarma was crowned the winner of the contest and recognized as a paragon of feminine beauty. A well-known waria and leader in her community, Sonny Sudarma was photographed together with Ali Sadikin and his wife at a waria performance at the

Jakarta Fair, a monthlong event held at Merdeka Square. This was one of a pro-liferating number of locations that cemented in the minds of the city's citizens an association between the polished performances of feminine beauty and warias.

As an event for promoting state-sanctioned consumerism and demonstrating national pride in technological progress, the Jakarta Fair was an opportunity for warias to establish a public platform for attempting to wrest the meanings of their visibility from moral impropriety to polished respectability. This allowed warias to participate more freely in public life in the city. Their advocacy emerged from a necessity grounded in threats of exclusion backed up by commonplace claims that they were "afraid to stand in well-lit places." In Sadikin's early con-versations with warias, he "offer[ed] them an opportunity to work at a stand or restaurant at the Jakarta Fair managed by the city . . . a way to sort out the real from the false, reducing their presence on the sides of roads, cleaning the city, and freeing it from indecent sights" (*Selecta* 1968, 19). The proliferation of platforms such as the Jakarta Fair, and the demonstration of femininity as a claim to authenticity that it allowed, led warias to see their loose integration into municipal governance not as a constraint but as enabling an expanded participa-tion in public life.

Warias were not only committed to their own performances of modern feminine beauty but came to have a reputation as individuals whom citizens could turn to in order to align their public presentation with an emergent set of expectations associated with modern gender. In this respect, warias provide a better understanding of the relationship between moral and technological prog-ress against a broader backdrop of social change in postcolonial Indonesia. In the 1950s and 1960s, both state and non-state actors increasingly told warias to limit their feminine visibility on the grounds that they were not compatible with national modernity (Peacock 1968). With the emergence of spaces for con-sumer capitalist and body-centered consumption in the late 1960s, warias har-nessed an existing reputation for bodily transformation in specific contexts to advance claims to recognition on terms that they were beauty experts. This leap was only partially successful, as warias continued to find that some publics were more amenable to their presence than others. As demonstrated through their well-recognized presence in professions related to beauty salons and as fashion designers, warias' belonging, never fully assured, was conditional on their ability to undertake forms of self-cultivation for public consumption.

In chapter 4, I argue that the technologies and forms of expertise that warias adopted to accomplish a more presentable appearance relied on an understand-ing of economic participation imagined in terms of improvements in the form of feminine beauty. While it was an authoritarian state ruled by the military, the New Order did encourage the kinds of individualized forms of participation advanced by international development agencies (Li 2007). This meant that the language and concepts of international development, what Christopher Kelty (2019, 231) called its "toolkits," were translated and adopted into Indonesian notions of the collective espoused by earlier generations of nationalists (see Moon 2015). Suzanne Moon described how, in reference to a broader condition of municipal governance during the New Order more generally, "the issue of local technological participation in rebuilding these neighborhoods was at least as important as the distribution of new and improved infrastructure" (Moon 2015, 187). Warias' commonly voiced desires to be "accepted by society" (*di terima oleh masyarakat*) were advanced through local technological participation in the form of the skills and training involved in achieving modern femininity. Training manuals and programs produced by city governments for warias, known as "guidance" (*pembinaan*), were part of a broader pattern of development that instilled a "desire for collectivity and for authentic participation" (Kelty 2019, 231), a form of liberation through the transformation of consciousness at the level of the individual, the success or not of which was tested every time warias walked down the street.

Seen as more proximate to the technological moorings of Indonesian postcolonial modernity, the practice among warias of *dandan*—of making up—presents rich insights into the meanings of recognition. On the one hand, dandan rested on skillfully executed technologies of feminization that transformed outer appearances, such as applying makeup, styling hair, and wearing women's clothing. On the other hand, warias' narratives about dandan stressed that it made visible their woman's soul (*jiwa perempuan*). The practice of feminization through the application of cosmetics and clothing described among warias as dandan therefore escapes Euro-American conceptualizations that the mind has primacy over the body. Tom Boellstorff observed that "warias do not always assume that the soul makes one wear women's clothes; the causality can be seen to work in the other direction or to be mutually constituting, thereby reflecting the widespread assumption in Southeast Asia that internal state and external presentation naturally align with each other" (2007, 91). Despite the centrality of the accomplishment of femininity to warias, dandan nevertheless involved practices that were largely temporary or could be put on and taken off on a daily basis. While dandan was a concept of self-improvement used commonly in Indonesian social life, the concept held specific meaning when practiced by warias as an effort not only to be visible but to control the conditions of that visibility.

In chapter 5, I argue that, in claiming technologies of gender for themselves, warias cultivated a distinctive style of national glamour that expanded the boundaries of what it meant to see and be seen as an "Indonesian." This chapter is the most richly illustrated in the book, containing images of warias' practices of dandan that are from a collection of photographs taken in the 1980s held by one waria named Tadi. I introduce photographs and oral history accounts with Tadi to trace a history of warias' aesthetics and practices of feminization that they describe as dandan. I argue that warias' practices of dandan demonstrate how gender is inseparable from class, nation, spatial regulation, and sexuality. Even as the city identified trans women's visibility as a problem of public order, and hence as a problem to be solved, warias asserted their own self-knowledge as a claim to authenticity. Dandan in particular, and its capacity to achieve self-hood through bodily cultivation beyond that authorized by the state, reflects the persistence of alternate systems of visual power throughout the New Order. This highlights the potential for gender, a symbol for linking bodily cultivation to the modern self, to establish competing opportunities to participate in a collective public. Reflecting warias' ambiguous and largely unrecognized relationship to the New Order state's visual power, the ability to harness dandan as an alternate claim to recognition shows how public gender continued to rely on spatial and temporal forms of regulation. This was most marked in the distinction made among warias between the styles of dandan that were suitable at night and those during the day.

Before and during the New Order, warias negotiated with an ambivalent and contradictory public gaze. The technological processes tied to the specific format of national development that the New Order state ushered in rested on a framework that symbolized the achievement of modernity through the pursuit of a clear-cut gender binary. This provided warias a new format for claiming recognition. The emergence of a distinctive set of possibilities for imagining public gender did not occur alone, therefore, but was shaped by a broader array of sociotechnical relations. Discussion of practices of dandan as contained in this photographic archive helps to clarify warias' understanding of binary gender as a means to accomplish recognition in ways that were never entirely under the control of the state. In distinction to the state's definition of sex and gender, warias described their experience of gender as a bodily transformation that reflected a process of refinement or the application of polish, which when done skillfully allowed an essential character to appear more brightly. Warias' gendering thus has a somewhat processual character, bringing to mind James Siegel's definition of dandan as that which "bring[s] out a quality that is somehow inherent in whatever is completed" (1997, 73). Practices of dandan among warias reflect how binary gender offered a means to accomplish recognition in ways that were never entirely under the control of the state. Chapters 4 and 5 advance the argument of the book as a whole that the availability of technologies of gender—always far more widespread and accessible than those efforts to impose cisgender normativity by the state—served as an alternate framework of knowledge through which warias could advance claims to recognition. Warias thwarted the state's efforts to make up gender as an essentialized format of an individual self and body in part because they were already recognized by community, kin, and one another.

During the New Order, warias claimed forms of recognition that rested on their utility to society. Their gendered form of bodily cultivation was harnessed to the self so that they could become productive members of national society and could assist other citizens to align with the state's desires for economic development. The accomplishment of binary gender was central to an understanding of citizenship as participation in a morally bounded community. Warias demonstrate technology's ongoing role in shaping the limits of belonging, extending to the surface of the body as a medium for recognition. The mixed successes of warias' efforts to seize sources of visual power and use them to command an audience challenge any simple notion that increased visibility facilitates greater inclusion. Rather, warias serve as a reminder of the need for historians and ethnographers of trans cultural life to attend carefully to the specific meanings of gender within the publics, conditions, aesthetics, and technologies through which that concept is wielded by the modern state.

A Made-Up State

This book centers the sociotechnical relations that both open and limit gender as a technology of classification with far-reaching consequences for the organization of human difference. This approach enables a perspective on gender as a way of differentiating the boundaries of participation within national and social collectives that naturalize dualisms of male/female, mind/body, and cisgender/transgender at the level of the individual self. The ways that warias engaged with and were subject to technological transformations demonstrate how the making of modern gender in Indonesia did not rest on technologies of the self that were focused on the inner life of the subject (C. Taylor 1989) but reflects other histories of personhood, national belonging, and citizenship (Boellstorff 2005). In turn, the technological mediation of gender in postcolonial Indonesia—and the emphasis on bodily cultivation tied to selfhood that underpinned it—established the competent accomplishment of masculinity and femininity as public performances that were key to making and unmaking who could be recognized as a citizen.

The centrality of binary gender to modern citizenship did not disappear at the end of the New Order. Following Suharto's downfall amid mass protests in 1998, the religious authority of Islam provided an important justification for political action. In the post-Suharto period some religious groups, but by no means all, have depicted warias as incompatible with a national identity that aligns more closely with a pious Islamic outlook (Wijaya 2020). Yet although the presence of warias in everyday life has long chafed with conservative Islamic publics, secular experts such as psychiatrists and state officials have been equally as strident in continuing their efforts to impose a definition of gender by drawing on binaries of mind/body, male/female, and cisgender/transgender. Rather than reflecting its origins in Islam, this essentialist paradigm of individual gender recalls the history of New Order development, which situated Indonesia as part of a global network in new ways. As Ariel Heryanto has described, the development of the concept of *pembangunan* by the New Order state sought to rearrange the relationship between technology and social life as "no longer a creative experiment in the expression of foreign ideas" but rather "a distinct response to foreign ideas" (1988, 11).

The gendered body, a key symbol of development during the New Order, continues to be an enduring symbol in the state's efforts to claim ultimate authority over recognition. From early 2016 onward, just after the moment when I concluded my extended period of fieldwork in Jakarta and Yogyakarta, a wide range of actors mobilized opposition to the claims to political recognition advanced under the broad format of "LGBT rights." Efforts to oppose LGBT rights appeared to be based on the assessment that such concepts marked a foreign threat to an essential Indonesian character. This public anxiety about the place of LGBT in Indonesian public life led to a corresponding constitutional court case and various efforts to revise the nation's criminal code (Butt 2019). While these efforts to explicitly criminalize same-sex sexuality at the national level failed, various regional regulations were hastily imposed to criminalize gender nonconformity. Seen from the history of warias' engagement with public gender contained in this book, these regulations resemble a troubling reversal of the utilization of the mechanisms of municipal and neighborhood governance to expand claims to recognition during the New Order. Warias' integration into Indonesian social life after Suharto reflects yet another instantiation of the integration of different currents of knowledge and technology, including a reconfiguration of the partial connection between waria and transgender. Attending to the historical specificity of gender as an effort not only to be visible but to control the conditions of that visibility helps us to understand how citizenship is forged through recognition as part of a technologically mediated public, one that is an unpredictable, unfinished, and made-up state.

BANCI, BEFORE WARIA

Approximately two decades before Indonesian independence in 1929, the capital of the Dutch East Indies, Batavia (now Jakarta), was home to fewer than half a million people. The population of the city reflected the diversity of both the colonial world and its heir, the postcolonial nation. Batavia's population was made up of individuals defined as belonging to one of three legal categories that structured social life in the colonial state: "Europeans," "natives," and "foreign Orientals."[1] In 1945, the independence leader and first Indonesian president, Sukarno, declared independence from the Dutch in Jakarta, the new name that had been granted to the former colonial capital during World War II. In the immediate postindependence period, Jakarta experienced rapid growth, as migrants from other parts of the country moved to the city in large numbers, bringing the population of Jakarta to approximately two million people in 1952 (Abeyasekere 1990, 171). These newcomers jostled with one another for the opportunities associated with the new Indonesian nation, shaping the kind of culture that would define belonging within it.

Against this backdrop, gender nonconformity emerged as an increasingly visible feature of urban life. Warias who were old enough to remember spontaneously reflected on the way that the collective visibility achieved during this period offered new possibilities and perils. The well-known waria performer Maya Puspa moved from a small town in Sumatra to Jakarta around 1950. As a member of the nation's ethnic Chinese minority and the child of relatively wealthy merchants, Maya had access to education and a degree of social and financial capital. She narrated her migration to Jakarta as part of a collective movement shared by many Indonesians, one that allowed her to seek out new opportunities. After arriving in the city, Maya encountered others similar to her, whom on this occasion she called bancis but could just as easily be interpreted as warias. But even as urban life in the new nation's capital offered unprecedented forms of freedom and a distinctive social life in the company of others like her, the presence of gender nonconformity on the city streets could be met with physical and verbal attacks.

From the 1600s onward, the twin effects of the growing dominance of Islam and European colonization contributed to a transformation in understandings of sex, gender, and sexuality throughout the archipelago. The ascendance of monotheistic religious and secular laws and regulations that held binary sex and gender as innate, natural aspects of the self was reflected in the gradual reduction of spaces for individuals who, as part of diverse indigenous cosmologies, played an important role in communal and ritual life by expressing ambiguity and combination through their bodies and appearances (Peletz 2009; Blackwood 2005a). Although colonial rule was based on racist assumptions about indigenous sexuality, efforts to control the public meanings of gender by state and nonstate actors accelerated in postcolonial Indonesia during the 1950s and 1960s. Against a backdrop of intersecting political and economic crises (Feith 1962), widespread efforts to reduce the visibility of gender nonconformity at this time were not limited to a distinct geographical area but appeared in different parts of the new nation.

The political integration of noble-led kingdoms in South Sulawesi into a centralized national government, and the political power wielded by Islamic movements, had a pernicious effect on the public role of *bissu*, ritual practitioners who mediate between the human and spiritual world within Bugis cosmology (Davies 2007, 86–87). In the city of Surabaya in East Java, James Peacock (1968, 49) reported that the leader of one large *ludruk* theater troupe recruited a psychiatrist to lecture trans feminine performers on homosexuality and encouraged them to marry and father children.[2] Accounts provided by these ludruk performers suggest that gender nonconformity was framed increasingly as an embarrassing faux pas that was in conflict with being a modern citizen. As one performer put it, "Like other players I once had hair halfway to my waist. I curled, arranged it like a girl—but then came embarrassment [*malu*] and progress [*madju*]. I cut it off" (Peacock 1968, 206–7). Gender was central to an emergent apparatus aimed at determining not only the limits of participation in public life but establishing the internal boundaries of citizenship in the modern state.

To understand how gender nonconformity emerged as a specific problem within Indonesian postcolonial modernity, I look to the meanings and effects of the term *banci* from the late colonial period through the first decades of

Indonesian independence. Addressing the shifting historical meanings of the term as used to index a specific experience of selfhood across this period opens new horizons for considering a more global perspective on the traffic in knowledge between categories for defining gender and those related to race. Rather than employing a model based on essentialized psychological or biological differences, efforts to define and regulate race in the Dutch East Indies were framed in terms of appearances, and particularly dress (see van der Meer 2020; Nordholt 1997). Drawing on the analytic strengths of placing trans in relation to waria outlined in the introduction, I assess the public meanings of gender in light of shifting modes of categorizing race in the Dutch East Indies. Pursuing a perspective on gender as a global classificatory scheme that signaled modernity on the surface of the body reveals how the colonial project of regulating the boundaries of public difference through appearances did not vanish following Indonesian independence. I argue that the colonial infrastructure of race, so fundamentally concerned with appearances in the Dutch East Indies, was smuggled into an emergent apparatus for governing publics via binary gender. The postcolonial state sought to assuage anxieties provoked by the indeterminate possibilities of racialized gender by drawing from rapidly developing scientific and medical expertise about the classification of sex and sexuality.

As outlined in the introduction, the term *banci* is used in contemporary Indonesia to refer to a range of ambiguity, most often in reference to gender and sexuality and usually in a pejorative way. It was the offensive calls of "banci!" from passersby in the city that led to claims that *wadam* and *waria* were more refined terms of identification and recognition, challenging the way belittling terms robbed them of control. Bearing this important caveat in mind, in this chapter I use the term *banci*, because that is the term that appears in archival and oral history accounts as a form of identification, and because it played a crucial role in placing warias in communication with one another, shaping in fundamental ways their experience of recognition as part of a modern public. Reconsidering published and archival accounts by scholars and administrators alongside narratives provided by warias themselves helps to better interpret how banci positioned themselves in the global currents of knowledge that emerged in the late nineteenth and early twentieth centuries. I also use the term to provide a sense of the momentousness of the shift in terminology from *banci* to *wadam* in 1968, a change that was described as one of vital importance among almost all warias I met who were old enough to remember.

This chapter articulates how banci emerged as a category that facilitated communication between different systems of knowledge, allowing space for new struggles over the classification of gender to emerge in the postcolonial nation. The experience of these struggles was most powerfully felt by those identified as or who found themselves categorized as banci. As this chapter argues, a lack of any clear legal or social sanctions against the public presentation of gender nonconformity and homosexuality in the colonial state must be interpreted in light of the dominant form of classifying human difference on the basis of race. Yet rather than premised on a biological essentialist account of human difference, "European status" was defined in terms of more culturalist definitions of race (see especially Stoler 1995, 10–11). Although this did not make colonial policies any less premised on white superiority, the meaning of race at this point in the Dutch East Indies, as Bart Luttikhuis has argued, reflected "a multidimensional hierarchy rather than a clear dichotomy of 'coloniser' and 'colonised'" (2013, 541). As in other colonial contexts, official attempts to separate the population contrasted with the social reality of mutability and mixing. As racial difference was parsed along cultural lines, the colonial state's classificatory regime struggled to retain its legibility, giving rise to anxieties premised on a disjuncture between appearances and authenticity. This racial history of citizenship, most fraught at its boundaries or where individuals were held under suspicion of disloyalty or inauthentic belonging, is illustrated by Ann Laura Stoler's description of a late nineteenth-century preoccupation with "interior frontiers" that were used to draw a "national essence . . . [as] a powerful trope for internal contamination and challenge conceived morally, politically, and sexually" (Stoler 1992, 516). Efforts to unmask frauds and expose moral failings, understandings developed via attention to mixed-race and lower-class white populations, not only revealed individualized forms of pathology but were deployed to delimit and defend a nation that was defined as a collective public.

   The shift from the colonial to postcolonial state witnessed a rearrangement in the meanings of gender as a central technology through which the boundaries of citizenship were managed. Anxieties about the public meanings of gender, in part established since the colonial period through patterns of comparison and exchange between the category "transvestite" and the term *banci*, did not disappear but were heightened following Indonesian independence. This highlights the imbrication of race and gender as categories that mutually constitute the meanings of citizenship in the modern state. This history reveals how the relationship between authenticity and recognition was defined in terms of access to public space, a site where the meanings of outer appearances were continuously assessed. Yet this quality also engendered in public space the possibility to lay alternate claims to authenticity and recognition. The public adoption of modern forms of feminine gender among banci, although certainly perceived as aberrant to the new nation's character, must therefore be interpreted within the history of this emergent Indonesian style.

Defining Banci as Transvestites

Although the precise origins of *banci* are unclear, by the dawn of the twentieth century, the term appears to have been in wide use in Malay. Lacking the hierarchical status of Javanese or the inaccessibility of Dutch, Malay served as the unofficial lingua franca between the populations who comprised the subjects of the Dutch colonial state. As Tom Boellstorff (2005, 218) observed, Malay was "not just the language of trade and administration, but a means by which information from outside the Indies entered the archipelago" (see also Siegel 1997). Despite the widespread circulation of the term *banci*, European observers largely referred to it within distinct, bounded, local cultures, rather than as a product of an emergent Malay-language superculture that was taking shape within the expansion of capitalism and colonial rule.[3] The equation of indigenous culture with the scale of the local in turn meant that colonial-era observers either did not or could not see banci beyond the discrete sites in which they had encountered them. Despite the tendency of scholars and administrators to address bancis at a spatial scale that collapsed "ethnicity and locality" (Boellstorff 2005, 43), the meanings of the term were nevertheless influenced by a global traffic in knowledge during the colonial period.

In the late nineteenth and early twentieth centuries, the term *banci* was integrated into globalized currents of colonial knowledge that framed homosexuality on gendered terms in ways that do not easily map onto contemporary theoretical understandings based on the category transgender. Aligning with the popular theoretical model of "gender inversion" (Hekma 1996, 213) developed in the nineteenth and early twentieth centuries, European scholars usually assessed bancis as one local instance of a diverse array of indigenous homosexualities (Boellstorff 2007, 85). As Rudi Bleys (1996, 180) outlined, by limiting their interest to "passive, effeminate roles," colonial-era scholars both reproduced and created the then-dominant understanding that physical signs of femininity on the male body could be interpreted as evidence of male homosexuality. For example, the Dutch physical anthropologist Kleiweg de Zaan, better known for his series of plaster casts of faces created as objective visual representations of racial difference (Sysling 2015), drew on observations of gendered behavior to separate out what he saw as the genuine homosexuality of what he called "passive boys" from their partners (cited in Bleys 1996, 180). In 1942, one dictionary listed the Dutch translations of *banci* (classified as a Javanese Batavian term) as "tweeslachtig, hermafrodiet, kwee (Orango bantji)," that is, "ambiguity, hermaphrodite, queen (banci)" (Mayer 1942, 37).[4] In accounts informed by prevailing theories of race, which framed same-sex and excessive sexuality as evidence of primitivity, colonial scholars and administrators often interpreted what they saw as nonconforming gender as evidence of what David Valentine called "the implicit deficiencies of all bodies which were not white, male, and procreatively inclined" (2007, 41).

These designations relied on a prevailing understanding of sex as a natural component of the body, but also an emergent understanding of the physical body as a sign of a person's inner state. In this respect, it is notable that the discovery of banci—with their women's souls (*jiwa perempuan*)—appeared at a moment of transformation in nineteenth-century scientific accounts of both sexuality and race, in which physical signs of femininity were increasingly assessed as an unreliable sign of otherwise indiscernible inner pathologies (cf. Foucault 1978). The book *De vrouwen op Java: Eene gynaecologische studie*, by Dr. C. H. Stratz (1898), was one example of the emerging logics through which the biological basis for race was gendered, reorganized through an emergent discovery in colonial science that there was a putative alignment between genital morphology, reproductive capacity, outer appearances, and inner self. In her discussion of Stratz's book, Ann Stoler described how "internal and skeletal body form reveals a woman's hidden racial characteristics even when her physical appearance is that of a European" (Stoler 1995, 185). In other words, this suggests a racial history of the concept of cisgender personhood as a marker of civilizational status as it emerged via currents of knowledge about banci and other gender-variant figures in the colonial world.[5] One effect of this entwined history of race and gender, including the incomplete process of mapping the European concepts of homosexuality and transvestitism onto banci, was its lasting influence on the meanings of public gender in colonial and postcolonial Indonesia.

Efforts to understand how banci experienced and narrated their own relationships to gender are challenged both by a lack of sources and the tendency to portray their femininity as a symptom of homosexuality. For this and other reasons, the complex interplay between race and gender in the Dutch East Indies has been largely overlooked. In the seventeenth and eighteenth centuries in Batavia, homosexuality was subject to capital punishment, corresponding with Dutch law at that time (Boomgaard 2012). The adoption of the French legal code in the Netherlands in 1811 saw penalties for homosexuality removed, however; the application of a new criminal code in the Dutch East Indies in 1918 contained differential age-of-consent laws for homosexuality and heterosexuality (Pausacker 2020). In one of the rare instances where age-of-consent laws were used in 1938–39, colonial authorities oversaw the arrest of over two hundred high-profile Dutch and other European men for sex with Indonesian men and boys. While the power relations of such relationships were undoubtedly shaped by the political and economic structures of racial inequality in the Dutch East Indies, Marieke Bloembergen (2011) considers this purge of prominent European homosexuals in the context of growing anxieties about morality, derived from increasing contact between Europeans and Indonesians in the latter part of colonial rule. In other words, concern for homosexuality was only clearly articulated in response to the possibility that such practices marked a threat to European male prestige. Available historical records suggest that the Indonesian men and boys who were the partners of European men—regardless of their motivations—were ignored or described as needing to be corrected through forms of rehabilitation. Looking to how the meanings of sexuality took shape at this time requires considering the parallel development of knowledge about race and gender as dominant influences that shaped legal, social, and administrative aspects of colonial rule. The history of banci is key to understanding the shifting modalities through which public participation was governed and lived.

From the 1930s onward, European scholars began to understand and distinguish banci from homosexuals as "transvestites," a category that was popularized over the first decades of the twentieth century. The German sexologist Magnus Hirschfeld, who identified and defined the category "transvestite" in his book *Die Transvestiten*, published in 1910, traveled to the Dutch East Indies in the early 1930s (for an account of Hirschfeld's journey to Asia see Bauer 2006).[6] In *Women East and West*, a book chronicling his travels throughout Asia, Hirschfeld offered an intriguing description of an evening on the streets of Batavia he spent with a group of "Malay transvestites" (Hirschfeld 1935, 139) in terms that are strikingly similar to accounts of banci. During his stay in the city, Hirschfeld also attended a lecture about "transvestites" presented by Pieter Mattheus van Wulfften Palthe, a prominent Dutch professor of psychiatry and neurology and a key figure in an emerging body of scientific thought that asserted racial difference (and, implicitly, European or white superiority) in essentialist terms (Hirschfeld 1935, 139).[7] Hirschfeld's encounter with van Wulfften Palthe in colonial Batavia highlights the shared genealogies of knowledge produced via the classification of trans and racial identity in the 1930s, the period during which racial difference was increasingly framed in essentialist terms.

Colonial-era efforts to interpret banci as transvestites via racialized scientific and medical knowledge emerged within the tumultuous political context of the final decades of Dutch colonial rule in the 1920s and 1930s. The colonial encounter had been transformed in the wake of the introduction of the Ethical Policy in 1901, encompassing a wide set of liberal reforms that included a "technological turn" (Moon 2007, 23), which positioned economic development as a crucial component of the civilizing mission. In this context, colonial-era psychiatry played an important role in lending legitimacy to European rule over Indonesians in light of a growing nationalist movement (Pols 2018; 2011). As Hans Pols observed, "Politicians came to advocate a psychological colonial policy in which scientists would study the nature of the native psyche as a guide for colonial policy" (2011, 145). Van Wulfften Palthe, the Dutch psychiatrist who had met with Hirschfeld to discuss transvestites in the 1930s, had himself contributed significantly to scientific definitions that both hardened the boundaries of racial classification and located forms of difference primarily in the mind.[8] Efforts to stabilize race through recourse to an essential mind emerged in dialogue with the twentieth-century development of transvestite as a racial category when applied to banci. Yet as was the case for race, an essentialist definition of gendered difference was hard to sustain in the face of the troubling and increasingly common sight of those whose appearances, thanks to the more widespread availability of modern fashions and dress, challenged the authority of both the state and psychiatric experts over recognition.

From the early twentieth century onward, popular and scholarly accounts of banci—read through the category transvestite—focused largely on how and to what degree their gender presentation could be read as an enduring aspect of the mind. Contextualizing banci within the wider context of shifting understandings of biological difference in the late nineteenth century offers an important analytical perspective on the shared relationship between the histories of knowledge about race and gender in the Dutch East Indies. Given the colonial relations within which such knowledge was produced, however, it is difficult to ascertain how and in what way gender was lived and articulated as a component of everyday life among banci themselves. I further elaborate the entanglement of race and gender by drawing on oral history accounts provided by elderly warias born from the 1930s onward, and newspaper and magazine articles that included bancis' own accounts of the colonial period. A recurring theme expressed by warias was the concern with movement in and subtle adjustment of public gender in cities. I argue that these experiences of gender defined as recognition within a public grew out of longer histories that emphasized dress as a visual symbol for defining the boundaries of racial status in colonial society. The particular emphasis on appearances as key to governing race, as well as the dissolution of these rules in the early twentieth century, played a crucial role in shaping the possibility for the appearance of bancis.

Despite some differences, both historical and oral history accounts suggest a degree of stability between definitions of banci in the colonial period and waria in the New Order. In 1932, an account in a newspaper column described in Batavia "banci who every night" were "very visible along the sides of roads together with women of the night, who [needed to] be suppressed until they disappear[ed]" (*Soemanget* 1932, 2).[9] Alterations in bancis' public visibility at this time were measured by the adoption of what were described as more modern styles of dress and appearance. More specifically, these accounts cited transformations in gender through which bancis developed a more stable association with the clothing, makeup, and bodily transformation of a modern, internationally legible feminine presentation. The presence of gender nonconformity was tied both to changes made to the individual body and the publics to whom bancis appeared.

Public Gender in Postcolonial Indonesia

A distinctive component of bancis' descriptions of themselves in the postcolonial period was the stress that they placed on narratives that they had a woman's soul (*jiwa perempuan*). It was this emphasis on interiority, rather than only alterations to outer appearances, that served as a tactic of narrativization through which banci asserted that their public gender was born from an innate quality that was unwavering. Possessing a woman's soul did not correspond to a need for a stable public femininity, however, as reflected in frequent cases where bancis were not able to perform dandan all the time out of necessity or a lack of skill. For example, Maya said that the public gender of banci in the 1950s and 1960s was often unmarked, but that nevertheless they were able to identify one another based on the evaluation of subtle corporeal and linguistic signs legible only to the trained eye or ear.

A series of accounts published in 1968 by the Jakarta government in the magazine *Mingguan Djaja* presents some insight into the lives of bancis in the 1940s and 1950s, in the form of narratives of the then-recent past.[10] One banci conveyed a historical shift in the meanings of public gender through the following recollection: "The difference is that in the past *béncong* [a contemporary vulgar usage for *banci*] were quiet and often operated outside of Jakarta, whereas now they are more in the light" (*Mingguan Djaja* 1968c, 4). This account suggests that prior to the 1960s, within ambiguous peri-urban spaces just outside Jakarta, bancis had largely been visible only within circumscribed settings within the fabric of rural life, such as during festivals and at weddings. The author of the accounts contained in *Mingguan Djaja*, who had carried out field research, summarized, "We were told that a long time ago, these béncong and her friends operated in the areas of Bogor, Tjibotabék, and Tjibulan [then rural enclaves and towns outside the Jakarta metropolitan area], particularly during the fruit and rice harvests. During those two seasons, many people of the village held celebrations for circumcision and weddings, and they would call a theater troupe or an orchestra. Béncong would visit the celebration and join the troupes or orchestra" (*Mingguan Djaja* 1968c, 4). These accounts highlight that, in the 1950s and early 1960s, a shift was under way not only in the locations in which banci were visible but in the very meanings of public gender. There could be several reasons for the increased visibility of banci at this time, including that Indonesians were freer to move into the city and that they had readier access to fashion and dress to transform their appearances in line with global styles of dress.

Warias who were old enough to remember the period recalled their increased visibility in the immediate postcolonial period. While warias cherished even the limited opportunities available to them to wear women's clothing and makeup in the company of other warias and at night, their appearance in public and during the day could prompt severe exclusion. One waria in Jakarta recalled that "we couldn't even go out in makeup during the day at that time. If we tried, we would be chased from the neighborhood. So we adjusted our appearance, only wearing women's clothing at night." Another waria, recounting their experience in Jakarta around 1949 in another *Mingguan Djaja* article, described the transformative possibilities that accompanied wearing women's clothing in public:

> A few years later when I was in my twenties, I began to be brave enough to wear women's clothing. I remember well, at that time, there was a night market. One night, I took a bra, woven cloth, and clothing from my older sister. I also bought a horsehair switch [*cemara*]. I put on makeup [*berdandan*] at the house of a friend and just for that night went to the night market dressed like a woman. Later, wearing women's clothing I helped with a Malay orchestra that played at Cikini Kecil. All who were there said how pretty I was, and I felt very happy. (*Mingguan Djaja* 1968d, 8)

The happiness that came with these expanded possibilities for the practice of dandan had to be balanced with increasing efforts made by authorities and ordinary citizens to limit the public presence of bancis. One waria born in the 1940s explained how she too experienced the performance of dandan in happy terms, as a form of recognition by community and the self. She explained: "By doing dandan I became visible. I grew my hair long, and would wear makeup and women's clothing either at night or during the day if there was an event. I wouldn't practice dandan during the day if there wasn't an event. I wouldn't get ready in front of my family, but at a friend's house. I would put on lipstick, foundation, and blush before I went out. Simple and clear!" Yet even such close attention to the practice of dandan, always relative to whom they were visible to, did not guarantee safety for warias, particularly when they encountered an emergent regulatory apparatus that defined gender in terms of public nuisance.

From the first years after Indonesian independence, local-level police concerned with public order targeted warias in raids on city spaces. In May 1951, the Morality Police (Polisi Susila)— a branch of the municipal police concerned with ensuring public order—arrested a group of banci in the center of the city during a routine raid on what the journalist called "female prostitutes" (*Siasat* 1951, 13). As reported in the well-respected weekly magazine *Siasat*, published by a group of artists and intellectuals that included some of the most prominent Indonesian writers of the period, the police had discovered no fewer than eight banci among the women. The journalist claimed that several of the banci had come from poor neighborhoods in the city where they were part of a group of performers who appeared in rituals for weddings and other special settings: "On the stage they play the roles of women, according to their talents and the calling of their soul [*panggilan jiwa*]" (13). In an echo of firsthand reports during the colonial period, the author described the role of banci within weddings or performances as harmless. In contrast, the declaration made by these banci that they had the "soul of a woman"—and hence that they not only appeared in women's clothing but claimed public recognition that they were banci—was presented as at best a novelty, and at worst a form of fraud.

As their presence in colonial-era Batavia shows, with respect to dress and presentation, banci were nothing new or remarkable in the city. Given that banci wearing female clothing in public places had featured as a part of social life in Indonesia stretching back to the colonial period, why would a story of their discovery among a group of "female prostitutes" be newsworthy? The primary concern did not appear to be related to their sexuality, as reflected in the journalist's rather casually posed rhetorical question about male homosexuality: "What is wrong if there is a concealed [*dirahasiakan*] relationship between two men, so long as they are both enjoying it, and there isn't any force, and both are adults?" (*Siasat* 1951, 13). Rather than simply addressing public homosexuality, this story was chiefly concerned with bancis' ability to skillfully move across boundaries of gender and status. According to the account offered by the police in this article, what was most notable was the bancis' adoption of modern and hence desirable feminine appearances to claim recognition in public.

Much was made of the bancis' successful accomplishment of modern femininity. The journalist included a lengthy description of the appearances of the bancis in question, accompanied by photographs that looked like those gathered by the police as evidence of criminality: "Their cheeks and lips are made up with blush and lipstick. They adorn themselves with necklaces, earrings, and bracelets. Some of them even wear bracelets on their ankles! They wear dresses that are half New Look, and walk or ride bicycles wearing women's shoes" (*Siasat* 1951, 13). The bancis' adoption of New Look fashion, a globally prominent style that, as historian Stephen Gundle noted, "proclaimed the desirability of conspicuous extravagance" (2008, 199) in the mid-twentieth century, situated them as figures who styled an outwardly glamorous appearance for Indonesian national modernity. Yet the fact that they dressed in such a way not during the day on the street but in a darkened park at night highlights the limited spaces in which bancis' gender was an acceptable part of public life.

In this respect, concern for bancis' modern femininity emerged against the broader terrain of the body, on which nationalist struggle had at least partially been waged. Modern styles associated with femininity were lively symbols of debate about the character of the new nation appearing, as Carla Jones noted, in revolutionary novels in which "female characters enamored of European-style clothes, lipstick, and perfume failed to find happiness or met tragic fates" (2010, 275). Reading anxieties about bancis as part of a broader historical concern about the relationship between modern femininity and authenticity helps to illustrate the centrality of technologies of bodily transformation in defining national belonging. That bancis' femininity was pointedly referred to as dangerous because of the potential it held to deceive Indonesian men into illicit desire is one example of how the emergent naturalization of heterosexuality relied on technological interventions that defined individuals according to male/female and body/mind categories that relied on modern binary gender for legibility.

It was precisely this relationship between technologies for determining public gender and the body to which the journalist drew attention when remarking on the key problem with banci. The anxieties triggered by the capacity for anyone—Indonesian or European, man or woman—to access New Look clothing, makeup, and prosthetics surfaced in the accusation that bancis had committed an act of "deception," described by the journalist as follows: "These banci have deceived [menipu] because they have worn women's clothing and because of this, the activities of banci must be punished by law" (Siasat 1951, 13).[11] The arrest of these banci in 1951—foreshadowing more forceful efforts to regulate the visibility of warias by Jakarta's municipal authorities from the late 1960s onward—revealed just how little authorities were concerned with gender nonconformity or homosexuality as practices in and of themselves. Rather, gender and sexuality were mapped onto an overarching anxiety about the recognition of authenticity, and who had the power to grant it.

The charge of "deception" leveled at banci in this account illustrates the enduring preoccupation with appearances that was the hallmark of the governing race in the colonial period. The Dutch colonial state went to considerable efforts to limit individuals' appearances within the bounds of racial status as a visual assertion of European dominance. Replacing existing municipal-level codes concerning dress, a regulation stipulating the alignment between clothing and the race or status of the person wearing it was implemented as part of the first colonywide laws in 1872 (van Dijk 1997). The regulations underpinned what Arnout van der Meer (2020, 112) called an "ethnic sartorial hierarchy," a means through which colonial subjects were placed on a visual grid of difference. Clothing in turn was an important vehicle for contesting the hegemony of colonial rule, as Javanese people drew on it to demand that they be considered civilized and modern (van der Meer 2020). Expanding what were originally spatial forms of regulation policed at the municipal level, colonywide regulations governing appearances dramatized differences between groups of people and sought to secure European status in a context where the color of one's skin was not a reliable indicator of status. Although regulations limiting who could wear what in public waned and began to be challenged and were officially overturned with the dress circular of 1905, clothing and appearances continued to operate as a lively cultural vehicle for debating the boundaries of race and social status.[12]

Even as access to European dress provided new opportunities for participation in public life, so too did it reveal new anxieties about the degree to which appearances were a reliable form of recognition. James Siegel (1997, 86) observed the relationship between appearances and recognition as a central recurring theme in Malay-language literature in the early twentieth century. Describing the Dutch East Indies as a "society of appearances," Siegel wrote that "dress, instead of guarding identity, would hide it" (1997, 81–82). Siegel draws on one book published in 1938, *The Book of Fraud*, which introduced various cases of fraud involving deception through public attire. The author Soerohadipoerno (1938) offered the example of a Chinese person dressed in Western clothing as acceptable, with the caveat that the police should investigate whether such dress was consistent and hence a part of the person's authentic identity. Such concern reflects how the state's efforts to stabilize race rested on the presumption of a stable individual legal identity, one that was consistent at night and during the day, and in public and private. This emphasis on governing the public meanings of race through appearances served as one influential model through which gender was later interpreted and deployed as a marker of authentic difference.

Despite the official removal of limitations on dress in 1905, regulations governing appearances remained in the form of existing police regulations governing fraud, the legitimacy of which was premised on the necessity of the state to confer recognition on a person's identity. Other sources produced during the colonial period provide an illustration of the entwined logics of race and gender that established the format through which public appearances were evaluated in Indonesia. One description of the legal meanings of fraud was contained in the 1905 edition of a Malay-language manual of police regulations for native prosecutors written by W. F. Hasse and W. Boekhoudt: "a person who disguises themselves by dressing up in a costume not of their race [*bangsa*], or not belonging to their sex, with the exception of masked parades" (1905, 152).[13] An injunction that individuals could not wear clothing *not belonging to one's sex* apart from specific occasions was prefigured in a colonial sartorial logic that had been predominantly directed at race. The addition of regulations related to public gender appears to have been an innovation born out of a concern regarding disguises for the purposes of fraud, one that was absent from the earlier 1872 regulations governing dress, which only referred to race, ethnicity, and rank: "whoever appears in public, disguised in a different dress than the one corresponding with one's ethnicity or position, with the exception of masked or costumed parades" (cited in van der Meer 2020, 114). The addition of gender alongside race as a way to verify the authenticity of a person's legal identity on the basis of fraud highlights both the shared histories of these concepts and their continuity between the colonial and the postcolonial state.

Performing Indonesian Authenticity

The colonial histories of race that stressed the transformative potential of appearances continued to shape the meanings of citizenship in postcolonial Indonesia. This reflects the persistence of an understanding of the power of appearances to not only represent but transform, an understanding that brings to mind the pre-eighteenth-century European understanding that clothing could "*make* identity, rather than merely . . . signify its anterior existence" (Wahrman 2004, 179). Rather than suggesting that banci are a premodern residue of tradition, however, I suggest that such an understanding reflects the performative process through which the state seeks to impose a monopoly on powers of recognition. The primary mode through which the state sought to secure the boundaries of citizenship was to naturalize a concept of personhood that relied on an essential identity that could be mapped onto a stable outer appearance. Despite these efforts, the experience of warias highlights how the relationship between appearances and recognition often exceeded state control. Alternative networks of community, kin, and society could, in fact, make possible alternate routes to recognition.

Against the backdrop of a changing and contested national public in the 1950s, banci were viewed in some quarters as a problematic sign of the times and by others as a symbol of a national modernity that had already arrived. In this setting, the boundaries of belonging to an Indonesian public were themselves in flux, connected to urban forms of bodily cultivation and signs of progress that were not necessarily shared by all (C. Geertz 1976, 377). The meanings of the public performance of femininity for women were themselves far from settled, and some Javanese women had only begun to appear publicly in European clothes following Indonesian independence (Taylor 1997, 109).[14] Thus, early efforts to decipher the bodies of banci for clues of authenticity must be interpreted within the broader contestations under way over the relationship between modern binary gender and national identity. After all, the primary problem with banci was not so much their femininity but rather the meanings associated with their public performance of gender. Part of what made the appearance of banci on the streets of the capital in the new Indonesian nation so troubling was their skill and motivation to make themselves up according to a modern, international, feminine style.

Bancis' skills in feminine beauty prompted an ambiguous mixture of admiration and concern. In the account of the bancis arrested in central Jakarta in 1951, the journalist described them as "wearing woman's clothes, and clutching breasts made of balloons filled with water" (*Siasat* 1951, 13), a representation that seemed to focus on just how realistic the modern femininity of banci appeared to be. Similar to Maya's assertion that in making herself up with modern technologies she became "more woman than woman," access to modern technologies of feminization made it difficult to locate the difference between women and banci. This positioned banci as ambiguous and thus potentially deceptive figures, particularly if they were encountered on a city street late at night in poor lighting. Banci stressed that their feminine appearances served as the basis for their claim to authenticity. As one put it, "Just look at my clothes. Aren't these the clothes of a woman?" (*Siasat* 1951, 13). In presenting themselves in women's clothing and makeup and adopting women's bodily mannerisms, bancis did nevertheless uphold a modicum of heteronormativity that aligned with an emerging Indonesian national identity. The accusation that banci were engaging in deception stemmed, therefore, from the fact that their feminine public gender roused the desires of Indonesian men. This gave rise to the possibility that bancis could corrupt a nascent national identity premised on heterosexual desire. In a reversal of the assertion of moral authority on the basis of essentialist racial difference wielded by the Dutch, the author of the *Siasat* article claimed that the only men who were attracted to banci were those from among the diminishing population of Europeans in the city. Indonesian men were, in this author's view, unequivocally not interested in banci. The legibility offered by the existing category banci threatened to blur not only the boundaries of gender but the boundaries between heterosexual desire and same-sex desire. It was this ambiguity—one that had migrated out of concerns over racial appearances—that made banci not only objects of concern but viable national subjects as well.

The concern expressed for locating the origins of bancis' gender as deception in this account brings to mind the distinction between the asli (original, authentic, indigenous) and the palsu (false), a master trope within Indonesian political thought. Drawing attention to its roots in the colonial encounter, Tom Boellstorff has observed: "It [asli] is the ultimate criterion for belonging; what belongs to Indonesia and is deserving of recognition is that which is authentic" (2005, 214). The racialized foundations of the concept are apparent in early formulations of

Indonesian nationalism, which emphasized belonging in the nation for all original inhabitants of the archipelago but excluded those not easily defined on such
terms, a distinction directed at the nation's ethnic Chinese citizens (see Coppel
1983, 2–3). From the founding of the republic, Chinese citizens were subject to
increased state surveillance, requiring documentary proof of their legal citizenship (Strassler 2010, 133). This distinction established ethnic Chinese as inauthentic and suspect citizens, serving as a biopolitical foundation on which the
Indonesian state positioned itself as possessing ultimate authority over adjudi-
cating citizenship and belonging.

The analysis of this genealogy of a "crisis of authenticity" (Hoesterey 2016,
214) in the Indonesianist literature provides a rich set of insights, albeit focused
largely on the period during and after the New Order. The neologism *aspal*
(a combination of the words for asli and palsu) during the New Order highlighted anxieties about authenticity in a context where official objects could
themselves be false (Siegel 1998, 54). What is less well described in this literature
is how notions of asli and palsu were mapped onto technologies of gender and
sexual classification. Whereas gay men whose gender conforms with dominant
expectations of masculinity refer to themselves as "asli gay," through which "they
implicitly challenge the state's monopoly on designating what will count as tradition in Indonesia" (Boellstorff 2005, 86), the publicness of warias' gendering generates a specific conundrum. Given that their gender relies on dandan, or acts of
making up, waria may be designated by the state as inauthentic and false (Boellstorff 2007, 112). Yet this burden of belonging defined in terms of the asli is not
shouldered by waria alone but also by a broader array of subjects for whom outer
appearances mark not only a claim to recognition but an articulation of a sense
of self. For feminine subjects, often charged with inauthenticity (Jones 2010), the
relationship between inner and outer parts of the self generates a specific kind of
problem that can be addressed but also exposed by technological intervention.

Efforts to determine the meanings of gender to citizenship did not emerge out
of forms of colonial and postcolonial statecraft tied to the regulation of sex and
sexuality alone. An early concern for gender nonconformity in the postcolonial
state emerged out of anxieties over the meanings of dress and the physicality of
the body as it appeared within public space. After all, what made the arrested
banci "deceptive" was that they appeared not on the stage as part of a performance but as participants within public life who privileged alternative forms of
knowledge other than that offered by the state. If they presented and narrated
themselves as banci, what was to stop those around them from recognizing them
as such? Bancis' educated and successful efforts to transform their bodies, and
efforts to interpret them, highlight an understanding of gender as a semiotic
system of classification. The centrality of public gender to citizenship, routed

through extant logics of governing racial difference as authentic and nonauthentic, was a crucial aspect of the postcolonial state's effort to obtain control over the conferral of authenticity. Bancis' appearances and claims to self-knowledge rendered them potentially inauthentic citizens and as such subject to surveillance in public life.

This specific historical understanding of gender in postcolonial Indonesia is likely why banci pointed to their feminine appearances to stake a claim to recognition. But these claims could be countered by assertions that, despite their skill, bancis' deception could ultimately be uncovered by shifting observation beyond dress to the physicality of the body: "Their falsetto voice and behavior . . . is a mimicry of the behavior of women. . . . In size and height, they are exactly like a man, their skin and the shape of their mouth like a man, their voices are loud like men's, but they talk a lot, they have let their hair grow long, and some even coil it up" (*Siasat* 1951, 13). Yet even as the state's agents and others invested in limiting powers of recognition strove to pin down more stable meanings of banci through evidence that could be viewed on the surface of the body, the reduction of bancis' essence to sheer physicality was refuted by bancis themselves on other grounds—namely, that they had a woman's soul. Alongside appearances, then, was a narrative formulation that was tied to an understanding of an inner and to some degree essential self. Rather than questions of sexual morality alone, bancis' appearances in public brought to light nascent anxieties about categorical purity and the monopoly of the postcolonial state over the recognition of public gender. Gender crossing—and the very ambiguity indexed by the term *banci*—marked an instance of categorical confusion, highlighting that there could be a mismatch between appearances and authenticity. Tracing a concern for public gender within the cultural history of appearances in Indonesia presents important insights on the relationship between national identity and the performance of authenticity. Considered in light of a transgender studies literature that locates the symbolic force of "gendered deception" (Beauchamp 2019, 10) as a broad condition of histories of citizenship in the United States, attending to efforts to classify banci and bancis' own desires for recognition helps to both clarify the meanings and locate the limits of public gender in the expansion of state power.

Approached in this way, widespread hostility toward banci and other forms of gender nonconformity throughout Indonesia in the 1950s and 1960s can be understood as tied to a much broader crisis of control over the recognition of authenticity. Recalling earlier spatial modes of racial classification governing access to public space, bancis' increased visibility drew widespread ire. The limited glimpses of bancis' own experiences of gender are touching in their candid expression of a sense of a diminishing place in a changing conception of public comportment in the new nation. They highlight how warias were viewed as a disruption of the smooth functioning of social relations and the role of gender classification as a powerful force used to draw public limits around citizenship in Indonesia. In 1950s and 1960s Indonesia, where social censure and the ambiguous legal status of gender nonconformity restricted bancis to a limited range of spaces, gender nonconformity was gradually subject to increasing forms of regulation that denied belonging to those who did not conform to the clarity of binary gender. But rather than retreating from public life and into the private sphere, bancis and warias utilized their performances of modern femininity in new ways. Warias pushed out into public space and against the limitations of a narrow conception of authenticity wielded by the postcolonial state.

The Limits of Inclusion

Banci appeared in Jakarta against the backdrop of the transformation of the city into a modern metropolis and the capital of Indonesia. According to accounts provided by journalists and by warias themselves, their presence was viewed as a sign of the times, part of a changing urban landscape recovering from revolution and civil war. Banci gathered in front of the construction sites of the modernist buildings flanking major boulevards and railway stations in the late 1950s and early 1960s, and they organized into theater troupes that provided entertainment for the neighborhoods where they lived and within which they appear to have been an accepted part of the city's pluralistic social fabric. What is clear, however, is that this shift was not a simple movement from rejection to acceptance. Many warias expressed considerable sadness at the rejection from public space that they experienced during this period, even as they found some comfort in the limited places in which they found acceptance. Yet if, on the one hand, the visibility of the banci who gathered in cities at the birth of the new nation prompted condemnation, on the other, their skillful use of the dress, makeup, and body modification associated with an international feminine modernity laid a path to a fragile form of belonging.

Public gender was not secondary but crucial to the shifting meanings of who could participate in public life and on what basis. Although early interest in the appearance of banci in Jakarta's public space revolved around questions of public morality and potential for fraud, warias responded by asserting that theirs was a genuine and pressing desire for recognition that stemmed from having a woman's soul. This led to corresponding claims among banci that they yearned for a more stable gender presentation, as many of them described it, one that was visible at all times of day and across spaces of the city. At the birth of the Indonesian nation, banci thus advanced public gender as a new kind of consciousness holding the potential to bestow recognition. The adoption of modern women's clothing by banci in the early 1950s was not necessarily couched in terms of a definitive claim to the category woman through the public demonstration of femininity. After all, the universality of the category woman was not necessarily settled or given for any Indonesian, seeing that it was a category from which indigenous women were largely excluded throughout the colonial period. To warias, modern gender surfaced as the demonstration of a desire to participate in public life. In this respect, contestations over the public meanings of banci in the 1950s and 1960s can be read as part of a broader reorganization of who belonged to the categories "man" and "woman" and could thus accomplish recognition as citizens in the postcolonial state.

Banci achieved greater visibility in the immediate postindependence period at the precise moment that the newly independent state began to evaluate citizenship according to modern binary gender. Beyond establishing national identity as part of an "imagined community," furthered through the mass media, the body became a key locus of technological intervention through which the meanings of citizenship were made. Becoming Indonesian relied on the adoption of styles of dress and consumption that classified individuals according to binary gender based primarily on appearances. The semiotic meanings of gender classification, inheriting many of the logics of colonial-era technologies governing race, were chiefly fixed not on the interiority of the individual but on how banci might be integrated into a modern public. Yet bancis' own demands for recognition rested not only on outer appearances but also on the basis that they had "a woman's soul." This narrative formulation, one that had acquired scientific legibility in part owing to the meanings associated with the category transvestite since the early twentieth century, served to consolidate an emergent understanding of the meanings of authenticity in gendered terms. Warias' claims to recognition were not opposed to the logics of the colonial and postcolonial state but were shaped by the entanglement of race and gender in placing limits on who could appear in public and under what conditions. This history, and the critical importance of public gender that it helps to make visible, is vital for interpreting how technologies of citizenship were both made and unmade in the Indonesian city.

JAKARTA, 1968

To the Jakarta municipal government in the late 1960s, the increasing visibility of bancis on the streets of the city could no longer be swept aside. Even as it had long featured as a component of urban life, gender nonconformity was increasingly discussed in the pages of the popular press and in the offices of city hall as cause for concern. In early New Order Jakarta, a broad cross-section of the city's residents remarked on the brazen visibility of what was seen as the gender nonconformity of bancis, mostly as a novelty or a problem to be solved. Sensational reports asserted that some fifteen thousand bancis resided in the city. Claims that the city was being inundated served as justification for an unprecedented campaign with the twin aims of educating the public and intensifying the regulation of public space. Complaints about gender nonconformity, consistent with those that had been raised since the colonial period, largely focused on its public visibility. The increased visibility of bancis, however, prompted the city to modify the strategies that were deployed to contain it. This view is reflected in one police spokesperson's statement justifying police raids on the grounds that warias created an unpleasant view along the sides of Jakarta's newly constructed highways, "especially for foreign guests" (*Kompas* 1969a, 3).

Far from a superficial matter, public gender served as a key means through which individuals could be included or excluded from participation in the city. Within the apparatus of governing citizenship, warias played a central role. In order to better evaluate and solve what the city framed as a stubborn problem, municipal authorities worked with psychiatrists and other medical experts to assess and interpret warias down to the minutiae of bodily appearance. These efforts at definitional clarity resulted in the introduction of new terminology in the form of the term *wadam*, a combination of the words for Adam and Eve. Ali Sadikin, the governor of Jakarta from 1966 to 1977, played a crucial role in this effort, popularizing the term *wadam* and formalizing its use within the city bureaucracy. Those who identified with wadam (and later waria) evaluated the creation and resultant proliferation of knowledge about the new term as an affirmative form of recognition tied to its connotation as more modern and presentable than the term *banci*. Warias commonly reflected on this period as heralding an opportunity to achieve greater clarity and a more respectful term of address, even as the city administration framed gender nonconformity in terms of two entwined sets of regulatory logics, those related to "public order" (*ketertiban umum*) and "public morality" (*kesusilaan umum*).

To those who identified as such, these new terms of address mattered chiefly because they contributed to what they saw as an improved public image. According to newspaper accounts and warias' own recollections of the period, the adoption of *wadam* and *waria* was accompanied by the adoption of higher standards of modern feminine appearance and its presentation across all public settings. Correspondingly, municipal policies no longer limited efforts at regulation to the wholesale exclusion of bancis from public places but made individuals responsible for the status of their own visibility and the publics that they imagined themselves a part of. City authorities encouraged warias to limit their appearances to more respectable settings and to improve their appearances through municipal training in vocational skills, such as salon work and bridal makeup. Thus, even as the ambiguous social acceptance achieved by wadam emerged in dialogue with regulations that positioned them on terms akin to a public nuisance, the recognition provided by the city administration marked a decisive historical break from the widespread rejection experienced by bancis in the 1950s and 1960s. For this reason, many warias remembered the beginning of the New Order as a welcome change.

This chapter charts the historical emergence of the terms *wadam* and *waria* by examining their origins in municipal-level innovations aimed at maintaining public order. Although the meanings of these new terms were shaped by an emergent body of national scientific and medical expertise about "transvestitism" and "transsexuality," a more far-reaching set of technologies for addressing nonconformity emerged via the spatial format granted by the specific texture of municipal governance.[1] Looking beyond more spectacular forms of bodily transformation through technologies of science and medicine—common fields in which the conceptual frameworks of Euro-American interpretations of trans history have been developed—clarifies how the meanings of gender emerged through processes of borrowing and translation. Warias' integration into the workings of municipal regulations revealed how public gender was assessed and managed as an aesthetic and moral problem alongside other city-level concerns such as sanitation, housing, and traffic.

In the view of the city government, the integration of gender nonconformity into a format of governance of public order rested on a specific problem of participation that required, to follow Christopher Kelty, "tool[s] to make sense of the existence of immediate, affective, and ethical intuition common to very different collectives, an existence that becomes visible through cases of perplexity" (Kelty 2019, 262). The earnest perplexity with which municipal authorities assessed the "problem of banci," as they commonly called it, soon came to be integrated within a broader set of governmental techniques that hinged on enrolling these citizens into a collective conceptualized as society (masyarakat). This was a largely depoliticized vision of collective participation underpinned by the sociotechnical imaginary of the New Order state. Accordingly, warias' engagement in civic life was defined in terms of an individualized form of self-improvement oriented toward economic development. Becoming more beautiful—as warias referred to their capacity to accomplish a modern international style of femininity—also aimed at integration into the economic productivity of the developmentalist state. It is relatively unsurprising that approaches to managing warias were first developed and tried out at the municipal level, given that cities are commonly a laboratory for developing new modes and methods of governing that exceed a binary of functionality or aesthetics (Valverde 2011; Moon 2015). And it was at the scale of the city, within its remit for regulating public order, where the boundaries of who belonged to what gender were commonly adjudicated and policed in other contexts too (Sears 2015). Yet in the Indonesian case, more important still was perhaps the emphasis placed on granting warias the skills and expertise they needed to improve their appearances. The city provided warias with training to attain these skills as the means through which they would be able to increase their participation in public life, and in turn fulfill their aim to be accepted by society. From their initial meeting with Sadikin and the integration into municipal governance through new terminology that followed, warias became experts at adeptly navigating municipal governance and the space for participation that it allowed. Warias' engagements with public gender, even when addressed at the level of the self, did not reflect the forms of internalization that Foucault has characterized as "the deeply buried truth of that truth about ourselves which we think we possess in our immediate consciousness" (1978, 69). Through a dynamic process of seeing and being seen, warias' participation in public gender developed forms of recognition and citizenship that challenge dominant Euro-American theorization of the political implications of the modern self as an endless process of individualization, which sees the decline of shared forms of community and no social units other than that of the individual.

Scrutinizing how trans femininity was addressed at the scale of the city contributes to a better understanding of the moral texture of technology in Indonesian postcolonial modernity. The status that Sadikin granted to gender nonconformity cannot be understood as wholesale acceptance, but rather as a conditional integration within the existing grounds of spatial regulation. The category of wadam was evaluated as a problem of spatial governance, on terms that framed it as a *legal but nonconforming* status, extending a conditional form of recognition on the grounds that it was not officially condoned. Referring to the history of planning law in cities in North America, Mariana Valverde (2011) described "legal non-conforming use" as a reflection of the ambiguity characteristic of governing cities. Exceptions to the law are in such instances built into the law itself. Given the complex contingencies of municipal governance, Valverde eschews a perspective of top-down rationality in favor of close attention to how "governing urban disorder through embodied, experiential, and relational categories is a necessary component of contemporary urban governance" (2011, 280). The ambiguous recognition granted to warias by the Jakarta government reflects an extension of this character of city governance to the individual body—a necessity to contend with practices that, for practical or economic reasons, could not be entirely excluded. The history of regulating gender nonconformity in Indonesia therefore departs from common theorizations both of state-led development (e.g., Scott 1998) and of gender (e.g., Butler 1990), which in different ways tend to stress a top-down format that grants a uniformity to the modern state and its legal regulations. Rather, in Jakarta, efforts to enforce standards of what men and women should look like proceeded through a necessarily uneven codification of gender nonconformity on spatial grounds, as a component of governance at the scale of the city. Warias achieved a fragile but productive form of recognition through participation in this form of the city and its politics.

The Politics of Presentation

The recognition of *wadam* as a legal but nonconforming status, specific to events that unfolded in Jakarta, took place against the backdrop of the early years of the Suharto presidency. The former military general had come to power by claiming to have suppressed a coup in 1965, a politically motivated maneuver followed by a paroxysm of mass violence toward real and imagined members of the Indonesian Communist Party.[2] A critical yet often overlooked aspect of Suharto's claims to political legitimacy, apparent from the founding of the New Order, was the role of gender as a key symbol for the expansion of state power (Wieringa 2002). During the thirty years of Suharto's presidency, the subordination of women remained a key component of the New Order state, underpinning the gendered basis for development and political claims to the maintenance of order on which it rested.

The gendered symbolism of the New Order not only operated at an ideological level but established the contours along which state citizenship and national belonging was lived and experienced on an everyday basis. In this context, citizenship was mediated through the demand that citizens participate in the nuclear family and the gendered and sexual forms of reproduction on which it was predicated (Boellstorff 2005). Centralized state organizations for the wives of civil servants and military officers were key institutions through which women were transformed into mothers and housewives, responsible for the domestic sphere but accountable ultimately to men (Suryakusuma 1996). Given that this state-sanctioned system of patriarchal control rested on a very narrow definition of femininity as wifehood and motherhood, the degree of acceptance extended to trans women is surprising. But the very conditions of city governance—invested in limiting the visibility of gender nonconformity in public space—paradoxically encouraged a more flexible engagement with power that extended beyond and indeed transformed possibilities for belonging within a resolutely heteronormative state ideology.

Efforts to craft a workable system through which to regulate those identified as belonging to the category of wadam in Jakarta in 1968 had a profound bearing on the integration of gender into technological systems of development on the national stage. The emphasis on appearances migrated out from urban governance, contributing to efforts to stabilize the meanings granted to masculinity and femininity around a specific aesthetic of dress and comportment linked to the reproductive role. Approaching the scale of the city as a microcosm of the nation offers a theoretical counterpart to the focus in Indonesianist anthropology on the heterogeneity of state development at its margins, as reflected in rich accounts of state violence and neglect directed at indigenous peoples and the rural poor (Tsing 1993; Li 2007; Chao 2022). What is distinct about the gradual integration of gender nonconformity (a marginal status, to be sure) into the technological texture of New Order development was that it relied on an understanding of gender in terms of an aesthetic standard tied to the adjudication of presentability in public. Rather than fixed moral positions harnessed to a deep and abiding interiority, the meanings associated with public gender were fast-changing and challenging to regulate. The naturalization of gender as a putatively normative yardstick for appearing in public space served to buttress dominant class and racial norms of comportment and dress. The city government's efforts to regulate wadam reveals that, rather than premised on an assessment of bodies as already definitively men or women at the level of the individual, the meanings of public gender rested on a shifting concept of status tied to a range of meanings including aesthetics, dress, physical body, and the social context within which it appeared. It was precisely the gaps and ambiguities in meanings associated with public gender that ultimately allowed for the integration of wadam as a legal but nonconforming status at the municipal level.

The broader sets of regulations of public order and public morality not only trained on gender nonconformity but were a key component of military rule during the New Order. Public order, on one hand, served as the initial justification for Suharto's ascendancy and remained key to political claims to legitimacy (Barker 2001). The regulation of public morality, on the other hand, was central to what Evelyn Blackwood (2007, 296) called the "deployment of gender," referring to the central role of reproductive heterosexuality as an organizing principle of social and political life.[3] These twin disciplinary norms of public order and public morality—and the "public" (*umum*) to which they referred— became most apparent on city streets, where city-level ordinances struggled to define the boundaries of conformity and nonconformity not in abstract terms but through enforceable procedures and rules. As a moral concern addressed on spatial grounds, gender nonconformity was ensnared in a wider logic through which the appearance of femininity in public space was adjudicated and disciplined. Warias and street-based female sex workers (referred to as prostitutes in municipal governance) in particular were framed by an overlapping set of regulatory logics that targeted both their movement through the city and what styles of clothing and makeup they adopted when they did so.[4] Reflecting its origins in the racial history of spatial regulation in the colonial period, efforts to contend with public forms of gender nonconformity were not born out of perceptions of an individualized pathology linked to an innate sex or sexuality. Instead, the city sought to govern the femininity of warias on the more encompassing yet flexible basis that their visibility was a disturbance to public order.

A concern for the visibility of gender nonconformity in urban public settings was not new. Inheriting the racialized logics underpinning spatial governance during the colonial period, the Jakarta government gradually took a series of steps to formalize the regulation of gender nonconformity from the late 1960s onward. Spurred by reports of an explosive expansion of the visibility of warias, in April 1969 the commission of the municipal representative body that was responsible for public order adopted a resolution on the "problem of wadam" (Jakarta Special Region 1969, 11–12). The minutes of the meeting record potential points of action raised, with several suggesting the participation of warias themselves in the process. The commission also referred to the Banci Research Project, which was based on the scientific evaluation of twenty-five banci by two psychiatrists at the University of Indonesia (Masdani 1968; Ling 1968). The actions proposed included limiting wadam to a single location to reduce their visibility, holding a public campaign in which they could showcase their talents, and extending to them the freedom to engage in their activities under the watchful eye of the city government.

The integration of wadam into a regime of regulating gender premised on public order was consolidated in the years that followed, on terms framed in relation to morality (*kesusilaan*). From at least 1972 onward, the number of warias was reported in monthly data collected by the city, alongside the number of "prostitutes" and "pimps" tabulated according to district (City of East Jakarta 1972). In that same year, a sweeping regulation on public order issued by the Jakarta government stated, "Any person whose performance of acts disturbing morality [*susila*] or public order [*ketertiban umum*] is banned from being on the street, the park, and in public places" (Jakarta Special Region 1972). Listed among behaviors referred to as a disruption of public morality were those as sedate as kissing and congregating in city parks at night.

The regulation of gender nonconformity in terms of public order did not lead to unequivocal acceptance but shifted concern to how the visibility of warias could best be managed. Warias could not be managed through exclusion from public space alone. The key disciplinary apparatus through which the city sought to reduce the visibility of gender nonconformity was the integration of wadam into the official governmental programs known as "guidance" (*pembinaan*), comprising vocational training in skills in fields of feminine beauty. Such programs for wadam were officially endorsed by the city's Department of Social Welfare in 1969. A keyword of paternalistic state development projects that sought to extend territorial control over peasant and indigenous populations for the purposes of resource extraction, "guidance"—also used in the passive construction "being guided" (*di bina*) and as the verb "to guide" (*membina*)—was premised on a hierarchical chain of command that reflected the military origins of the concept (see Li 2007; Tsing 1993). Waria leaders, such as Maya, commonly referred to themselves as "being guided" by the governor and the city administration, with various intermediaries between them and those in power.

In this respect, warias encountered a regime of paternalistic forms of social welfare that paralleled the forms of discipline targeted at women, including through organizations for the wives of civil servants (Suryakusuma 1996). Whereas guidance for women was predicated on their relationship to the family and the domestic sphere, guidance aimed at warias was premised on encouraging an improved presentation through participation in the public realm of work. Guidance for warias therefore took the form of programs teaching skills associated with feminine beauty that could be translated into professional vocations, including tailoring, bridal makeup, and hairdressing. In interviews, senior warias often spontaneously shared the city's assessment that vocational training would allow them to escape street-based forms of sex work and hence to avoid disrepute associated with public sexuality. Warias stressed that guidance—both of one another and by the city—could improve individuals' appearances through the cultivation of a more polished femininity. These individual efforts could in turn play a role in elevating the presentation, and thus the status, of warias as a group.

These more modernized efforts to regulate gender nonconformity via "guidance" through improved aesthetic standards of feminine beauty relied on the recruitment of warias into the administrative function of the city. Maya described how the city had asked warias to create local organizations and nominate a corresponding leader in each district in the city. These organizations mirrored Jakarta's administrative structure, with one in each of the five separate city districts— North, South, East, West, and Central Jakarta—that composed the special region. Each leader was responsible for maintaining control over those who lived in her area, which meant dealing with petty crime undertaken by members of the group, overseeing the regulation of sex work on the streets, and mobilizing warias to participate in municipal activities such as dance performances. Again echoing the city's own structure, a system emerged around this time for nominating a single waria who would be a leader for the whole of Jakarta and who would serve as a community representative accountable to the governor. Maya explained that this system allowed warias to establish personal relationships with individuals in various powerful organizations and within the state apparatus, connections that over time allowed them to advocate for greater social inclusion.

The objective of loosely integrating warias into the structures of city governance primarily served the political and economic interests of public order, even as it allowed warias to improve their social standing. This aspect of managing city space parallels a broader characteristic of New Order governance that Joshua Barker called a "bureaucratic surveillance machine" (2001, 26), which rested on the ambiguous integration of state security forces and criminal gangs at the neighborhood level. During the New Order, criminal gangs often collaborated directly with security forces and local governments, a means to enable an image of order while concealing the origins of state terror (Barker 2001). In a similar manner, the city did not condone warias but rather oversaw them from a distance by entrusting the enforcement of discipline to warias themselves. This system of governance emerged in dialogue with exceptional forms of violence meted out to other nonconforming groups, the most well-known example being the "mysterious killings" of the early 1980s, during which time New Order military and paramilitary groups murdered an estimated five thousand petty criminals (Bourchier 1990).[5] Although warias appear to have largely escaped this more violent register of state governmentality, they did gain recognition on parallel terms to it. Their visibility and responses to state governmentality were therefore shaped by broader concerns over who could occupy public space and under what conditions during the New Order.

Whatever benefits warias received through their participation in vocational guidance programs linked to feminine beauty, it is important to bear in mind that such programs were frequently coercive on some level. Participation was often but not always punitive, and I heard of many occasions when it served as a component of detention for "rehabilitation" following capture during routine police raids. The city thus framed guidance programs not necessarily as an embrace of warias or as a reward for their presence, but as rehabilitative mechanisms reserved for individuals who disrupted public order. Seen from the vantage point of protecting the public from moral disorder and as a form of discipline that sought to encourage acceptable participation in the economic life of the city, encouraging warias to work in salons would restrict their appearance to certain locations that heightened idealized standards of masculine and feminine gender presentation. It is difficult to evaluate the extent to which such programs benefited warias. Nevertheless, decades later, many warias reflected on these forms of guidance not as an intrusive manifestation of state power but as an important means through which they made themselves more presentable and in turn earned greater recognition and respect. And this opportunity for important if piecemeal recognition rested, along with an effort to cultivate an improved presentation and display it to one's neighbors, on the idiosyncratic relationship that waria developed with the city's governor, Ali Sadikin.

The Governor of Waria

On the evening of August 2, 1968, a delegation of twenty-two wadam held a meeting with Ali Sadikin. The respected national daily newspaper *Kompas* reported that a representative named Lidya had addressed the governor directly. At the governor's official residence, located in an exclusive enclave in the center of the city, Lidya made a plea for assistance. She stated that wadam were subject to intolerable forms of exclusion and abuse at the hands of their fellow residents. When they appeared during the day in public places wearing women's clothing, Lidya explained, wadam faced verbal and physical abuse. To avoid this abuse, they gathered clandestinely, meeting at night in obscure locations, such as along highways and railway tracks. Because of this, the public associated them with moral impropriety and public indecency. In response to their predicament, Sadikin—an innovative and charismatic urban reformer and respected former naval officer—not only declared that Lidya was a member of a group "whose social rights must be protected" but also called on the city's residents to come together to assist them (*Kompas* 1968a, 2).

As an early demonstration of official interest in the conditions of gender non-conformity in the city, the results of this meeting resonated in the years and decades that followed. Although more than fifty years had elapsed since this initial meeting in 1968, the warias I met who had been in Jakarta during the late 1960s and early 1970s frequently referred to Sadikin using terms of endear-ment such as "Uncle Ali" (Bang Ali) and "The Governor of Waria" (Gubernur Waria). Drawing on a powerful shared narrative of 1968 Jakarta as the begin-ning of a "golden age," warias remembered the governor as playing a pivotal role in assisting them to become "accepted by society."[6] Many warias credited Sadikin's support for the "guidance" programs run by the city, drawing on the official term used in legal regulations and policy documents. Access to training in vocational fields such as salon work and bridal makeup had allowed warias to demonstrate their use to society, participating in forms of economic activity that allowed neighbors and kin to evaluate them as citizens (Boellstorff 2007). Over time, older and higher-ranking warias became responsible for providing this vocational training and delivering it as representatives of the city. But despite a common refrain of admiration for Sadikin, these forms of vocational training were by no means entirely benevolent. As reflected in warias' frequent complaint that police raids had always and would always be a part of urban life, the desired aim of the municipal government was to ensure that the visibility of waria and other gender-nonconforming citizens—among which the city included beggars and sex workers—could be managed in a way that did not cause offense to the general public (*masyarakat umum*).

Directly appointed governor in 1966 by the first president, Sukarno, Sadikin remained in the position until his retirement at the end of the first decade of the Suharto presidency in 1977. Although the position of the Jakarta governor was close to that of a city mayor in some respects, the city's status as the capital city and administrative designation of province meant that since the founding of the city it was an important political post that was implicated in national politics (Malo and Nas 1997; Nas and Malo 2000). Particularly during the New Order, the Jakarta governor was "responsible to the head of state rather than the urban citizenry" (Kusno 2014, 21). Despite this, Sadikin exercised a considerable degree of independence, both tackling problems in the city and even extending a vocabulary of rights and social justice for marginal citizens despite the restricted environment for political participation in the New Order (Simone 2014, 37). Nevertheless, Sadikin's description of the city as a "battlefield" (Budiman 1969a, 75), reflects the strong emphasis that he placed on discipline in his vision for modernizing the metropolis. His interest in warias, therefore, emerged at the intersection of spatial anxieties about the public visibility of nonconforming bodies and an emergent governmental style for managing the population.

Sadikin implemented far-reaching reforms in Jakarta during his tenure. They included regulation of migration flows from the countryside, modernization of the city's appearance, and implementation of various administrative changes that improved government efficiency. Sadikin also applied his modernizing zeal to the regulation of gender and sexuality, including the conversion of informal red-light districts for female sex workers into state-sanctioned complexes offering access to health care and other support services (Abeyasekere 1990). For example, Sadikin oversaw a pilot birth-control project premised on "total community mobilization" (Hull and Hull 2005, 20–21), an approach that would later serve as the template for the New Order's family planning scheme—lauded on the international stage even as participation in it was often compelled—in cities, towns, and villages throughout Indonesia (Niehof and Lubis 2003; Dwyer 2002). Such innovations extending state control over women's and trans bodies were double-edged, both offering fragile forms of recognition and resulting in pernicious surveillance.

Each of these efforts attracted strident criticism from conservative Islamic groups and those aligned with them, who considered Sadikin's efforts to regulate sexuality as representative of a broader problem of moral decay that was in part caused by the openness to international development in the early New Order. Willard Hannah (1968), writing in the American Universities Fieldstaff Reports in 1968, conveyed that Sadikin's apparent endorsement of the new term *wadam* caused a major scandal among conservative Islamic social groups in the city. One magazine editorial, responding to a 1969 constitutional court review of pornography, listed wadam as "pornographic" alongside prostitution, partying all night, nightclubs, sex work, and dancing in dance halls (*Varia* 1970, 25). This stance condemning the visibility of wadam does not appear to have been a minority view. The prominent Islamic scholar Buya Hamka ([1975] 1981, 275), writing in the mid-1960s in his famous five-volume *Tafsir Al-Azhar*, a commentary on the Quran, criticized those whom he called banci for flaunting themselves in front of the Al-Azhar Mosque in the southern reaches of the city, brazenly "facing the public."[7]

The governor's controversial if ambiguous endorsement of warias, and criticism of him for it by Islamic leaders, must be understood as unfolding against a broader reorganization of the visibility of warias in the city. In some accounts— including from those who remembered him—Sadikin couched his interest in warias in terms of a desire to encourage greater social acceptance of them by the city's residents. The official magazine of the Jakarta government framed these efforts on paternalistic terms: "If it wasn't for Governor Ali Sadikin, who sees all citizens of the capital city as his children, they would be fated to live out their days as isolated and miserable wretches" (*Mingguan Djaja* 1968e). This comment highlights the developmental subtext that was the basis of Sadikin's interest; *wadam* was a term that designated the status of trans visibility as a legal but nonconforming status, framed in pursuit of a broader vision of a respectable society founded on public order. Seen in developmental terms, warias' accomplishment of a more stable femininity was thus seen as holding the promise to prevent social stigma in ways that recall mid-century Euro-American models of sex (Gill-Peterson 2018, 119). In this respect, Sadikin's invitation to warias to participate in their own process of development not only reflected his attitude toward the management of the aesthetic of the city more broadly, but reflected the emergence of a modern regime of public gender as a model for asserting authority over the recognition of who was and who was not a fully developed citizen.

Details of Sadikin's support for warias surfaced later in 1968, when the tabloid magazine *Selecta* published an account of Sadikin and his wife Nani attending a waria performance. Accompanying the article was a photograph that showed Sadikin seated alongside Sonny Sudarma, who a year later would win first place in Jakarta's inaugural beauty contest for warias, which I discuss in chapter 4 (*Kompas* 1969b, 2). The same account also reported that Sadikin had dispatched his representative Haji Sapi'ie to a meeting with warias held at city hall (*Selecta* 1968; Sadikin 1992, 484). This meeting, along with the publication of a photograph of the governor of Jakarta assembled with a group of glamorously dressed warias, demonstrated a recognition of their emergent position within the public life of the city.

Even as Sadikin's engagement with warias marked an important shift, the emphasis on spatial governmentality was inseparable from the historical dynamics of municipal governance originating in the colonial period. Efforts to improve the appearance of cities were an early site of political mobilization following the establishment of municipalities in Indonesia in 1905 (Nas 1990). The emergence of municipal governance revealed explicitly how the participatory promise of citizenship was problematized by racial hierarchies, with privilege granted to the European male population (Malo and Nas 1991; Roosmalen 2015).[8] Revealing the entanglement of morality and aesthetics in the Dutch East Indies, European citizens were also preoccupied with "native" villages "situated within the limits of their municipality, but which remained outside municipal jurisdiction" (Nas 1990, 102), particularly when the lack of sanitation of neighboring or indistinguishable nonconforming Indonesian villages became a threat to the health of the European citizenry. Recalling sumptuary laws governing appearances on the basis of racialized hierarchy during the colonial period, the apparently neutral domain of the sociotechnical apparatus of civic improvement during the New Order was key to establishing public gender as a constitutive feature of the boundaries of citizenship.

The spatial management of gender nonconformity demands reckoning with the municipality as defined by more than administrative or political boundaries. Viewing warias from the scale of the city reveals that their capacity to articulate desires for acceptance in the early New Order was built on a strategic negotiation with regulations governing city space. Given warias' experience of strict social sanctions on their public visibility in the 1950s and 1960s, Sadikin's extension to them of a limited legal but nonconforming status highlights the unique opportunities that municipal regulations provide to bestow recognition. The recruitment of the citizenry in these efforts brings to mind Nikolas Rose's (1999, 136) description of "government through community," one premised on a "vision of the building of responsible communities, prepared to invest in themselves." Yet rather than a shift toward an individualized form of ethics as "the active and practical shaping by individuals of the daily practices of their own lives in the name of their own pleasures, contentments or fulfilments" (Rose 1999, 179), limited to the private sphere, warias' engagement with Sadikin on the terms of their visibility highlights the centrality of a collectively defined public as a crucial scale of modern governance. In Sadikin's Jakarta, the social collective was governed as a seeing public, one that was stabilized through the mobilization of gender as a sociotechnical imaginary.

In some respects, warias accomplished a degree of recognition that was unthinkable in the United States at the same time. Esther Newton describes how white, middle-class, gay men in the late 1960s carefully negotiated public performances of femininity to protect their privileged status, given its widely recognized symbolic relationship to homosexuality (Newton 1979). Those for whom public gender was more than performance faced significant social and legal sanctions (see also Valentine 2007). In the United States too, since the nineteenth century, municipal governments played a crucial role in regulating public gender in the form of misdemeanor offenses for gender crossing (Sears 2015). Public gender was a key locus for social discipline linked to visibility that drew on norms of sexuality, race, and class in ways that combined what Clare Sears called a "voyeuristic compulsion to see with the regulatory desire to control" (2015, 92). Rather than reflecting isolated local concerns, these legal regulations established "gender normativity as a precondition for full belonging, denying access to the city and nation to those who fell outside its bounds" (Sears 2015, 138). In the United States, the effects of legal and social sanctions on gender crossing at the municipal level operated to push white, middle-class, trans individuals into the private sphere, a condition that influenced a broader emphasis in normative political claims to gender and sexuality as private rights (Valentine 2007, 241–43). In Indonesia, however, the municipal regulation of wadam and waria—and policies directed at those identified as such—enhanced their visibility, even as the city sought to extend spatial and temporal control over public gender with greater precision.

Indeed, even as the Jakarta government addressed warias as a problem to be solved, by the time that Sadikin retired in 1977, they occupied a far more reputable social position than had been the case when he had entered office just over a decade earlier. Sadikin took pride in this achievement. In one biographical account, he wrote: "When I began to guide waria, who in the past would be showered with stones and abuse on the street, I was criticized. But I guided them [*membina mereka*], and now they are accepted by society" (cited in Roem 1977, 2:230). In part because of Sadikin's interest, warias developed a national reputation as skilled workers in beauty salons and as hairdressers, finding in this work a level of recognition that provided conditional acceptance. This reputation was scaled up to the level of the nation, no doubt in part because Jakarta, as the capital and as a region with the legal status of a province, had (and has) an outsize degree of influence in Indonesian political and social life. Indeed, it appears that legal innovations in the city facilitated warias' increased acceptance at the national level, rather than the other way around. This acceptance relied on the disciplinary apparatus of guidance, underpinned by the emancipatory promise that technologies of femininity could be harnessed to efforts to achieve development rather than causing collective moral decay.

The Jakarta Fair

The first Jakarta Fair, held in June and July 1968, was a watershed moment when warias demonstrated a public relationship to the New Order state's sociotechnical imaginary. The fair was a stage in the heart of the capital from which body-centered forms of consumption spoke directly to national development, and warias drew on it to fashion themselves as a part of Indonesian national modernity.

Although the fair combined the trappings of a commercial trade exposition with modern forms of entertainment, to warias it was a milestone when they asserted an association with polished, if at that time unusual, norms of modern feminine beauty. The 1968 Jakarta Fair was established by Ali Sadikin as a festival accessible to all citizens, in part designed to bring the people more closely into a national project of development that rested on social order (Kusno 2014, 21). Writing in his autobiography, Sadikin reflected on the fair as an opportunity for the city's residents to come together around a shared cultural imaginary

(Sadikin 1992, 195–96). For warias, it was one of the earliest moments at which they were visible to a respectable public audience and hence could start to imagine the possibility of more widespread social acceptance. The understanding that vocational training in fields related to feminine beauty was key to the advancement of warias appears to have been influenced by the role that they played at the inaugural Jakarta Fair. The fair saw the first professional performance groups of warias at two venues, Sasana Andrawina and Paradise Hall (*Mingguan Djaja* 1968d). Although these venues did offer a new opportunity for warias' economic advancement and collective identification as a group, they also enhanced a suite of policies that sought to manage the visibility of warias in the city through disciplinary sanctions.

The presence of warias at the first Jakarta Fair shines a light on the role that public gender played in shaping state citizenship. It was at the level of the city that warias were first recognized, if as a legal but nonconforming status, giving rise to a possibility that male and female were not the only categories of gender classification possible within the boundaries of modern citizenship. The adoption of the new terms *wadam* and *waria* and the vocational training programs that accompanied warias' integration into state development offered them the means through which they could contest their classification as a public nuisance. Warias' deft manipulation of this ambiguous status is reflected in the way that their ability to improve their appearances exceeded the narrow purview of gender as it was governed through city-run guidance programs. Rather than framing vocational rehabilitation in terms of discipline, warias asserted that it helped them satisfy their own desires to become experts in the application of technologies required to achieve modern femininity.

An early means through which this altered understanding of warias was communicated to a wider public was in the form of an information campaign about their presence. Running through October and November of that year, following the Jakarta Fair, a series of articles titled "The Problem of Banci" was published in the city's official weekly magazine. The series was made up of dozens of didactic essays that conveyed to Jakarta's residents both the steps being taken by the city and the role that ordinary citizens could play in managing the increasing visibility of warias on the streets. It included interviews and investigations based on observations of the everyday lives of trans women in Jakarta (*Mingguan Djaja* 1968e); translations of Western psychological and medical taxonomies of gendered and sexual difference (*Mingguan Djaja* 1968c); historical accounts of "transvestites" in Europe, such as Charles d'Éon (*Mingguan Djaja* 1968a); and a translation of a sensationalist article decrying same-sex sexuality between women first published in the United States (*Mingguan Djaja* 1968b). Possibly emerging out of Sadikin's meeting with waria leader Lidya in August 1968, this campaign reflected an unprecedented public effort by the city to communicate and redefine what it framed as the problem of warias to residents of the city.

In these accounts, the government reiterated its official position that gender nonconformity was best addressed through vocational rehabilitation. Firsthand reports containing the narratives of warias were sympathetic, making a clear attempt to educate the readership that being waria was no fault of their own. The articles offered one of the earliest definitions contained in an official publication that the appearances of warias was an inescapable aspect of who they are, their femininity residing not just in their clothing but in practices and behaviors linked to an inner sense of self: "They don't only wear men's clothing, but their ability to chop vegetables and fry food can't be beaten by genuine women" (*Mingguan Djaja* 1968d, 7). This same account, one of the last to appear in the series of articles, included a plea from a waria that was addressed directly to the governor for resources for warias to acquire the skills required to enact a more presentable femininity. Warias' efforts to accomplish recognition rested both on improvements to appearances and acquisition of skills required to achieve a convincing modern femininity.

It follows that a key concern pursued by warias was the discrimination that they faced in obtaining employment. A crucial component of warias' request to Sadikin, advanced since their first meetings, was that he mediate between them and an employer who had not paid them in full for their work as entertainers (*Selecta* 1968, 18). But the economic aspects of work were not all that appeared to matter to warias. Rather, participation in fields of employment related to feminine beauty was also tied to the cultivation of an ethical self in public, practices that bring to mind what Tom Boellstorff (2005, 209) characterized as "a kind of personhood-as-career where 'success' carries momentous implications for recognition and belonging." In some settings, such as beauty salons, the work that warias undertook could not be separated from *prestasi*, a term used to refer to morally worthy good deeds that are both tied to self-improvement yet are a way in which individuals advance participation in a collective understanding of national belonging (Boellstorff 2007, 105). It was these forms of activism and mobilization, emerging at the intersection of economic advancement and ethical cultivation, that resulted in the first formal organizations for warias and the intensification of their connection to city governance.

Sadikin's successor Cokropanolo, who became governor in 1977, continued to advance policies that stressed warias' improvement through the cultivation of vocational skills. In this way, the city continued to link self-cultivation through public gender to economic productivity. Cokropanolo stated that his plans were to expand warias' participation in training programs in sewing and flower arranging so that they could be "of use" within society (*Kompas* 1977, 3). In 1982,

Kompas reported that, in one three-year period, 271 warias had graduated from training courses in fields related to beauty: "Upon completion, the warias received a number of beauty products and other tools, as well as enough money to start their own salon. Many of them already have experience working in salons and in show business. As many as eighty participants returned to their region of origin and opened a business there" (*Kompas* 1982, 3). The citywide leader of warias at the time, Myrna Bambang, was quoted as stressing this improvement in ethical terms: "Skills are very meaningful for warias, because with it we can demonstrate we have prestasi, be valued by society, and live off the proceeds of our skills." In the years that followed, salon work became closely associated with warias, an occupation through which they could transform citizens into "better representatives of proper modern Indonesian womanhood and manhood" (Boellstorff 2007, 111). Guidance policies developed and implemented at the municipal level played a profound role in shaping warias' position within national society.

Even as this transformation continued to unfold across the 1970s and early 1980s, aided by an increased access to technologies related to modern femininity and a burgeoning consumer culture, in the popular imagination warias remained a consistent symbol related to public disorder. Two cartoons in as many months published in *Kompas* in 1979 depicted warias on terms that linked them to public sexuality. One cartoon illustrates an offensive caricature of a waria who propositions an approaching man on the street corner before fleeing out of the frame, wig askew and stiletto heel kicked off to reveal hairy legs and an oversized body beneath the clothes (*Kompas* 1979a, 2). In the final frame of the cartoon, the cause for alarm becomes clear; the person approaching is a municipal officer responsible for enforcing public order. The other illustration depicts two warias in a part of central Jakarta well known for sex work, wearing revealing clothing and garish makeup, propositioning a European businessman in English (*Kompas* 1979b, 2).

These cartoons, which depict warias in the context of public sexuality on city streets, underscore the role of public gender in shaping the meanings of full belonging. Despite the promise of inclusion that accompanied individual acts of self-improvement, warias continued to face violence—often from the security forces associated with the state—for the simple act of walking down the street. The introduction of guidance programs did not therefore eradicate older forms of discipline premised on the exclusion of warias from public space. Warias who gathered on Jakarta's streets continued to face the likelihood that their presence would be met by overt forms of rejection and violence on similar terms to the harassment faced by trans women by state security forces in the name of public order in other parts of the world (Valentine 2007; Ochoa 2014). Nevertheless, in Indonesia during the 1970s and 1980s, warias gradually obtained a widespread

FIGURE 3. "One evening in Krakatau Street," part of the "Our Jakarta" series of cartoons, published in *Kompas*, 1979.

Source: Kompas Newspapers

FIGURE 4. "An incident in Lawang Park," part of the "Our Jakarta" series of cartoons, published in *Kompas*, 1979.

Source: Kompas Newspapers

reputation that valorized them for their skills in beauty and related fields. In turn, this reputation enabled new forms of political engagement that contested the terms of public order within which warias had staked a fragile claim for inclusion.

Experiences of violence at the hands of city authorities also served as a catalyst for warias to participate in new forms of advocacy. Warias established a host of organizations with semiofficial status in response to police raids that appeared to increase in frequency and severity in the early 1970s. In 1973, one waria organization named Wadam of the Capital (Para Wadam Ibukota) took the noteworthy step of issuing an official letter of complaint to Jakarta's municipal police force in response to its policy of raids on public places (*Kompas* 1973a). The letter demanded that police immediately release the warias who had been detained and cease raids altogether, because those arrested had not committed any crime.[9] The municipal police nevertheless justified ongoing raids and detention as a response to complaints that the presence of warias "disturbed public order by being too visible in public places, especially along the sides of major roads" (*Kompas* 1973a, 3). The police clarified that they had not technically arrested the warias during the raids but rather had detained them temporarily, an ambiguous distinction that framed gender nonconformity not as illegal but as subject to regulation and discipline at the level of the municipality. Six years later, in 1979, the drowning deaths of several warias while fleeing municipal police raids in Jakarta led to similar protests by another organization, the Association of Wadam of Jakarta (Himpunan Wadam Jakarta). On this occasion, too, warias called for an end to the ineffective and violent tactic of raids by municipal police on well-known places where warias gathered (*Kompas* 1979c; see also Atmojo 1987, 11–12). Given that these vocal protests took place in a military state that had no qualms about violently removing nuisance bodies, this early organizing among warias was a courageous effort to expand participation in public space. This tenacious advocacy, centered on the perils and promise of public visibility, demonstrates how warias leveraged the ambiguous recognition they had achieved in the city by virtue of their legal but nonconforming status.

Governing the City, Governing the Nation

The Jakarta municipal government's efforts to regulate gender nonconformity in public space during the New Order resulted in unlikely coalitions. Various actors, including warias, the city governor, the municipal police, and social welfare officers, made every effort to restrict gender nonconformity to certain settings and strict conditions. To warias, this integration into the mechanisms of city governance was a vehicle for obtaining recognition. But given that their integration rested on sustaining the grounds on which public order and public morality were defined, the successes of warias in accomplishing belonging were fragile and piecemeal. The meanings of gender nonconformity remained ambiguous, with it representing an exemplar of feminine beauty in some contexts even as it posed a threat to public order in others. Living in the shadow of regulations that produced warias' visibility even as they were designed to limit it, warias navigated their designation as a disturbance to public order by demanding recognition from the city governor. Similarly, even as guidance programs were intended to discipline gender nonconformity and guide them toward a more presentable appearance, warias participated in such programs to achieve a respectable position in society.

Focusing on the technological format through which warias negotiated modes of recognition in a spatial and visual guise provides insight into a history that may too readily be interpreted in terms of the expansion of all-seeing surveillance. James Scott (1998, 55) described the advent of modernist planning in cities in terms of "straight lines and visible order," with the aim of producing "a simple, repetitive logic . . . easiest to administer and police." Jakarta in the New Order, a capital certainly planned and built along modernist lines, might be characterized in this way. But the bodies of those subject to such disciplinary regimes are rarely as malleable as the spatial efforts to discipline them presume them to be. As the history of warias' regulatory integration through a legal but nonconforming status suggests, the spatial and visual modality of municipal governance also furnished possibilities for struggle. Considered from the vantage point of what Valverde (2011, 277) called "seeing like a city," the history of gender nonconformity in Jakarta allows for consideration of alternate ways that citizenship can be won and lost through everyday practices of defining a public. The city's codification of public gender—a subjective aesthetic standard that it struggled to define—reflects an understanding of morality that is not fixed to inner essence but instead subject to change and appropriation over time and within social and historical contexts. A focus on the preoccupation with gender nonconformity by city officials therefore complicates the homogeneity imagined to be characteristic of top-down, expert-driven governance such as that imposed during the New Order.

The city government's codification of the locations and times where warias socialized, and of the aesthetics that they adopted in public, reflect just how central the governance of space was in efforts to enforce cisgender personhood as a marker of modern citizenship. The development of strategies to discipline public gender, and warias' tactics to engage with them, emerged in dialogue with city ordinances designed to maintain public order. Even as *waria* became a term that had national valence, used widely throughout Indonesia, that category remained entangled with the regulation of space that remained enforced largely at the level of the municipality. The efforts of city governments to govern warias' movement through space via temporal and spatial prohibitions reflected one concrete strategy through which authorities adjudicated individual bodies according to appearances based on cisgender and heteronormative ideals. Municipal authorities drew on the prevailing concepts of morality and order to establish new standards of gender presentation in public, a history that provides rich insights into how the state has constructed the normative boundaries of citizenship in Indonesia.

That warias would publicly articulate desires to pass through public space unhindered, and celebrate their successes in achieving this goal, was understandable. In the period immediately after independence, in the 1950s and early 1960s, warias' visibility had been subject to considerable social and political censure as various groups launched struggles over claims to speak as and for national publics. Even as it may have marked the beginning of a golden age, however, the year 1968 was not a complete revolution in the public meanings of gender. If warias gathered at night, the municipal police would continue to target them in raids along with other nonconforming individuals in public places. Warias remained positioned on a disciplinary grid, such as had been operating since the colonial period, that sought to control public participation through forms of governance positioned at the intersection of aesthetics and functionality. What the experiences of warias in New Order Jakarta highlight above all, then, is the crucial importance of the scale of the city in shaping the meanings of public gender as a technological system of classification. The recruitment of warias into efforts to regulate space did not make them disappear, but had a bearing on struggles to determine an adequate definition of the relationship between gender, sex, and sexuality as the product of an individual self in the years and decades that followed.

THE PERFECT WOMAN

During the 1970s, the Indonesian state gradually consolidated a more stable set of definitions of sex, gender, and sexuality in relation to the mind/body dualism central to one modern concept of individual personhood. In addition to the first legal recognition of a change of gender in a Jakarta court in 1973 and the first "sex reassignment surgery" undertaken by a team of Indonesian doctors at a Jakarta hospital in 1975, "transsexuality" emerged as a sustained topic of public interest and debate in the national media.[1] In part, the medical, legal, and popular rearrangements related to transsexuality in Indonesia that took place at this time reflected a neglected transnational component of what Susan Stryker (2017, 117) dubbed "the 'Big Science' period of transgender history" across the same period in the United States, when major universities set up programs that combined medical and psychological research with the provision of clinical services (see also Meyerowitz 2002).[2]

Despite some similarities, Indonesia's pursuit of medical transsexuality as a national concern, and the specific understanding of gendered and sexual personhood that it rested upon, were not precisely the same as those developed in the United States. Rather, working within the transnational currents of scientific thought, Indonesian psychologists, psychiatrists, and other doctors played a crucial role in translating and defining internationally circulating concepts related to transsexuality and intersex bodies in particular.[3] Although the category "transvestite" had been used to refer to bancis since the colonial period, an expert engagement with transsexuality during the 1970s folded existing national terms such as *wadam* and *waria* into Indonesian postcolonial modernity in a more consistent way. Working within a broader framework of scientific authority linked to technological development that was key to New Order rule, many scientists and doctors saw themselves as pursuing technical solutions to problems through the transfer of expert knowledge. Seeking out solutions to problems associated with sex, gender, and sexuality was no exception.

Integrated within a broader format of state-led economic "development" (*pembangunan*), gender nonconformity achieved new visibility via a state-sanctioned interest in transsexuality, a biopolitical concern that proceeded parallel to the immense state investment in heterosexuality and reproduction within the nuclear family. Unlike its concern for the nuclear family, however, by the end of the 1970s the Indonesian state's brief surge of official interest and even legitimation of medical transsexuality on narrow grounds had dissipated. In its place emerged a definition of public gender that was premised almost entirely on reproductive capacity, establishing even more clearly a format of cisgender personhood as central to attaining full citizenship. Although popular and expert opinion had been stirred by the possibility that modern science could make perfect what nature had left incomplete, this was abandoned, with a growing consensus that warias and other trans women could not give birth to children. This did not mean, however, that transsexuality as a biopolitical apparatus entirely disappeared from the Indonesian state's toolkit for governing public gender. Rather, the legal, medical, and psychological procedures defined in relation to transsexuality were redeployed piecemeal, as onto the bodies of intersex people, leading to a degree of overlap that persists in Indonesian medical and legal decisions regarding trans people to this day.

The application of technologies for categorizing and disaggregating human difference through the entwined categories of transsexuality and intersex in the 1970s reflects another aspect of the "deployment of gender" (Blackwood 2007, 296) as a component of New Order governmentality. Although Indonesian doctors and scientists did engage with trans men as patients and subjects, as well as with intersex people, their interest overwhelmingly lay with warias and trans women. In part this reflected the historical visibility of categories associated with trans femininity since the colonial period, which had emerged as an established format for defining and governing public gender. But state experts' intense interest in trans femininity at this time must also be interpreted within the parallel development of gender as a pillar of state ideology, in which what the state portrayed as the natural meanings associated with femininity and women were oriented toward the social roles of housewives and mothers (Suryakusuma 1996; Brenner 1999). Carla Jones described how this form of "gendered citizenship combined cultivation with coercion" (2010, 278), conditions under which feminine selves emerged as an ambiguous locus of discipline and pleasure. Delving into the state's abrupt engagement with transsexuality during this decade—one that had an enduring impact on the relationship between public gender and citizenship—helps to better understand how definitions of warias were refigured through an encounter with global transsexuality, albeit in terms that did not entirely reproduce the forms of Euro-American personhood upon which its disciplinary apparatus relied.

The integration of waria as a legal but nonconforming status in Ali Sadikin's Jakarta was a vehicle for exhilarating new claims to national belonging. As a limited means to achieve recognition, imagined and deployed at the scale of the city, warias' embrace of technologies of feminization provided an opportunity for them to demonstrate their usefulness to society on economic terms. The mastery of femininity as a suite of technological skills in turn facilitated a claim to entry into a specific rendering of state citizenship at the level of the city. As warias became visible in places and at times of day in which they had been previously invisible, they served as a catalyst for new efforts to define and defend the boundaries of preexisting concerns for public order and public morality in new ways. Efforts to remake public gender, which continued to be preoccupied largely with appearances, emerged out of a conversation between municipal efforts to control public order and transnational scientific and medical knowledge that was dominated by the fields of psychiatry and psychology. This process of transfer and exchange between publics who were imagined at different scales played a vital role in translating the gendered boundaries of citizenship from the city to the nation.

This chapter considers the role played by globalized knowledge about transsexuality during the 1970s in shaping the meanings of public gender and its relationship to the self in Indonesia. As was the case in previous decades, public gender was a chief means through which the boundaries of national belonging were condensed and naturalized. Up until the 1960s, definitions of gender nonconformity more generally had been largely restricted to bodily comportment, with little regard for genital morphology. Although the meanings of "man" and "woman" were of course unstable and contextual, the adjudication of the successful accomplishment of public gender relied on appearances, incorporating the adoption of clothing and makeup as well as physical attributes such as hairstyle and tone of voice. In the 1970s, technological interventions with their origins in Euro-American procedures related to transsexuality—chief among them a set of psychological and surgical procedures referred to as "sex reassignment surgery"—raised the possibility that outer appearances were giving way to a stress on genital morphology. This shift prefigured the appearance of individual "sex" (*jenis kelamin*) on binary terms as a meaningful category for recognizing citizenship, including its appearance as one piece of data on the state identity card that was first established at the beginning of the New Order.[4] In response to these technological possibilities and drawing on the work of their contemporaries in the United States, a dedicated cohort of Indonesian doctors and psychologists interpreted and advanced the view that it was combination of psychological state *and* biological difference that established the meanings of sex and gender as natural forms of bodily difference.

This engagement with medical transsexuality by psychologists and doctors working under the auspices of the Indonesian state emerged at a historical moment of unprecedented investment in technology. Sulfikar Amir referred to this period of the New Order as a "technological state," in which technology was not just an outgrowth of but critical to the maintenance of authoritarian power, "drawn from the belief in modern progress which was entangled with the obsession for techno-logical supremacy that became the basis of legitimacy for the regime" (2013, 161). Yet this legitimacy, and its moral underpinnings in technological progress, did not go unchallenged. Rather than only pursuing a singular agenda set by the state, various doctors and scientists oriented themselves toward what they understood as advancing universal forms of scientific knowledge in the pursuit of national progress (Barker 2005; Goss 2011; Pols 2018). And, distinct from other areas of technological intervention, such as the aerospace industry, which was the focus of Amir's (2013) theoretical account of state power through technology, efforts to produce and apply knowledge to the body and the self produced unexpected and less-conclusive findings as to what technical expertise could and should achieve. As a result, the relationship between sex, gender, and sexuality—as well as the specific form of individual personhood it indexed—remained inconclusive.

Technological Gender in the New Order

Indonesian psychiatrists and doctors developed and conveyed a clearer concept of gender nonconformity in terms of medical transsexuality that reflected an extended engagement with technological development adopted by the state. Throughout the 1970s, in the context of the expanded mass media of the New Order, writers with and without explicit endorsement from the government con-tributed to a range of official and popular publications that connected warias to global transsexuality. A tacit yet ambiguous state engagement with trans femi-ninity on Indonesian terms rested on a transfer of knowledge between experts and the popular domain, one that reached the public through an array of repre-sentations in popular films, magazines, and newspapers.

One result of this proliferation of knowledge via globalized circuits of scien-tific knowledge appeared in the reorganization of the meanings associated with the term *wadam* in 1968. Although a central factor involved in the establishment of wadam was a desire to expand participation in public space in the New Order city, the emergence of a distinctive model of medical transsexuality and corresponding vocabulary with which to describe men and women at the level of the individual self influenced the meanings of existing terms. From the outset, discussion of wadam in the popular press in Indonesia positioned the term as not entirely distinct from Euro-American accounts of medical transsexuality based on medical and psychological expertise. Wadam and waria drew on and redeployed the modern binary gender by capturing male and female in a single body. Yet this possibility was not entirely indigenous to Indonesian thought but was facilitated by the growing circulation of transnational theories, often from the fields of psychology and psychiatry, which sought to define gender based on one Euro-American model of individual personhood premised on the assumption that difference lies between bodies and that the continuous person is located in an individual body with a corresponding locus of rationality in the mind. This understanding of personhood crystallized in the model of gender identity as a core of the self (Meyerowitz 2002; Valentine 2007). In reaching an understanding of gender in terms of the self, Indonesian experts drew on and translated the work of psychologists and doctors involved in the growing institutionalization of an emerging field of medical transsexuality centered in the United States, including the influential writings of the endocrinologist Harry Benjamin (*The Transsexual Phenomenon*, 1966), the psychiatrist Robert Stoller (*Sex and Gender*, 1968), and the psychologist John Money (*Transsexualism and Sex Reassignment*, 1969). In official reports produced by various Indonesian government departments and in popular reporting contained in newspapers and magazines, this medicalized national discourse on transsexuality consolidated a definition of trans selfhood and applied it to warias.

Indonesian psychologists played a particularly prominent role in introducing an understanding of medical transsexuality into their own national context, creating modern Indonesian taxonomies to define waria in terms that relied on translations of Robert Stoller and John Money's definitions of gender identity as "mental sex" (*sex kejiwaan*). Such an understanding helped to further articulate a longstanding conceptual separation that held waria distinct from male homosexuality, in one account described as "active banci [also] known as homosexuals" who were "only Dutch . . . [and] are never Indonesian" (*Siasat* 1951, 13). In contrast to the putative foreignness of male homosexuality and same-sex love, warias' femininity as a condition of the self was discussed in open terms by Indonesian experts, who believed that it could be domesticated as a familiar, if disquieting, presence in postcolonial modernity. Psychologists drew on culturalist arguments to advance a view that modern warias could be described as heirs of bounded, indigenous traditions, even while they framed their increasing visibility in urban contexts as a problem to be solved through the application of modern scientific and medical expertise.

In 1969, one psychologist at the University of Surabaya, Tjiptono Darmadji (1969, 3), wrote in *Kompas* that a willingness to tolerate wadam among the Indonesian lower classes in particular was one effect of preexisting ritual and performance practices found throughout the archipelago.[5] Darmadji defined wadam as a specifically Indonesian "problem" which could in part be solved through the integration of techniques from modern psychology and psychoanalysis with a concept of culture based on anthropological theories. He described the appearance of wadam as part of a broader problem concerning the development of gender as social roles within the family, writing, "It is just that they are experiencing the consequences of psychosexual development most likely encountered during their childhood" (Darmadji 1969, 3). Darmadji drew on a common trope from psychoanalytically inspired accounts of childhood development to suggest that young men must be shielded both from seeing wadam and from overly feminine influences—particularly their mothers—in order to avoid such a transformation. On the front page of the same newspaper, the prominent Harvard University–trained psychologist Arief Budiman (1969b, 1) similarly looked to theories from "the psychology of the abnormal" (*psychologi abnormal*) to announce the arrival of wadam as transvestites who were distinct from homosexuals. Drawing on a set of Euro-American medical definitions of transsexuality and related assumptions about personhood—including a separation between the bounded, material body and the mind—he defined wadam as those with a "self identity" as the "opposite sex," describing their experience as legitimate and therefore deserving of sympathetic engagement (Budiman 1969b, 1).

The tone and analytical concepts deployed in these accounts suggest that this increased visibility did not mark the acceptance of warias by the state. Rather, reflecting a parallel effort to the mechanisms deployed by city officials, state officials drew on available psychological theories as they grappled with a loss of control of public gender. The twin concerns of safeguarding morality and applying expertise to everyday problems stimulated interest in assisting wadam. Despite widespread censure of the public visibility of warias, however, most psychologists stressed that little could be done for adults who had already "developed in the wrong direction" (Darmardji 1969, 3). In the name of a psychologized form of "prevention," then, Darmadji's account appears to support an emerging consensus that society should not ostracize warias (1969, 3). Rather, reflecting a broader rehabilitative logic echoed in Sadikin's support for vocational training, "It is enough to provide them opportunities to work, consistent with their desires and abilities" (1969, 3). Far from settling the facts of gender and sexuality, however, the terms used to refer to waria introduced a new vocabulary through which the meanings of modern binary gender as constitutive of individual personhood came under increasing scrutiny.

Although these accounts suggested a consistent concern with a medicalized discourse of transsexuality, they did not primarily emerge around a concern for transformation in the context of the clinic, as was the case in the United States (cf. Stone 1992; Meyerowitz 2002). For one, there were insufficient institutional resources through which to establish adequate health care services in a nation that was impoverished by decades of instability following centuries of exploitative colonial rule (Pols 2018). As a result, engagement by psychiatrists and doctors with globalized concepts of medical transsexuality often emerged where they found well-established presence of warias: on the streets of major cities. After all, interest in gender nonconformity had first been shown by the municipal rather than the national government. Engagement with a medical discourse of transsexuality in Indonesia was refracted through the historical disciplinary concerns of public order and public morality.

Rather than being separated out, a municipal-level concern for defining public gender grew in tandem with the deployment of expertise about medical transsexuality. One evening in the late 1960s, Jakarta's police arrested twenty-three lower-class warias who had gathered in the center of the city. Rather than detaining them briefly, as had been commonplace in the previous decades, on this occasion the police transported those who had been arrested to a psychiatric facility. There, they were held for two weeks as part of a study, the Banci Research Project, undertaken by Johanna Masdani and Tjiauw Ling of the psychiatric department of the University of Indonesia (Masdani 1968; Ling 1968).[6] Masdani, a lecturer in psychiatry who published widely on women's social roles and reproductive health, and Ling, a young student psychiatrist who later completed his residency at the University of California, Los Angeles, declared their project to be the first to investigate scientifically the meaning of bancis, rendered in this account as transvestites.

At the psychiatric clinic of the large, public Dr. Cipto Mangunkusumo Hospital in Jakarta—which would also be the site of the nation's first sex reassignment surgery in 1975—researchers subjected the warias to an array of psychiatric and physical examinations. As in the United States, in postcolonial Indonesia the state's efforts to know and thus to manage public gender was integrated into extant inequalities based on class and race, which addressed subjects of knowledge in coercive and unethical ways (Snorton 2017; Gill-Peterson 2018). Disseminating the results in the journal of psychiatry *Djiwa*, Ling (1968, 48) underscored the disjuncture between warias' bodies and their appearances in exaggerated terms. Writing in objectifying terms, he contrasted their "over-the-top makeup and breasts made of rubber and foam" with their "masculine bodies, identified by hair growth (body, mustache, beard) consistent with the norm of Indonesian men and external sex organs in the normal range." Masdani (1968, 45) drew this data into conversation with a global medical literature, announcing that even as *banci* as a term was used in ways that ranged from broad gender ambiguity to homosexuality, "transvestite" was the most adequate translation for warias. Although the fate of the warias captured in the raid was never mentioned again, Masdani and Ling's research encountered a regime of public gender even more explicitly when it became the basis for the Jakarta municipal government's strategies of guidance under Ali Sadikin.

Indonesian psychologists and psychiatrists such as Budiman, Darmadji, Masdani, and Ling pioneered engagement with international knowledge and technologies related to medical transsexuality and transvestitism within the national context. The fields of psychology and psychiatry underwent significant growth during the 1950s and 1960s, with large numbers of Indonesian doctors and psychologists receiving training in the United States (Pols 2018). Later, some of the nation's most prominent psychiatrists, including Kusumanto Setyonegoro, the head of the psychiatry department at the University of Indonesia from 1961 to 1972, played an important role in generating interest and engagement with a medical discourse of transsexuality.[7] Apart from psychiatrists, prominent experts in surgery and other scientific fields wrote candidly about trans femininity in the context of broader efforts to interpellate gendered citizenship according to reproductive roles based on the nuclear family. Although established as a central framework for determining both social difference and the disciplinary form of public order during the New Order, a concept of gender based on the psychological individual as congruent or incongruent from broad social expectations as a bounded entity had to be actively enforced. Medical transsexuality, introduced in relation to warias, was one point through which the Indonesian population was plotted onto a normalizing grid of minoritarian trans and majoritarian cisgender concepts of self, body, and society in the 1970s.

A Woman's Soul

A particularly important node in engaging medical authority regarding transsexuality in Indonesia emerged through efforts by state officials to translate and restrict access to the emphatic narrative among warias that they possessed a "woman's soul." The integration of transsexuality within Indonesian psychiatry and medicine during the 1970s extended efforts to adjudicate public gender through wadam and banci in terms that had been employed since the colonial period. The colonial and postcolonial state's claims to medical and psychological

expertise as guiding principles for recognition formed part of a struggle to elimi-
nate the legitimacy of both individuals' own self-knowledge and those of the
networks of neighbors and kin they lived alongside. To this end, psychiatrists
and doctors compiled and published an array of taxonomies and lists that pur-
ported to separate real from false warias and bancis, an effort to secure public
gender as defining the boundary of full belonging in a way that brings to mind
earlier anxieties over authenticity represented in racialized appearances during
the colonial period.

The series of accounts published in the Jakarta municipal magazine *Mingguan Djaja* was one such example. Its authors translated and provided an extensive taxonomy listing the various possible scientific definitions of banci, which
incorporated a variety of terms. These included translated accounts that defined
"hermaphrodites" as "people with combined men's and women's genitals,"
"homosexuals" as "men who interact intimately [*berhubungan kelamin*] with
other men . . . and wear women's clothing for this purpose," and "bisexuals" as
"men who have sex with women and other men, especially those who perform
or dress as women" (*Mingguan Djaja* 1968c). The author noted that although
the term *banci* could possibly be translated as any one of these terms, the most
suitable was "transvestite," defined here as "a man who is physically a man, but
with the psyche [*psychis*] of a woman. She does the work of a woman and wears
women's clothing because of the force of her soul [*dorongan jiwa*]." Drawing on
the prominent American sexologist Alfred Kinsey, the authors in this account
highlighted that transvestites could be distinguished between those who were
"permanent" and those who were "partial," designations that could primarily be
sorted through discovering to what extent individuals were committed to wearing women's clothing, by which it was possible to adjudicate their "self-identification as the opposite sex" (*Mingguan Djaja* 1968c, 10).

This early taxonomy deployed in a popular translation of a scientific account
facilitated the popularization of an emergent definition of self-identification as
banci, wadam, and waria according to a hybrid formulation. Accounts of the
English term "transvestite" and later "transsexual" referred to banci as having a
"woman's soul," at times using a translated term for mind, *psychis*, but more often
by using a long-standing Indonesian word for interiority, *jiwa*. The selective process of translation and incorporation of concepts from Euro-American psychiatry
worked to connect warias' public gender to individualized interiority. The key
defining factor through which the meanings of authentic expressions of being
waria were established therefore rested on the longstanding concept of a "woman's soul" (*jiwa perempuan*), which animated a much more profound and lasting
relationship to an individual's gender presentation. The integration of medicalized knowledge resulted in three defining aspects of trans selfhood that would

have a profound bearing on popular and official understandings of warias in the decades to come. First, possessing a "woman's soul" was defined as the primary driving factor for public gender, in the form of manifestations of femininity. As a result, warias' public gender could not for the most part be repressed or changed. Second, experts drew on psychoanalytic and psychological theories to define becoming waria as a process, determined to a degree by social and familial influence. Third, these factors meant that waria was defined as distinct from male homosexuality, although the line between who was waria and who was homosexual was able to be crossed, and homosexuals were understood along the lines of false waria, or those who were dressing in women's clothing not owing to an abiding woman's soul but for some other reason (such as economic necessity). In Indonesian national modernity, the predominant manner through which selfhood was understood rested not predominantly on sexuality but on a relationship between public gender and authenticity.

Twin concepts of a "woman's soul" and, to a degree, the possibility of belonging to the "opposite sex" appeared as key to defining the meanings of the modern concepts of transvestite and transsexuality in Indonesia. The application of a pair of dualisms specific to the individual as a prototypical modern self—incorporating body/mind and male/female—served to clarify an emergent boundary between cisgender and transgender bodies at this moment in critical ways. Anthropological accounts discussing subjective understandings of selfhood among trans women in Indonesia have most frequently translated the Indonesian term *jiwa* as the English words "soul" or "spirit" (Boellstorff 2007, 101; Blackwood 2010, 88), giving these terms a certain religious inflection that is perhaps not unintended.[8] Yet the use of *jiwa* in these Indonesian translations of accounts by authors such as Harry Benjamin and Robert Stoller highlights the influence of medical transsexuality in shaping the meanings of the term as a narrative formulation relevant to evaluating and recognizing warias. When writing about transsexuality, Indonesian psychiatrists and psychologists in particular moved between three concepts pertaining to a sense of interiority: jiwa; the English-derived term *psychis*; and the Islamic concept of *roh*. Each of these terms reflects a specific history of personhood and its relationship to bodily cultivation, and they all are incomplete in their mapping of that interior sense onto the concept of the self (*diri*). The state's interest in warias here reflected an emergent apparatus for defining gender as lying at the core of individual interiority. The integration of psychiatric and psychological expertise, drawing on concepts from medical transsexuality, reflected the state's effort to confer a stable or authentic inner self crystallized through public gender in Indonesia.

The integration of jiwa into a series of concepts related to the modern self—including gender identity—reflects one way in which the medical model of transsexuality emerged as a biopolitical formulation with global reach. The process of defining warias proceeded through efforts to naturalize an individual model of gender conceptualized in terms of a disjuncture between mind and body, a disjuncture that in turn shaped what Sandy Stone called the emergence of "a binary, oppositional mode of gender identification" (1992, 156). To be sure, this formed part of a much longer process through which diverse indigenous cosmologies related to the body were displaced under modern regimes that framed gender as innate in Indonesia (Blackwood 2005a). But in a less totalizing reading, it is also possible to see the ways that Indonesian psychiatrists—and warias and other trans people themselves—translated internationally circulating concepts via historically and culturally specific forms of personhood relevant to them. Distinct formulations of personhood as interiority generated a national discourse of transsexuality in other contexts, too. Recalling the definitional insta-bility between jiwa, roh, and psychis employed in Indonesian psychiatry, Afsaneh Najmabadi (2014, 190) observed that in Iran, "the slippage between soul and psyche . . . has produced a creative space for extensive discursive and practical col-laboration on the issue of transsexuality." As efforts to define banci and wadam through psychiatric and psychological taxonomies of sex, gender, and sexual difference suggest, incorporating knowledge about medical transsexuality was a process of translation and integration rather than the wholesale displacement of previous forms of knowledge. Codifying warias' narratives of self-identification as *jiwa perempuan*, a woman's soul, was one means through which public gender was interpreted in relation to the self by the Indonesian state.

Writing in 1973 in the official Department of Health magazine *Majalah Kese-hatan*, a publication intended for dissemination among doctors and other medi-cal professionals in hospitals and offices throughout Indonesia, a psychologist named Karsono described bancis (no justification is given for the use of this term rather than wadam) expressly as "transsexuals" on account of the fact that they were individuals "whose mind was in conflict with their body" (Karsono 1973, 89). Central to Karsono's account was his translation of Robert Stoller's theory of "gender identity." In the United States, the concept of gender identity played a pivotal role in developing a conjoined medical and psychiatric frame-work through which to address transsexuality in terms of an essential self. Stoller first published on the concept in 1964, based on his research and clinical work at the Gender Identity Clinic at the University of California, Los Angeles. As Joanne Meyerowitz (2002, 115) wrote, gender identity bridged biological and environ-mental explanations for transsexuality, as well as "more clearly differentiat[ing] the subjective sense of self from the behaviors associated with masculinity and femininity."[9] But Karsono's use of a theory of gender identity was not necessarily comprehensive, and neither did it reflect a dedication to parsing rigid, binary poles of behavior and identity. Rather, in the process of parsing out banci's relationship to "the self" as *diri* and "psyche" as *kejiwaan*, Karsono's account promoted a more unidirectional understanding of the relationship between outer and inner parts of the self than the Euro-American concept of gender identity permitted.

Despite this incorporation of a concept that appeared likely to lead to the normalizing effects of medical transsexuality, in what was to emerge as a consensus for the length of the New Order, Karsono concluded that the overlapping mind/body and individual/society disjuncture that warias experienced in the form of public gender could not be resolved via medical or psychiatric forms of intervention. As a result, the possible forms of rehabilitation proposed to the authorities were not surgical or even strictly psychological at the level of the individual. Rather, Karsono proposed that warias should participate in beauty contests and undertake vocational training in fields associated with emergent norms of feminine beauty. This view reflected a harnessing of transnational knowledge to preexisting terms to generate new, hybridized Indonesian concepts for defining warias and other trans people, what Asfaneh Najmabadi described in Iran as a "productive looping effect, a generative traffic, between the vernacular and the more academically generated knowledge within biomedical and psychosexological professional domains" (2014, 50).

Despite its hybridity, the definitional work and process of translating Euro-American concepts nevertheless invested in a biopolitics with its basis in naturalizing the biological individual as gendered. A concept of "mental sex" (*sex kejiwaan*)—the Indonesian translation of a concept of gender identity—was increasingly deployed not only to describe a subjective state but to confer on men's and women's social roles a stability that could be located in the self. Despite its translation via a medicalized discourse regarding transsexuality, the notion of having a woman's soul cannot be understood as only an imposition of medicalized transsexuality; it was also used as an important strategy of self-narrativization deployed by warias in strategic ways. As a narrative formulation used among warias, the concept of a woman's soul predates the intensive integration of transsexuality that unfolded during the 1970s. Both as it appears in the historical record and as I encountered it during fieldwork, the narrative of having a woman's soul was so commonplace that it cannot be dismissed as a Euro-American imposition. In any case, the concept takes on different valence in the Indonesian context; to have a woman's soul is not seen as a mode of individualized accomplishment or articulation tied to a psychological state located in the mind. Rather, reflecting a more encompassing meaning of the Indonesian word for "soul," to have a *jiwa perempuan* was a key means through which warias advanced themselves as legible to an audience. Warias' narratives of having a woman's soul, even where they were incorporated partially into a cisgender and heteronormative project of state citizenship, also worked to assert a claim to self-knowledge as a basis for recognition. When coupled with the adept application of modern technologies of feminization, the narrative of a woman's soul established a means to claim recognition that rested on an expanded vision of what public gender could and should mean.

Competently acquiring the skills required to achieve a stable form of public gender served as an essential demonstration of belonging during the New Order. At the same time as warias became objects of psychiatric expertise, the state-implemented invasive program of restricting women's fertility through reproductive health programs had served as the material means through which women were encouraged to understand themselves as "procreators of the nation" (Suryakusuma 2011, 101). The organization for the wives of civil servants, and Indonesia's revised marriage law—key routes through which women's roles came to be defined in Indonesia—were both established by 1974, the latter explicitly institutionalizing definitions of binary gender in relation to social roles in the nuclear family. The marriage law defined men as "heads of the household" (*kepala rumah tangga*) and women as "housewives" (*ibu rumah tangga*). I suggest that the translation and selective incorporation of knowledge about transsexuality, and the central emphasis on defining a stable gender identity, did not stand apart from but was central to establishing the relationship between citizenship and public gender.

Over time, this process of sorting out banci, wadam, and waria gradually excluded them from possible belonging to the category "woman" altogether. One corollary of this development was that waria were increasingly defined by the state and wider society, as Tom Boellstorff wrote, as an "abject masculinity" (2007, 109). Even as experts drew on warias as visible subjects for theorizing and interpreting the modern self in terms of public gender, they did not reject entirely the possibility that bodily cultivation could enact a more lasting transformation to the inner self. Rather, and in a way that brings to mind ethnographic accounts of Indonesian trans life that hold that "the physical body is of utmost importance and cannot be superseded by quotidian practices" (Davies 2010, 21), Indonesian psychiatrists and doctors never reduced warias to an essentialist definition based on biological sex. By the mid-1970s, state experts had established a somewhat surprising consensus that, so long as warias could make use of the technologies they had available to cultivate their bodies, then they too would be able to accomplish partial acceptance.

A key difference in the adoption of a discourse of medical transsexuality in Indonesia was that biological sex, as conferred by genital morphology, appeared to not hold the same weight. In the United States, a focus on genital morphology animated a whole field of knowledge about sex change, which grew from the entwined histories of intersex and transsexual medicine that was concerned with correcting the developing body so that it would grow into a male or female gender identity, reflecting a conservative medical and legal paradigm (Kessler 1998; Gill-Peterson 2018, 67–70). The dominance in the Indonesian context of the fields of psychiatry and psychology coupled with histories of personhood that emphasized bodily cultivation meant that there was initially little interest or engagement with genital morphology as the primary site for stabilizing sex. Popular and expert interest in the bodies of warias and trans people in Indonesia tended instead to emphasize appearances, particularly the face and hair, as the primary site for the adequate accomplishment of gender.[10] This is not to say that genital morphology was entirely unimportant to the Indonesian state's definition of men's and women's social roles. Increasing biopolitical interest in women's reproductive capacity, an unprecedented investment in high technology, and a surge of popular interest in transsexuality led to newfound consideration of the relationship between gender and genital morphology.

Vivian Rubianti and the Perfect Woman

Popular interest in transsexuality in Indonesia emerged most evidently during the first widely publicized case of sex reassignment surgery performed for an Indonesian citizen, Vivian Rubianti, in 1973. Vivian had traveled to Singapore, where she had undergone surgery at the Kandang Kerbau Hospital by the esteemed surgeon Sittampalam Shanmugaratnam (commonly abbreviated to S. S.) Ratnam.[11] Vivian obtained widespread attention in the Indonesian national media after successfully petitioning a Jakarta district court to change the gender listed on her state-issued identity documents to female in October of the same year following her return from Singapore (*Kompas* 1973b).[12] Vivian's international reputation and glamorous appearance attracted an extraordinary degree of attention, including reports of a visit from President Suharto and First Lady Ibu Tien following her court case. This reflects how media interest transformed Vivian into a minor celebrity, a process that culminated in the production of a film about her life—in which she starred alongside star Kris Biantoro—released in cinemas in 1978 (Murtagh 2013, 41–42).[13] The degree to which Vivian's story was covered, unfolding across a period of significant crackdowns on press freedom (Sen and Hill 2006, 37–39) and film censorship (Sen 1994, 124), indicates if not explicit then certainly tacit support from state authorities.

Vivian was a well-known hairdresser and stylist. She stated that she had undergone gender reassignment surgery in Singapore and wanted her gender listed accurately in her passport to avoid confusion when traveling (*Tempo* 1973a). A secondary motivation for her legal case was a desire for legal recognition as a woman, given that she felt especially "insulted by being referred to as a banci, which troubled her mind [*jiwa*]" (*Kompas* 1973c, 5). She was represented by the prominent defense lawyer Adnan Buyung Nasution, the founder of the nation's first legal aid and human rights organization, the Legal Aid Foundation (*Tempo* 1973b). The case was settled on November 14, 1973, in Vivian's favor. The judge declared her "mental sex" (*seks kejiwaan*) to be that of a woman, and as such she was issued identification documents that listed her gender as "woman" (*perempuan*) (*Kompas* 1973d). The ruling in the case also rested in part on Vivian's legal status as a Chinese Indonesian citizen, a population that since the founding of the nation had been "at the vanguard of state policies of surveillance, control and identification documentation" (Strassler 2010, 131). The legacy of more intensive civil registration requirements for ethnic Chinese citizens—and laws from 1966 and 1967 that urged assimilation through the adoption of Indonesian names— emerged as a component of the legal case advanced by Vivian's lawyer for her change of name (Manshur and Iskandar Al-Barsany 1981; Nasution 1978, 621). Although the capacity to change name was covered under existing regulations, no existing law permitted a change in gender. As a result, the decision rested on the jurisdiction of the district court over the recognition of social change in "a development or progress in medical technology (*teknologi*), in particular the possibility that a person's sex (*jenisnya*) can be perfected in order to be categorized as male or female" (Nasution 1978, 626). The judge agreed with this argument, issuing an instruction to the office for civil registration for Chinese Indonesians to add a notation to Vivian's birth certificate that listed her new name and gender.[14]

Early public commentary on the case in the press was supportive, reflecting a widespread enthusiasm for technological progress within a rubric of national development. Magazine articles applauded the judge's decision, asserting that Indonesian "law must go along with the developments of the era" in order to "facilitate and assist development" (*Tempo* 1973a, 14–15). Newspaper reports described the judge's verdict in terms of a relationship to social justice and the triumph of medical science. The initial account in *Kompas* reporting the decision declared in lofty terms, "As someone with a mental affliction [*menderita jiwa*] the law must help Vivian . . . because the law must uphold welfare and justice" (*Kompas* 1973e, 1). An author named T. H. Lim published an editorial in *Kompas* claiming, in overtly nationalist terms, that the case reflected how Indonesia was "more liberated compared to Holland, and more flexible toward the development of a society which continues to change" (Lim 1974, 4). Lim emphasized that unlike in Indonesia, where judges were able to recognize Vivian's gender through a degree of flexibility in regulations governing civil registration, the rigidity of definitions limited to biological sex in Dutch law made the case difficult to argue in that context. Although this claim may not have necessarily been true, it does reveal the way in which Vivian's case was seen as a matter of national progress.

A boon for Vivian was the support offered by the prominent Islamic scholar Buya Hamka. In his role as an expert witness, his support for transsexuality and for Vivian was unequivocal:

> Basically, this is a person who doesn't know who they should be: they are not a man, and also are not a woman! People who are like this, who experience a long period of mental anguish, are often teased by others, so their mind is a mess. They are a man. However, their behavior, comportment, and even their mind is that of a woman [*jiwa perempuan*]. In the modern era, there is an operation that releases them from their anguish. If wadam then decide to obtain gender reassignment surgery, then so be it!" (*Kompas* 1973e, 1)

Reflecting a now common theme in which transsexuality was related to national technological progress, Hamka reasoned that all individuals should be able to access the science and technology enthusiastically adopted by the state. According to Hamka, Vivian's access to surgery was warranted as a way for her to alleviate her "mental suffering" (*tekanan jiwa*). Hamka justified his support for her status as a transsexual in relation to the concept of *khunsa*, an Arabic term used to refer to both intersex and transsexuality. Hamka's borrowing of *khunsa* to develop an Islamic justification paralleled a similar formulation justifying the legality of and state support for transsexuality in Iran. In the 1960s and 1970s, Iranian experts' discussions drew on Islamic legal interpretations of *khunsa* to stress an affiliation between medical procedures for intersex and those for transsexuals (Najmabadi 2014, 47).[15] Although Hamka's comments may have superficially reflected a consensus of sympathy toward trans people—one that did not extend to bancis or to warias—the capacity to receive assistance and support rested on a necessity to submit to forms of state expertise beyond the reach of most Indonesians.

Interest in Vivian's case led to widespread discussion of the capacities of modern technology to transform public gender, usually in the form of a speculative concern for "sex change surgery" (*operasi penggantian kelamin*). One consequence lay in the demand for greater efforts among state experts to clarify the difference between transgender femininity and cisgender femininity. The tentative acceptance of Vivian in effect rested on the way that she eschewed the terms *banci* and, to a lesser degree, *wadam* reflected how gender was inseparable from a class-based respectability tied to a consistently performed femininity worthy of state recognition. This increasingly manifested in the focus on fastening the meanings of the category "woman" more closely to a capacity to bear children. The judge in Vivian's case had noted that, although she could not give birth to children, she should nevertheless be considered a woman legally (*Kompas* 1973e). In another account, the judge outlined the justification of the judgment as follows: "Among women there are those who may be born less than perfect [*kurang sempurna*], such as those who do not have a womb or ovaries, but they are nonetheless called women" (*Tempo* 1973c, 15). Nevertheless, in these accounts, the meanings of what the state defined as a "perfect woman" were clarified beyond doubt: one who had the capacity to bear children. At the same time, a lack of clarity as to the relationship between genital morphology, inner self, and the ideal performance of gender surfaced repeatedly, confounding attempts to settle the matter beyond doubt.

Such commentary reflected the importance of the role that the more psychologized concept of jiwa established in the preceding years—one originally linked to a concept of the soul—had played in lending the legitimacy of medical and religious authority to Vivian's efforts to obtain medico-legal recognition of her gender. Drawing on expert testimony from doctors, psychiatrists, and Islamic scholars, the judge reasoned that given Vivian's "woman's mind," the alterations that she had made to her body meant that she fulfilled the Indonesian state's definition of a "woman." Yet even as such a definition was possible for Vivian, her case did not necessarily reflect the expansion of recognition to warias. If anything, Vivian's repeated claims that a primary reason why she sought state recognition was so that she could separate herself entirely from the pejorative meanings of banci and wadam serve as a reminder that the state's investments in medical transsexuality reflected an attempt to assert control over binary gender at a moment of transformation. This view reflects Vivian's middle-class position and Chinese Indonesian status; reporting in the popular press emphasized that she wished to distance herself from bancis and wadams, who reflected a lower-class and sexualized subject position beyond productive and respectable participation in society. As a nationally inflected version of what Susan Stryker called the "spectacular whiteness" (2013, 544) linked to the globalization of transsexuality, a relationship to middle-class respectability figured centrally in Vivian's claims to respectability and her disavowal of banci and wadam. These shifts facilitated the grounds for a clearer delineation of boundaries between the categories banci, waria, and woman, in turn reshaping how public gender was defined as the basis for citizenship.

Nationalizing Transsexuality

A narrowed definition of gender based on physiology and reproductive roles—rather than the possibility that outer appearances could transform inner state—had profound consequences in the last half of the 1970s. Nevertheless, an increasing emphasis on the reproductive basis for gender, one that was entwined with the state's insistence on cisgender selfhood as normal and natural, was not necessarily exclusionary or settled. Experts and commentators in the popular press debated whether waria could bear children, often presenting inconclusive results. One Jakarta Department of Health official and medical doctor working in the field of reproductive health, Dr. Herman, was quoted in a newspaper article saying that the success of "an operation creating perfect genitals" could only be measured against the criterion of whether it had provided "the capacity to later have children" (*Kompas* 1973f, 1). These definitions emerged alongside the kinds of technical and medical procedures that had been developed for use on intersex bodies, suggesting the way that knowledge about medical transsexuality and intersex bodies were never entirely separated on conceptual terms. For example, Dr. Herman noted that operations that could "change [*merubah*] genitals that were 'half and half' to those of a man" were already possible in Jakarta. Although drawing on a definition that seems more appropriate for intersex, Dr. Herman described the unnamed patient whom he referred to in this article by using the term *wadam*, highlighting one way that terminological slippage between transsexuality and intersex served as a route through which the meaning of femininity was related to genital morphology and, in turn, reproduction as a natural basis for recognizing and calibrating the modern meanings of gender in the Indonesian setting.

The most significant investment made by the Indonesian state in science and medicine's capacity to transform sex and gender came two years later, when Indonesian doctors undertook the nation's first gender reassignment surgery in June 1975. The availability of surgical interventions related to transsexuality, though never widespread in Indonesia, emerged as a yardstick for measuring national scientific progress. The first Indonesian surgical patient, Netty Irawati, was reported to have become "complete in every sense" following what *Tempo* magazine referred to as "genital refinement surgery" (*penghalusan kelamin*) (*Tempo* 1975a, 38).[16] Netty described having experienced "psychological suffering" (*penderitaan jiwa*) and "felt like she was a woman since she was a child." Recalling Vivian's comments to the press, Netty was reported to have said, "I hate being called a banci! Won't I be a woman [after the operation]?" (*Kompas* 1975a, 3).

Netty's case was the subject of significant attention and sympathy from Indonesian society, with well-known newspapers and magazines soliciting financial support from readers for her postoperative hormonal treatment. After the operation, and in the context of this support, Netty was reported to have said, "I feel as though my self-esteem has risen and I can become a proper person" (*Kompas*

1975b, 1). But the fact that she was unable to bear children cast a shadow over the success of the operation, raising the strong possibility of coercive or unethical medical practice, like that which had occurred in the context of Masdani and Ling's Banci Research Project just under a decade earlier. Indeed, Netty had claimed that she had undertaken the surgery in part because she thought it would enable her to bear children, and was reportedly surprised when she found out that this was not the case (*Tempo* 1975a). Much as in Vivian's case, journalists and doctors presented Netty's medical intervention as a means for unruly trans bodies to join respectable forms of femininity as defined against the category wadam and banci, marked by the association between lower-class status and visible gender nonconformity in public space.[17]

Netty's surgery generated sufficient interest at the intersection of medical practice and policy for the Indonesian Department of Health to convene a seminar in March 1978 (Indonesian Department of Health 1978; Manshur and Iskandar Al-Barsany 1981). The religious scholars, doctors, scientists, and psychiatrists invited to discuss the matter squarely addressed the role of science and medicine in defining the boundaries of gender normativity for the first time. The consensus reached at the seminar and in the subsequent report rested on evidence offered by biologists who argued that the latest scientific definitions of masculinity and femininity did not rely on physical appearance and function of the genitals alone, but must be measured in terms of genetic makeup and reproductive capacity. In line with this view, the seminar report concluded—in what marked an alarming reversal of past sentiment—that the "mind" (*psychis*) of banci, wadam, and waria should, in fact, be treated with psychotherapy so that their behavior might reflect their biological sex. The seminar report denounced the "operations to change the genitals" that had been performed in the mid-1970s on individuals like Netty Irawati and Vivian Rubianti, framing its objective instead as a concern for intersex people, referred to with the Islamic term *khunsa*.[18] Despite these proclamations that appeared to diminish the integration of medical transsexuality into state biopolitics, the results of the seminar were ambiguous in practice. The 1979 Department of Health decree that followed from the seminar, titled "Instructions on Operations to Change the Genitals," was hardly conclusive, conflating the diagnosis and treatment of transsexuals with operating procedures for intersex children.[19] Reflecting this conflation, trans individuals received surgeries at state-run hospitals as late as 1989, even as official legal and medical regulations restricted such access to intersex children on paper at least.

Although largely unstated, the social and legal definitions of the categories "male" and "female" in Indonesia prior to the 1970s had accommodated an understanding that inner and outer parts of the "self" (*diri*) need not necessarily be in alignment. To describe oneself as having a "woman's soul," in addition to showing some signs of femininity on the body, was thus a sufficient if fragile claim to belong to the social category "woman." The consensus reached at the 1979 seminar on transsexuality, incorporating a greater emphasis on a biological basis for binary sex, marked a significant departure in the state's medical and legal definition of gender and corresponding effort to assert a monopoly over its recognition. In addition to the role of gender as a combination of physiological and biological factors, reproductive capacity—for women, the capacity to give birth—emerged as a critical factor in determining the boundaries of cisgender personhood.

This shift, which abruptly concluded enthusiastic forms of engagement by the Indonesian state with transsexuality in the mid-1970s, highlights the ongoing role of public gender in struggles over the moral project of defining what was "normal." Given that citizenship itself was reframed as a moral category tied to the construction of the cisgender body as normal and natural, those unable to conform to it for various reasons would find themselves in an ambiguous position. Both unable to escape entirely the stigma related to the term *banci* and largely unable to access state expertise for support to accomplish cisgender normativity, gender-nonconforming Indonesians of all kinds would have to develop their own strategies to forge livable lives in the shadow of the understandings of medical transsexuality and intersex that emerged within the technological ambitions of the New Order state.

For the vast majority of trans Indonesians, the high technologies associated with transsexuality and their narrow focus on conservative forms of surgical and psychological intervention were either inappropriate, irrelevant, or simply unavailable. Thus, even as the state mounted a claim to stabilize one definition of sex and gender on individualized terms as the primary category through which bodies were recognized as citizens, a more general ambivalence toward state authority facilitated opportunities for trans women and warias to advance the centrality of their own desires for self-knowledge and recognition by community and neighbors. Throughout the 1970s and the decades that followed, warias almost completely bypassed the state's emphasis on making up gender according to an idealized alignment between genital morphology, appearances, and psychological state, instead advancing a claim to recognition within public domains associated with feminine beauty. The state's enrollment of medico-legal technologies to claim a monopoly on recognition of the meanings of gender according to a cisgender/transgender binary proved inconclusive. At the same time, warias' attainment of the position of beauty experts—a possibility that had grown out their participation in vocational training provided at the municipal level—enabled a divergent set of possibilities for alternative claims to recognition on the basis of public gender.

BEAUTY EXPERTS

In March 1969, the second annual beauty pageant for warias, called the Queen of Miss Imitation Girls, was held at the Hotel Duta in Jakarta. The event provided a stage on which warias could demonstrate a capacity to accomplish a polished form of feminine beauty and thus participate in a national public.[1] The inaugural Queen of Miss Imitation Girls competition had been held the year before and was an important site at which warias first became visible to Governor Ali Sadikin. After witnessing their potential for accomplishing a polished feminine beauty, the city government bestowed recognition to warias to minimize the disruption that they posed to public order. As one account of the 1968 meeting between warias and Sadikin outlined, "In a similar way to some women, banci also prostitute themselves because of economic need and other pressing reasons, including that they feel an imbalance in themselves" (*Selecta* 1968, 19). The solution that Sadikin put forward, one that was tied implicitly to an understanding of self-improvement in the service of economic development, rested on what the government called guidance programs. Guidance programs sought to improve warias' appearances by providing them with training in skills related to feminine beauty and became a central component of the municipal government's efforts to discipline waria by encouraging them to participate in projects of self-improvement. The municipal government asserted that this effort would allow an "understanding of which banci are genuine and which are false . . . because most banci in Jakarta are men who dress up as banci and 'prostitute' themselves only for economic needs, . . . If banci are provided with economic activities, it will decrease the number of banci on the streets of the city and clean up the city from the unpleasant view that they create" (*Selecta* 1968, 19).

Warias responded to this call, engaging in projects of self-improvement that positioned them as authentic citizens against a backdrop of national development in the early New Order. Yet unfortunately for the city government, this strategy did not diminish the public visibility of warias but rather led them to mobilize to further reduce the temporal and spatial restrictions on their presence. Jakarta was the location where Indonesia's return to an emphatically global form of capitalist development was staged following the instability and insularity that characterized the rule of first president, Sukarno. Experts and technocrats, most notably US-trained economists, oversaw a process that Bradley Simpson (2008, 3) described as "military modernization," dismantling overt state controls over the economy and quelling dissent to facilitate foreign investment. Although this period witnessed the military playing a greater role in political and social life, the New Order also saw the incorporation of Euro-American popular culture and fashion and a related anxiety about the impact of unruly youth cultures on Indonesian national identity (Anderson 1990, 186–87).[2] Despite the violence with which Suharto maintained his grip on power, the New Order state witnessed the growth of spaces for middle-class consumption and leisure, where politics and the potential for unrest that that term conjured up were kept at bay (Leeuwen 2011, 4). Warias, whose emergent visibility was facilitated by this intersection of military rule and emergent forms of body-centered consumption among the middle classes, reveal the ways in which gender shaped the boundaries of technological participation in national mass publics with a mixture of discipline and pleasure through practices related to self-cultivation.

The centrality of outer appearances in shaping who could participate in national mass publics was evident at the first Jakarta Fair in 1968. President Suharto, who inaugurated the opening of the fair, described it as an opportunity for Indonesians to display their "greater utility to work for progress and the development of the economy" (Suharto 1968). Warias appeared in this context as theater performers, film stars, and proprietors of small and large beauty salons. Their carefully composed feminine beauty reflected a capacity for self-improvement, anticipating an obsession with "talk of improvement" (Li 2007, 1) that has come to characterize contemporary Indonesian culture. Press photographs taken at the Queen of Miss Imitation Girls competition reveal the kinds of feminine beauty that warias drew on to mediate between national and global visual symbols of modernity. The winner holds a large trophy and mace and wears a crown in the style of a US beauty queen of the 1950s. She and the warias who surround her demonstrate a studied commitment to the skills of styling hair, applying makeup, and designing and selecting the clothing required to achieve a polished femininity (figures 5 and 6). When performed in circumscribed contexts, warias' recognized position as beauty experts was a demonstration of an authentically Indonesian modernity.

Interpreted in this way, the integration of warias into national modernity was unremarkable, inasmuch as it reflected a broader pattern that harnessed the meanings of public gender to a project of development. Warias' skillful practice of femininity allowed them to become emblematic of beauty as a demonstration of possibilities for self-improvement widely observed in other postcolonial settings (Ochoa 2014; Jackson 2003; Besnier 2002; Cannell 1999). But the integration of Indonesian warias into national development digressed from an individualizing framework that rested on a capitalist production of the individual self in pursuit of nothing but its own success. Despite state experts' incorporation

FIGURE 5.   Contestants at the second Queen of Miss Imitation Girls competition held at the Duta Hotel in Central Jakarta, 1969.

Source: Antara Photography Archives and the Indonesian Press Photography Service (IPPHOS)

FIGURE 6.   The winner of the second Queen of Miss Imitation Girls competition in 1969, Sonny Sudarma, is presented with a ceremonial mace and trophy.

Source: Antara Photography Archives and the Indonesian Press Photography Service (IPPHOS)

of Euro-American concepts of gender and sex premised on pairs of mind/body and male/female dualisms, warias' narratives of gender did not rest on the view that the inner and outer parts of the person comprised an opposing pair. More often, warias framed the body as akin to an interface between self and society. As one waria explained, in terms that would have been similar to those current in the early New Order, public gender was like an obstacle that all warias had to work to overcome: "To live as a woman in this way is to live with a contradiction within your body. From your nature, style and everything else, how on earth should we present ourselves? How should we live a worthy life like a woman? What there is, there comes a time to make yourself more feminine, and this is not spontaneous. It has to be learned. And so, those waria who are still dressing up with a style that isn't yet stable like a woman, this is what becomes an issue in society." In terms that bring to mind anthropological descriptions of personhood in Java as an "awareness of vulnerability in interaction" (Boellstorff 2004, 475), warias' participation in development during the New Order rested on a concept of bodily cultivation that sought to grapple with a self that was always in dialogue with its social context.[3]

Interpreting ethnographic and historical accounts of the role of public femininity in claims to recognition offers a way to approach warias not according to discrete concepts of gender and sexuality at the level of the individual but rather as part of the broader emphasis on visual forms of power that have shaped how belonging in postcolonial Indonesia has been imagined and experienced in everyday life (Steedly 2013; Strassler 2020). I develop this theoretical insight by showing how, in certain spaces, modern feminine beauty for warias during the New Order was understood not as a form of self-expression but of participation in society (*masyarakat*). Despite their collective orientation toward society, warias nevertheless emphasized individualized acts of self-improvement. Yet what warias called a "contradiction in your body" was not precisely the same as the "wrong body" discourse that came to be the common narrative consolidated via medico-legal definitions of transsexuality described in the previous chapter (Stone 1992). The contradiction expressed by the waria quoted above instead indexed an understanding of appearances as a site for navigating a relationship to a public—and hence an understanding of citizenship—that facilitated other opportunities to pursue partial integration into the sociotechnical imaginary of state rule to accomplish recognition. For the state, the benefit of warias becoming beauty experts rested on a logic that in doing so they could limit the disruption that warias' gender nonconformity caused. This is perhaps why warias' expertise in feminine beauty resulted in a relatively conditional form of acceptance, a form of recognition for which warias were responsible but over which they had little control.

This chapter describes how warias came to occupy the role of beauty experts in the early New Order. To be sure, warias' integration into these schemes was a form of discipline, a counterpart to the raids by municipal police, as a strategy that aimed to manage risks associated with public gender when it threatened to disrupt public order. Yet warias commonly reflected on the history of their integration into vocational guidance programs in salon work, fashion design, and related fields in positive terms, saying that it facilitated forms of recognition that translated into citizenship. Warias were objects of expertise, then, but they were also active participants in governmental technologies that combined functionalist and aesthetic logics to defend public order. In this respect, warias' capacity to accomplish social acceptance rested on a set of logics that were similar to other components of New Order rule. Suzanne Moon described urban improvement in the city of Bandung in the 1970s as constituting a "technologically systematic integration of people" through processes applied to other municipal problems, which made "them and their work necessary and desirable to others within society" and therefore "integral to the smooth material functioning of the city" (2015, 192). In addition to being adjudicated on their capacity to be "of use to society," a turn of phrase common among warias themselves, the relationship between self-improvement and citizenship reflected a tenet of spatial governance that Nikolas Rose has described as "a double movement of autonomization and responsibilization" (1999, 170). Rather than simply being coercive, authorities produce "a web of visibilities, or public codes and private embarrassments over personal conduct," one that results in "*government through the calculated administration of shame*" (Rose 1999, 73, emphasis in original). Efforts to manage public gender was part and parcel of the process of "rendering technical" (Li 2007, 7) society (*masyarakat*) at the scale of the city. Warias leveraged the affective charge of public gender to other ends. Competing in a pageant, or working in a beauty salon, was not only about developing skills in a particular area to express an inner sense of self but served as a form of participation as an economic unit in the city and the nation. This individualized format of participation, the results of which were never assured, meant that warias were ultimately responsible for the success or failure of their integration within a collective public.

Gendered Publics

From the earliest years of the New Order, warias were recognized as individuals who were both applying feminine beauty to the body and dispensing it as digestible advice to other citizens. Such skills were in particular demand for weddings, public rituals that connected gender to projects of national belonging. Identifying the centrality of expertise in fields of feminine beauty, Tom Boellstorff observed: "The ultimate expression of this salon work is wedding makeup and hairstyling, where the bride, and also the groom, are 'made up' as prototypes of the true Indonesian, the idealized citizen-subject" (2005, 105). A similar sentiment was expressed by Maya, who like many other warias of her generation described salon work—and makeup for weddings in particular—as a prototypical form of *prestasi* or "good deeds," through which she saw herself as able to obtain a more respectable position in society. But even as Maya framed her achievements in the skills associated with wedding makeup as culminating in a public recognition of her refined status as an authentic waria, she also conceptualized *prestasi* in terms of achievements that were limited to her as an individual. In this respect, hers was an individualized form of participation in society, one in which both the achievements associated with beauty and the risks of failure were articulated on moral terms. Accordingly, Maya insisted that her skills in feminine beauty were her own—achievements through which she revealed an essential or innate character with greater clarity and which did not extend to any other waria.

This emphasis on individualized accomplishments that could be accumulated over time to achieve further successes recalls the relationship between beauty contests and self-cultivation in post–New Order Indonesia. Writing in the context of a beauty pageant that was an important demonstration of a coherent regional identity, Nicholas Long observed *prestasi* as reflecting "not a momentary event or performance" but demonstrating a "quality of people, a revelation of character and capability that can be accumulated through time to increase one's agency in the social world" (2007, 111). This understanding that the "institutionally unbound" (Bartky 1990, 75) quality of feminine beauty (and beauty as a feminized realm more broadly) makes it an ambiguous vehicle for accomplishing recognition is a view shared by feminist theorists. Sandra Lee Bartky described how becoming a beauty expert is a form of "discipline that can provide the individual upon whom it is imposed with a sense of mastery as well as a secure sense of identity" (1990, 77). Such experiences appear to be particularly charged at moments of great political and economic uncertainty. Feminine expertise performs a crucial role, given that it provides "confidence from following rules through technical mastery of the world" as well as "revelation and truth in conditions of uncertainty" (Jones 2010, 271). Attending to warias' participation in state citizenship reveals how, even during the authoritarian New Order, state power did not only take a unilinear and surveilling guise. As a form of selective display that was oriented toward a public, and a prototypical form of *prestasi* that warias performed on others in the course of their work as beauty experts, the adoption of feminine expertise could have unpredictable results. For warias, the paradox of visibility was experienced through everyday acts of seeing and being seen that required constant image management, the results of which they ultimately had little control.

Warias' position as experts in modern beauty was consolidated by the beginning of the 1970s, as they established reputations as some of the nation's most skilled beauticians and salon workers. The centrality of this form of participation in national society through the symbolic universe granted by heteronormative gendering during the New Order is usefully summarized by Tom Boellstorff (2007, 111): "Warias signify their gender by making themselves up, but when they make up Indonesian women or cut the hair of Indonesian men they 'make them up' as better representatives of proper modern Indonesian womanhood and manhood, without which what the state terms its family principle of heteronormative governance (*azas kekeluargaan*) would not be intelligible." This view was echoed by one sixty-five-year-old waria who recalled that the beginning of the 1970s saw a transformation in the position of warias that was partially the result of their successes in transforming themselves. This understanding rested on a delicate play on the relationship between gender as both innate and as constructed: "Our role as beauty experts goes to greater limits and is better [than that of non-waria women or men], because we do it in our own style. Because we embrace beauty work with all our soul, customers are really happy with the results." She cited this innate skill in the field of feminine beauty as the chief reason why "people prefer to be served by waria." Adding that "society knows that many waria are interested in salons, in beauty, are experts [ahli] in fields of fashion, design and others," she highlighted that warias' acceptance rested on their capacity to be "of use to society." Warias' engagement with beauty as a field of technical expertise, however, revealed the more unruly possibilities of recognition by mass publics.

The key concept that warias used to describe their role as beauty experts in the modern nation was dandan. As a commonly used term among warias in narrative accounts in everyday life, *dandan* refers to everyday yet often temporary forms of gendering, most commonly through hairstyling, the use of cosmetics, and dress (Boellstorff 2005, 93). Yet dandan was also central to warias' performance of gender as a component of their understanding of the self. It was through dandan that warias not only showed that they possessed a woman's soul but also made that interior sense of gender more complete. Describing this relationship between dandan and the self, one waria explained that "if you are a waria you dandan, you wear women's clothing, and change your voice [to a higher pitch]. . . . I learned how to do dandan by myself, just with a mirror and some makeup." These practices, when put together, served as the means to enact an improved public presentation. Warias are not the only individuals who practice dandan, which refers to a broader condition of making up and being made up, particularly for special occasions. Yet for warias, dandan is an important practice closely tied to visibility in public, a process wherein they apply expert knowledge to appearances in order to be seen by an audience. In this respect, the relationship between warias and dandan is exceptional but not unique. It parallels Marcia Ochoa's description of *transformistas* in Venezuela, where the use of plastic surgery, makeup, hairstyling, and technologies like hormone and silicone injections was not understood as the fulfillment of an a priori identity but seen as "[utilizing] technologies to allow the feminine body to emerge" (2014, 158), a possibility that arose within distinctive histories of national modernity.

It was this feature that made dandan for warias different from that performed by gay men. For gay men, the practice of dandan took place in particular circumscribed contexts and in ways that in some respects accentuated the artificiality of its manufacture (Boellstorff 2005, 167). As used among warias, dandan exceeded an emphasis on appearances, articulating a more thoroughgoing form of self-improvement. Warias described dandan to me not as altering or transforming the natural or preexisting biological reality but as a necessary part of externalization of a hitherto concealed self. This understanding of gender as a form of knowledge that, when applied to the body, makes an inherent character apparent differs from dominant theoretical considerations of gender that frame it as related to processes that lead to stabilization of sexuality and gender as identities (Butler 1990). Distinct from gender as a constantly iterated or performative practice that naturalizes heterosexuality on individual terms, the practice of dandan among warias, as I interpret it, reflects an understanding of personhood similar to the interplay between inner and outer parts of the self, akin to aesthetic allusions revealed or concealed, a concept present in classical Javanese literature (e.g., Florida 1995).[4] Emerging from a history in which the bodies and faces of Indonesians served as a semiotic object that had condensed race and class norms since the colonial period, dandan was a technology through which the boundaries of belonging to a modern Indonesian public were established and governed.

The practices that warias called dandan, which linked them to a distinctive aesthetic format related to global norms of feminine beauty, was present from at least the 1950s. The history of dandan reflects a form of discipline that served as a counterpart to the state's biopolitical efforts to establish authority over the natural grounds for sex on the grounds of physiology and reproduction. During the New Order, an invasive program of restricting women's fertility through reproductive health programs had served as the material means through which women were encouraged to understand themselves as "procreators of the nation" (Suryakusuma 2011, 101). Femininity at this time served a malleable set of symbols for debating and contesting social change. It was a supposedly apolitical domain in which "tensions and anxieties that accompanied political repression, rapid and uneven modernization, and economic inequality and instability were displaced onto the figures of woman and the family" (Brenner 1999, 36). Attending to dandan, even while focusing attention on norms of public comportment, both reveals warias' position within a broader effort made by the state to assert authority over the recognition of public gender and stresses the force of images of femininity that did not originate in domesticity or the nuclear family. The position of warias as participants in this more public register of femininity is reflected in one archival photograph taken in the early 1970s of a group of "wadam of the capital" who are gathered with Martha Tilaar, the prominent owner of the Sari Ayu cosmetics company (figure 7).

Warias' appearance here in the orbit of Sari Ayu, a well-known Indonesian cosmetics company that was a "representation of the face of the nation in a transnational age" (Saraswati 2013, 76; see also Barendregt 2011), reflects how

FIGURE 7. A group of "wadam" in Jakarta, gathered together with Martha Tilaar, the owner of the cosmetics company Sari Ayu.

Courtesy of the National Library of Indonesia

warias' participation in femininity must be contextualized within the broader texture of Indonesian national modernity. More important, warias' role as beauty experts—primarily revealed through warias' own recollections but also in glimpses of them in the historical archive—demonstrated how gender functioned not only as an individualized form of expression but also as a technological mediation that facilitated participation in national publics. To refer to warias' practice of dandan as oriented toward a national public, however, may give a sense of a single or unified frame of vision and audience to whom their expertise in fields of beauty was addressed. As had been the case in other settings and in previous historical periods, warias' ascendance to the role of beauty experts continued to be limited to circumscribed contexts where their potential for self-improvement, tied closely to a specific experience of bodily cultivation, was recognized and valorized. It is important to stress that warias could not easily move between different publics with the same degree of comfort. This was not a condition limited to warias. Beauty pageants for women during the New Order did not go uncontested and were at times a catalyst for volatile public debates over the relationship between appropriate sexual morality and national identity (Pausacker 2015). Similarly, warias' participation in public life continued to have an unpredictable quality, reflected in the fact that their skillful practice of dandan led to both forms of recognition as well as efforts to reduce their visibility to general society.

Dandan was an important vehicle for crafting a legible if aspirational claim to recognition as part of Indonesian national modernity. The warias who were present during the New Order recalled their ability to accomplish the status of beauty experts as a critical means through which they could demonstrate that they were "authentically waria." What this meant was that their claim to authenticity through the application of expertise rested, in important ways, on the recognition of that expertise by an audience. The gendered body was not secondary but a crucial medium through which the boundaries of participation in public life were made in Indonesia. In this sense, warias' experiences show that even during the authoritarian New Order, the state's control over the population was subject to ambiguity and flux at moments when claims to shared meanings broke down. Public gender shows how what Daromir Rudnyckyj (2010, 159) has described as a postauthoritarian state of "governing through affect" that rests on a relationship to the self as an "ethics of shared sentiment" has a history that extends at least to the New Order. Through the transfer of technologies of feminization onto methods of self-fashioning, warias engaged with "Indonesia" not as a singular or stable entity but as part of an unruly seeing public.

Authenticity and Imitation

One of the first stages on which warias skillfully wielded technologies of feminization to forge a sense of belonging within a national public was the Jakarta Fair, where warias were invited performers from at least 1968 to 1972. One waria, Tini, recounted that a group of performers had first worked at venues affiliated with the Jakarta Fair called "Sasana Andrawina" and the "Paradise Hall" (*Mingguan Djaja* 1968c, 4). Among warias, the spaces affiliated with the Jakarta Fair provided a glimpse of the possibility of working in professions through which they could cultivate their skills in feminine beauty, and in doing so contribute—with the oversight of city social workers through city-run guidance programs—to a broader project of development. Once the fair had concluded, however, it was unclear whether warias' presence on the city's streets would be tolerated as a component of public life. A common complaint voiced by warias in the popular press concerned the difficulty of finding ongoing, respectable forms of paid employment. This was also the most frequent justification given by warias as to why they sold sex on the streets of the city late at night, and in turn why they faced such fierce discrimination as a result. This negotiation with the meanings of public order had positioned them as part of a long-standing problem of gender nonconformity that stretched to the birth of Indonesia.

Warias also reflected on the Jakarta Fair as a crucial step in consolidating a collective and coherent sense of self-identification as a group. One seventy-year-old waria remembered the Paradise Hall not only as a place of work, where warias were able to accomplish recognition as beauty experts and to earn a living, but as a gathering place where warias came together to enjoy one another's company. She recalled, "From the ticket sellers, the bartenders and the hostesses, to the dancers, all of the employees were waria! There were waria strippers, waria pole dancers, and waria snake dancers." Although warias, she explained, were "undisciplined" at this time—referring both to their public presence and to their designation as an object of nuisance laws who required "guidance"—the advent of the Paradise Hall meant that, for the first time, they had a location in which to work and to forge a sense of solidarity imagined as a collective.

Although venues like the Paradise Hall operated on an irregular basis, they served as a location where warias asserted a presentable form of femininity that distanced themselves from an association with public sexuality. These contexts, which gradually resulted in the establishment of more permanent settings such as nightclubs and bars, generated substantial if voyeuristic interest in warias among the citizens of the city. The relationship between trans femininity and forms of bodily cultivation through performance in Indonesia was not unprecedented within Indonesian culture and throughout Southeast Asia at this time. Warias were an important component of political communication during the 1960s, appearing as "outspoken proponent[s] of new ways and ideas" (Hatley 1971, 100). Even prior to the advent of visual forms of communication and the rapid growth of consumer capitalism during the New Order, warias were observed as communicating with a national public. As James Peacock observed, "[The] transvestite singer . . . regularly and directly exhorts an audience to be *madju* [progress-oriented] and loyal to the nation. . . . The transvestite addresses a system, the Nation" (1968, 208–9). Describing the performance of femininity associated with *bakla* in the Philippines, Fenella Cannell similarly queried the centrality of expression of individualized sexual or gender identity, describing performances of femininity akin to the mediations that were performed by a shaman in ritual practice. Seen as "recapturings of power, not literally through possession, but through a wrapping of the body in symbols of protective status," such performances served as a "transformation of the personal by proximity to the power it imitate[d]" (1999, 223). Understood as the mediation of the body through gender and as part of wider universe of symbols that facilitate political communication, warias' appearance at the Jakarta Fair highlighted how disciplinary mechanisms of public gender gained power through a relationship to an affective experience of public spectatorship.

Warias' access to the skills and locations for performing urban-centered forms of feminine beauty during the New Order positioned them as a component of the technologies through which they asserted that they were public symbols of the nation's place in a modern, global order. These possibilities were facilitated by new locations at which warias could convey desires for improvement, ones that channeled the functionalist and aesthetic logics of New Order developmentalism into public gender. But by making up themselves and others, not only as a project of self-cultivation but as a means of participating in the unruly processes of forging a relationship to a national public that always contained the possibility of exceeding the nation, warias demonstrated the potential mutability of all gendered bodies and forms of social status that facilitated or prohibited participation in public life. At the beginning of the New Order, warias asserted that the body of the person who was performing was not a barrier to the expert application of femininity or to the assertion of a modern sense of selfhood tied to the possibility and promise of becoming an authentically national subject. Nevertheless, the possibilities of technology to enable access to citizenship remained conditional, entering into a traffic in images—one that included the body itself—which could evoke different reactions, depending on which public had assembled to see them.

This play on differently assembled publics and the prospect of authentic participation through the technology that makes them up is reflected in the "Queen of Miss Imitation Girls" beauty pageant. The use of the word "imitation" insinuates artifice, bringing to mind Stephen Gundle's description of midcentury beauty pageants in the United States, "the artificial creation of a fantasy event" at which the "illusion of substance rested on all concerned, organizers, spectators, press, and contestants, taking it seriously" (2008, 257). Yet the first winner of the competition should not be dismissed as an inauthentic parody of femininity. The cultivation of appearances was a distinctive stance that was primarily framed in terms of spectatorship as a means to bind together publics through a shared experience. Warias were not the only Indonesians who participated in beauty pageants during the New Order; pageants were and continued to be a popular commercial pursuit, a stage from which to establish spectatorship along the lines of a safe, carefully constructed, multicultural fantasy of the representation of difference (Long 2007). In this case, a sense of interiority was not necessarily linked to gender but rather to a sense of emergence within a national public that was not only imagined but demonstrated and felt through the body.

The experience of recognition draws attention to the specific meanings of imitation in this context. Judith Butler has famously theorized gender as performative to claim that "the original identity after which gender fashions itself is an imitation without an origin" (Butler 1990, 137). Yet the specific genealogy of the imitation in relation to gender for warias must be considered in light of its relationship to the terms "authentic" (*asli*) and "false" (*palsu*), keywords of Indonesia's experience of colonial and postcolonial history. As discussed in chapter 1, *asli* is central to how individuals understand themselves in terms of Indonesian national identity and belonging: "It is the ultimate criterion for belonging; what belongs to Indonesia and is deserving of recognition is that which is authentic" (Boellstorff 2005, 214). *Palsu* in turn refers to something that is manufactured through technology and as such subject to human intervention, in ways that the *asli* can never be. This anxiety about authenticity reflects the relationships between Europeans and Indonesians that emerged during the colonial encounter (Siegel 1997). Recall that the distinction between the authentic and the false underpinned a racialized discourse of difference that framed who was permitted to wear modern, Western clothes in public in the nineteenth and early twentieth centuries. In the late nineteenth century, some quarters of Dutch colonial society viewed the increasing numbers of young Indonesians who wore Western clothing as inadequate imitations or failed subjects of an inauthentic modernity (Mrázek 2002; van der Meer 2020). Members of colonial society rebuked these young Indonesian men through newspaper articles and other public forums, holding them up as counterfeits who had abandoned their authentic cultural roots to participate in the modern world.

The designation of warias as "imitation girls" in the early part of the New Order must be assessed in terms of a historical resonance with responses to the adoption of European clothing by Indonesians during the colonial period. As Arnout van der Meer described, the act of donning European clothing by non-Europeans in early-twentieth-century Indonesia was "both empowering and disruptive, as it raised questions about how one's appearance reflected one's ethnic, religious, and national identities" (2020, 14). The recognition of warias' femininity, a gendering that was (as was all gender) "crafted through human action" (Boellstorff 2007, 111), placed it under suspicion of falsehood. What was seen as discontinuous was not anatomical sex and outer appearances, but the very form that the style of public participation in postcolonial modernity should take. Warias' participation was not an effort to mimic or reproduce "woman" as an essentialized biological or individualized form of gender on ontological terms. In any case, such an ontological or biological reality was not yet fixed for anyone. Rather, warias were Indonesians who performed an alternative vision of global modernity, reflecting a connection to a transnational femininity and a future that rendered them under suspicion of belonging to the *palsu*, the false. Within this historical horizon of appearances and its relationship to a mass public, authenticity was not concerned with the accomplishment of a prior sense of self—a mirror or alignment between inner and outer parts of the person—but rather highlighted the central role that public gender played in making up what it was to be and become Indonesian.

The Fantastic Dolls

Emerging via the public profile that participation in the Jakarta Fair enabled, warias established several independent performance groups in the city in the late 1960s and 1970s, leveraging diverse spaces and audiences for the performance and positive evaluation of transgender femininity.[5] In Jakarta, I met several founding members of the Fantastic Dolls, a performance group founded in the late 1970s, the most famous and enduring group of waria performers in Indonesian history. Warias of different ages, ranging from fifty to seventy, whom I met in the course of fieldwork responded with a mixture of delight and pride when I asked them whether they had seen the Fantastic Dolls perform, and warias in each of my field sites and from many different parts of Indonesia fondly recalled the group's iconic status, which for many represented the pinnacle of warias' ascendance to the position of national beauty experts.[6] The Fantastic Dolls also attracted widespread interest in the national media, lauded as an exemplary group of warias who strived for acceptance and to be understood as a part of Indonesian society. One former member of the Fantastic Dolls and a senior waria leader, Nancy Iskandar, recalled the enormous popularity, glamorous reputation, and fees corresponding with high ticket prices that the group commanded for their performances in cities throughout Indonesia.

The Fantastic Dolls were established in 1977, having grown out of an array of performance groups that had been founded earlier in the decade by the well-known community leader Myrna Bambang.[7] One original member of the Fantastic Dolls, Meifei—who was born in 1947 and raised in Jakarta—had first started working in 1967 as a performer at the Taman Ria amusement park located in the city's central square. It was around this time that Meifei became a member of the Kichi-Kichi-Ka Dance Group, which predated two better-known performance groups, the Bambang Brothers and Wadam All Stars.[8] Both these groups were founded by Myrna Bambang, who in 1972 ascribed the commercial success of the Bambang Brothers to the fact that they had received a contract to perform at the Tropicana Club (*Kompas* 1972). In a 1979 newspaper article—published in the context of the death of several warias in a police raid—Myrna described how admission as a member of the Fantastic Dolls was rigorous and limited to the most talented on principles of "expertise" (*keahlian*). Myrna referred to warias' position in a taxonomy of feminine beauty, which she offered as a distinctive hierarchy that paralleled translations of Western psychological and medical taxonomies of gendered and sexual difference that circulated in the national media at the time.[9]

Rather than assessing authenticity via psychiatric and psychological forms of expertise, however, Myrna sorted warias according to skills associated with feminine beauty. Myrna set out four "classes" of waria, which were evaluated by their ability to apply the skills and knowledge associated with feminine beauty: "High-class waria, who work as designers and who have a high position, those who have enough expertise and work in salons, and as artists and so on, those who are pretty [cantik cantik] but don't have any expertise, and those waria who don't have a pretty face and don't have any skills" (Kompas 1979c). Myrna's account paralleled my own observations during fieldwork, when warias sometimes evaluated one another based on a rather harsh criteria of "quality" that rested on their ability to align themselves according to beauty standards expected in a given situation. This at times painful evaluation of quality among warias tied public gender to citizenship in ways that Tom Boellstorff characterized as "indicators of a shifting state of being accepted by society" (2007, 105). Myrna's emphasis in the 1979 newspaper article both reveals the centrality of economic improvement to gendered recognition and helps to locate it within an emergent governmental framework in which appearances were adjudicated within a regime of public order.

For warias, citizenship also rested on the capacity to acquire, deploy, and demonstrate the expertise of accomplishing public gender in the service of others. In this environment, the role of performance groups like the Fantastic Dolls in shaping the meanings of waria as a category of affiliation cannot be overstated. During my fieldwork, warias would spontaneously narrate the way in which the Fantastic Dolls represented a paradigmatic example of improving themselves in pursuit of acceptance. In a newspaper article that focused on the efforts of waria to accomplish acceptance, Nancy Iskandar explained that the primary objective of the Fantastic Dolls was to "introduce waria to society" (Kompas 1990, 5). Part of the relationship between cabaret performances and recognition emerged out of an emphasis on what warias called authenticity (asli), a claim that appeared grounded in whether or not they were recognized as warias when offstage as well. Part of the possibilities for recognition therefore concerned the more general publics for whom warias' performances were intended; the group was asli in part because it was famous throughout Indonesia for being composed of warias, recognized across all segments of society in a way that transcended a partial or privatized "queer counterpublic" (Paramaditha 2018, 75). The relationship between recognition and public gender expressed by warias appears to have grown out of the emphasis on the relationship between authenticity and appearances since the emergence of Indonesian national identity in the colonial period.

This historical discourse of the surface of the body as a locus for anxieties about authenticity was revealed in the emphasis, both expressed in everyday narratives of warias themselves and in reporting about the Fantastic Dolls, on warias' capacity to transform themselves not in terms of gender but in terms of national identity: "There are those among them that are made up [*dandan*] as Cher, a Hollywood actress who has won an Oscar. There are those that are in the style of Boy George, the male singer from England who often dresses up as a woman" (*Kompas* 1990, 5). For warias, the practice of dandan established recognition as a kind of drawing and crossing entwined boundaries of gender and nation.

The only video recording of the group that I have seen was of one of its final performances at the Millennium Hotel in Jakarta in August 2004, provided to me by Nancy Iskandar. Although it does not, of course, date from the New Order period, which is the historical focus of this book, it offers some valuable insights that suggest the aesthetic style and content of the group's performances in the 1970s and 1980s. Newspaper reporting and firsthand accounts I collected of the group's performances suggested that the Fantastic Dolls' performances consisted of an array of acts that included singing, dancing, magic, striptease, and comedy, usually glossed as cabaret. In the recording of the 2004 performance, the audience appears to be mostly male employees from a corporation or a government department. The performance starts with Myrna taking the stage, her makeup and clothing presenting more explicitly the logic of combination invoked in the very term *waria*; the left side of her body is dressed as a military general in uniform, complete with mustache and beard, and the right side of her body is a feminine, glamorous diva. Holding a microphone, she moves to the front of the stage, and with the side of her body decorated as a general facing the audience, she drops the pitch of her voice to a gruff growl. Switching the orientation of her body along with her voice, she introduces the Fantastic Dolls with their tagline: "Singing [in a low-pitched voice], dancing [in a high-pitched voice], and joking [again in a low-pitched voice], without *nungging* [bending over] [finally, in a high-pitched voice]."[10] She then switches to English to announce an "all-Indonesian female impersonation show," continuing on to oscillate between a low- and high-pitched voice at the beginning of each sentence. Yet even as this performance relied on a juxtaposition of a binary format of male and female, it more precisely reflected a concern born out of a pair of symbols tied to the authoritarian New Order: a unification and hence effort to overcome forms of military and state power, reflected in the General and the Diva.

Several routines followed this act; warias sang in sequined evening gowns, danced in Brazilian carnival costumes, and shook their bodies in the garb of Egyptian belly dancing. One waria sang a *dangdut* performance, a kind of Indonesian popular music, but did so wearing a Japanese-style kimono. Through appropriating caricatured symbols of national identity, this performance established a symbolic universe that showed warias' prowess at imagining other ways of transcending and becoming authentically Indonesian. I want to stress that my reading of the Fantastic Dolls' performance should not be interpreted as a theory of gender per se, but rather as a means to reflect on the performative qualities of citizenship. What the Fantastic Dolls articulated was a hope for a kind of minor belonging in the context of the forms of state citizenship offered during the New Order, drawing on gendered symbolism to pursue the possibility of an authenticity that transcended state control. If imitation was a component of the hundreds of performances by the Fantastic Dolls and in beauty pageants since the early New Order, it was an imitation of national identity and not gender. Warias knew their gender; after all, it was recognized by community and kin, even if not by the state. What their appropriation of various, highly stereotyped national outfits suggested was the tenuousness of state control over the meanings of authentic Indonesian national identity. Theirs was an expression of hope in alternative possibilities through which recognition might be imagined and practiced.

When considered in light of longer histories of recognition in Indonesia, warias' description of dandan not only reflects the imposition of Euro-American understandings of the modern self through a biopolitics of gender, but also suggests how gender is positioned within a broader condition of visual power. The performances by the Fantastic Dolls bring to mind what Lauren Berlant has called "diva citizenship," a form that "does not change the world . . . [but is] a moment of emergence that marks unrealized potentials for subaltern political activity" (1997, 223). The kinds of performances at work here had less to do with expression of the self, but rather gesture to the historical preoccupations of "authenticity" and "imitation" that have been central to imagining citizenship in Indonesian postcolonial modernity. The centrality of seeing and being seen to the forms of recognition sought by warias through the Fantastic Dolls and other performance groups means grappling with more unstable and pleasurable operations of visual power, beyond the anxious gaze in which "state surveillance . . . produced suspicion, first of all of oneself" (Siegel 2006, 160). Rather than only an object of the forms of state surveillance and violence that characterized New Order rule, appearances—and public gender—were also locations for more unruly and hopeful forms of participation in mass publics.

A Procedure for Public Order

To be sure, beauty pageants and performance groups were sites where only a limited number of warias could participate in public life. Among many warias

I spoke to, as well as in descriptions of the motivations for performance groups such as the Fantastic Dolls, a consistently expressed objective of participating in such groups was a desire to dispel the association between warias and forms of public sexuality on the streets of the city late at night. A corresponding concern was a desire to expand the locations where warias felt comfortable. Even though the early part of the New Order saw warias become increasingly visible, their experience of public space remained fraught with challenges. The acceptance that they struggled to achieve was always partial, dependent on the audience who recognized them. Although a glamorous femininity granted warias visibility in some quarters of the national media, in other places their very presence was met with the accusation that they were pornographic and therefore incompatible with the nation. Ultimately, these contestations over what it was to look like an authentic Indonesian were a concern that focused as much on appearances as it did on the space that warias were permitted to occupy.

As introduced in chapter 2, from the late 1960s and intensifying in the late 1970s, the extension of forms of recognition to warias was largely considered in terms of whether they could meet a set of standards associated with the norms of feminine beauty. Warias emphasized the importance of the guidance (*pembinaan*) programs offered by the Jakarta city government under Governor Sadikin, considered a watershed moment for its bestowal of the potential role that they could play in society. Public gender was central to the everyday management of the modernizing project of development. Binary gender was a form of self-improvement tied to bodily cultivation that symbolized and enacted economic forms of development at the level of the individual. Yet the history of warias highlights moments when the body was not a docile subject of state discipline but rather an unruly medium for alternate claims to modes of recognition, which shifted the stakes of citizenship from an imagined community to concerns over space.

After the end of the New Order in 1998, gendered forms of self-cultivation remained a crucial technique used to address what regional governments throughout the country have assessed, in familiar terms: that warias posed a disruption of public order. The *pembinaan* vocational training programs have continued to operate as a crucial form of discipline through which not only warias but a range of nonconforming citizens were provided with the tools to facilitate their rehabilitation into society.[11] One guide for the provision of social services to warias, published in 2008 by the national Department of Social Affairs, is an example of the format of the guidance programs warias have participated in since the late 1960s. The cover of the booklet is a photograph of a group of warias onstage at a beauty pageant, each wearing a crown, and the winner with a trophy. This photograph resembles in many respects the press photograph from the 1969 Queen of the Miss Imitation Girls competition. The guide stresses that accomplishing a polished modern femininity is not only concerned with self-cultivation but positions the individual waria as a participant in a wider social collective. It presents this conceptualization of personhood on economic grounds: "As individuals or as a part of society, warias possess a potential within them, which enables development of a more constructive direction, to facilitate empowerment of waria in the development of the nation" (Indonesian Department of Social Welfare 2008, 3). Reducing gender to a process aimed at maximizing participation through a set of procedures, the guide presents a series of universal "indicators" through which social workers and other trained experts could evaluate warias' capacity to participate in their own improvement and in doing so become participants in a project of national development.

Both this guide, and the vocational training furnished by municipalities that sought to achieve these aims, reflect a view that addresses public gender on technological terms, a counterpart to the municipal regulations directed at prohibiting or limiting warias' movement in public space. Both the guide and vocational training present feminine beauty in terms that Christopher Kelty has called a "procedure," a "set of rules, techniques, and tactics for organizing people, issues, and things in the service of collective and equitable decision-making, getting things done, and/or changing the way things are" (2019, 3). The implementation of these schemes relied on a disavowal of warias' own self-knowledge—a struggle over the possibilities of recognition—that Sandy Stone has attributed to medical transsexuality in the United States, "a taxonomy of symptoms, criteria for differential diagnosis, procedures for evaluation, reliable courses of treatment, and thorough follow up" (1992, 162). Although concerned with facilitating transformations at the level of the individual self, warias in their position as beauty experts presented that self as embedded within a specific experience of collective belonging, made possible by the scale of society. Even as the locus of improvement was the individual self, the measurement of progress toward its accomplishment is an individual's position within society, a criterion of acceptance over which individuals have little control. The participation of warias as beauty experts in a national public and the self that it indexes reflects the application of technology to limit the possible alternate routes to recognition through public gender. The vision that warias presented of society was an alternative collective to that of a state with its emphasis on order. Despite the potential for making and seeing as a part of alternative publics, the specific connection between public gender and the self during the New Order transformed warias into a potential disruption. In this way, they were placed under a suspicion that never entirely disappeared.

NATIONAL GLAMOUR

In the photograph, a waria stands in a dazzling black-and-gold dress, one hand on her hip and the other resting on the hood of a red sports car (figure 8). She holds her gaze steadily, looking with purpose into the distance, as if called to the nighttime festivities in which warias have participated and a form of visibility tied to their gender performance that has been an object of surveillance since at least Indonesian independence. For the waria in the photograph, the image does not merely serve as a record of the past; it is a way to keep alive her memories and to seize control over how she wishes to be seen by an audience.

This photograph was one of hundreds contained in the personal collection of Tadi, a waria who was in her mid-seventies when we first met during fieldwork in Yogyakarta in 2014. Tadi frequently invited me into the living room of her home in the city, located approximately five hundred kilometers and an eight-hour train ride to the east of Jakarta. In her house, we would talk late into the balmy tropical night to the chirping of crickets and roar of motorbikes. Hers was one of hundreds of houses perched precipitously on a hill above a river that swelled with rain in the wet season and was completely parched in the dry months, a simple two-room dwelling constructed of bamboo and plywood. Tadi lived in humble surroundings and mostly spent her days alone, at a remove from the extensive community circles of waria in the city. Her life at the time that I met her did not adequately represent the richly populated, highly social one that she had lived over the time depicted in this collection of photographs, taken over a period spanning approximately a decade from the late 1970s to the late 1980s.

FIGURE 8. A waria in a glamorous sequined dress poses beside a car in Yogyakarta around 1980.

Source: Tadi's personal collection

But through her collection of photographs and narrative accounts of life at the height of the New Order, it was possible to situate her among the dense social worlds of warias in Yogyakarta and beyond.

The photographs consisted of scenes from everyday domestic life, life on the streets at night, large group gatherings before and during events, and formal portraits taken in rented rooms of local studios. With few exceptions, every photograph depicted warias in makeup and dressed in women's clothing, corresponding with an understanding of the practice of dandan as the broad utilization of technologies of feminization to accomplish public visibility. Warias in both Jakarta and Yogyakarta agreed that in the 1980s public practice of dandan was at its most visible.[1] The photographs were a visual record of both the practice of dandan among waria and its relationship to shifting aesthetic norms of feminine beauty more broadly during the 1980s, the decade in which Suharto perfected the cultural display of Javanese tradition as a symbolic counterpart to the "regime of order" central to the technological security state.[2] John Pemberton described the selective occlusion and display of carefully staged rituals by the New Order state as an "exemplary exercise in orderliness" and a demonstration of a "state in which nothing happen[ed]" (1994, 315). But as the photographic images in Tadi's collection and the centrality of them to her understanding of being and becoming a waria show, the state never achieved a total monopoly on visual power. Warias' practice of dandan emerged instead as a way of seeing and being seen that harnessed other collective imaginings and practices of identification in public extending beyond that authorized by the state. Dandan was a form of bodily cultivation that enabled public participation in the modern life of the city and the nation. More than this, however, the practice of dandan among warias reflected the centrality of class to the meanings of public gender in shaping sociotechnical imaginaries during the New Order. Understanding these photographs of dandan not only as representations but as constitutive of its potential for multiplication and enhancement helps to understand how gender in the New Order was at once hopeful and dangerous, imagined as a way of seeing and being seen that was in dialogue with the affective intensity of mass publics.

This final chapter introduces Tadi's photographs and the narratives that accompanied them. It draws on the photographs alongside oral histories for an ethnographic encounter with the past, an approach that allows for a more thoroughgoing interpretation of the ways in which trans femininity was shaped within a specific experience of postcolonial modernity characterized by authoritarian rule. The 1980s was a period that witnessed the consolidation of the New Order state's distinctive visual format of power, with increased access among Indonesian citizens to visual technologies, including film and television. In describing the centrality of emergent visual technologies during the New Order,

Saya Shiraishi depicted the president as synonymous with the act of unilateral state power to see without itself being seen, as when he "appeared on TV, standing in silence ... with his dark sunglasses" (1997, 91) or in a more benign role, holding a video camera during family holidays (see also Strassler 2009). These visual signs conveyed a sense of state power that lay in the use of technologies to make the objects of its gaze visible, an all-seeing gaze that denied access to the source of that gaze or the capacity to ascertain its authenticity.

I attend to photographs taken by and of warias in everyday life as a way to interpret the processes involved in making Indonesian modernity at the intersection of visual technologies, the body, and the meanings of state citizenship. Warias' rich historical engagement in Indonesian publics, and vexed visibility, can contribute to Karen Strassler's pathbreaking interpretation of the use of popular photography in Indonesia to graft "an alien and yet-to-be-achieved modernity" onto more intimate and personal domains, "generating new conceptions of time, truth, authority, and authenticity" (Strassler 2010, 18). Focusing attention more broadly beyond warias' enmeshment within photographic images and visual technologies, I propose that dandan is also a practice that works to mediate between visual forms of representation at the level of the nation and everyday affective registers of navigating public space. The previous chapter described how the possibility to become beauty experts emerged in the shadow of city and state projects of governance that limited the meanings of participation in public life. Nevertheless, warias consistently stressed the centrality of their participation in vocational training schemes in fields related to feminine beauty as helping them to acquire skills for self-improvement that enabled acceptance by society (*di terima oleh masyarakat*). This chapter looks to the opportunities that public gender offered that were not as restricted as the disciplinary projects pursued by city governments or that always had the state in mind as a single arbiter of the authenticity of citizenship. Practices of dandan were also addressed to other audiences, emphasizing the instability and potential for alternate forms of participation that flickered at the corners of visuality as a public domain over which the state sought to wield control. Photographs of waria practicing dandan in the 1980s reveal that cisgender is not an inevitable or natural basis for determining authentic citizenship, but rather is a divergent set of meanings shaped through struggles over participation in the technologies that make visible claims to recognize authenticity.

This chapter returns to a question that has arisen at different points in this book: What are the meanings of gender as an effort at cultivation and curation that is central to being a citizen who participates in the publics made possible by the modern state? Considering the historical centrality of participation in mass publics among Indonesian warias (Peacock 1968; Hatley 1971; Geertz

1976, 295), I turn to the role of photographic technologies as a crucial component of practices of dandan and gender as they were shaped within the broader economic context of Indonesia during the 1980s. An ethnography of historical photographs from the New Order period further pushes back against the limitations of Euro-American theories premised on the cisgender/transgender binary, while also pinpointing it as a model that shifts a concept of biological sex to psychological gender, retaining the limitations of naturalizing citizenship as the property of a biological individual understood in terms of a mind/body dualism. The history of warias introduced thus far has outlined both the analytical shortcomings and exclusions that follow from an assessment of citizenship as naturally following from individual personhood. Rather than a natural state, warias' participation in public gender shows just how constructed and hence limited a concept of citizenship framed within the concept of the biological individual has been. During the New Order, an understanding of an awareness of the self as a national subject was increasingly recast in terms of development and the attainment of middle-class status. Widespread forms of national development, including those that were focused on poor and rural populations, held that economic underdevelopment was a lack that individuals needed to become aware of in order to overcome (Tsing 1993). The aesthetics and practices of dandan as a form of national glamour are much more portable, sensuous provocations that facilitated movement across boundaries of class and nation and which needed no authorization, apart from that provided by the viewing public. Attending closely to warias' practice of dandan helps in understanding the way that public gender opened citizenship to possibilities apart from the grid of state bureaucracy, generating affective incitement to participate in social life in ways that could transcend the state's exclusionary format of development. The practice of dandan instead made legible an understanding of citizenship as a set of claims and struggles waged within a more fractured domain of belonging to a national public in the authoritarian state.

Authenticity and Evidence

Tadi was born in 1946 in Yogyakarta, the same year that the city was announced as the capital of the newly declared Republic of Indonesia. Although a clear biographical arc was difficult to establish, from our conversations I pieced together that she had spent her early life in Yogyakarta, and although she had traveled frequently, had returned to settle down there when she was in her early twenties. Unlike many waria, Tadi did not work in fields associated with beauty but rather for the Indonesian state railway company as an assistant in train restaurant cars. This constituted an important feature of her life, given that it marked a clear delination between her public performances of dandan and the standard-issue uniform she was required to wear at work. Yet this did not appear to have posed a major problem for Tadi; as she explained, everybody at her workplace knew that she was a waria anyway. Before her retirement, she worked in this position for more than twenty years, during which she traveled between cities on the island of Java. Tadi was particularly proud of her rare accomplishment as one of the few warias who had been able to gain formal employment within a state-owned industry.

Part of what made Tadi's collections of photographs so important to her was that her employment meant she was not able to practice dandan in all contexts and at all times of day. Rather, because of strict policies that required a uniform public presentation while at work, Tadi limited her femininity to particular times and locations, mostly in salons and at night in the context of sex work, for which she had been arrested in raids by municipal police several times.[3] Given that her performance of dandan was necessarily limited by the nature of her employment, she always carried a photograph of herself to prove that she was in fact an "authentic waria." As she explained, "When I was at work I brought a photo in case I met a man. I always brought a photo, so if I saw a man, I'd approach him and show it to him. If I didn't bring a photo, he might not believe me [that I was waria]." Echoing Maya's stress on her capacity to transform herself into a more beautiful version of famous actresses, Tadi insisted that these photographs served as "evidence" (*buktinya*) and that I could "see for myself" (*bisa lihat sendiri*) that what she was saying was true. Her appeal to visual evidence in support of claims to truth mirrored a specific kind of "documentary history" (Strassler 2010, 270) common to historical practices during the New Order, one that emerged out of broader anxieties over the relationship between truth and authenticity. If anything, Tadi's description of the importance of carrying a photograph of her performing dandan seemed to amplify her capacity for making claims to authenticity and through it recognition.

To Tadi, the photographs thus not only represented a treasured artifact of a lifetime of memories but served as documentary evidence of her claims, as reflected in her studied treatment of them as precious objects. Stored in sturdy albums and printed on quality paper, the photographs reflected a considerable investment in a neighborhood where many residents struggled to meet even the most basic of economic needs. When I asked her why she had started taking photographs in the late 1970s, Tadi simply explained that it had only become affordable at that time and that once she started, she had found it to be an enjoyable hobby. She was clearly no expert in photography, appearing ambivalent about the technology even as she actively and enthusiastically used it. One reason why she permitted me to both record and reproduce the photographs was that, as she framed it, ownership over the images was not a straightforward matter of property. While many of the people in the photographs were identifiable, Tadi referred to the collection as an archive of "Indonesian warias" whom she imagined on collective terms, bringing to mind alternative yet nevertheless overlapping possibilities of belonging to the publics made possible by the limited and bounded imaginary of the nation-state (Anderson 1996). My participation in reproducing these images, and contextualizing them in this book, was seen as one further step in expanding the grounds for participation in a collective public, raising hopes for recognition as authentically "Indonesian." This framing highlighted how efforts at taking, curating, and reproducing the images was not an idiosyncratic or individualized form of self-styling but reflected a hope of shared recognition as part of a collective public that was constituted for and by warias, one through which they could exercise greater control over the means of technological reproduction.

The photographs also help the viewer to see a more everyday aspect of warias' entanglement within the historically specific visual regimes of Indonesian postcolonial modernity. The aesthetic styles related to the practice of dandan apparent in the photographs—a counterpart to my historical description of how warias began to gain a reputation as beauty experts from the early New Order— show how dandan was gradually transformed into an aesthetic that I characterize as a form of national glamour. In referring to the styles of clothing, makeup, and other aspects of public gender presented in the photographs as national, I do not mean that the practices of dandan in these photographs are explicitly nationalist (although some do draw on national symbols of affiliation), or that they are explicitly condoned by the state. Rather, I do so to further illustrate how dandan reflected a format for femininity that connected the state's promotion of self-cultivation to feminine symbols of consumer capitalism in the market-based logic of the authoritarian New Order. Dominant accounts of glamorous femininity at times insinuate that it is akin to a façade, what Stephen Gundle called a "project or canvas on which a variety of socially significant meanings may be inscribed" (2008, 11). I want to link glamour to citizenship in a different way. Rather than outer appearances as markers of inauthenticity, I follow Marcia Ochoa's interpretation of glamour as an aesthetic which (in Ochoa's case) Venezuelan *transformistas* used "to draw down extralocal authority, to conjure a contingent space of being and belonging" (2014, 89; see also Berlant 1997). My interpretation of national glamour, and the centrality of it in making spaces for belonging at this time, must also be understood in light of the widespread understanding of personhood in Southeast Asia in which outer appearances are not signs of insincerity but key to the accomplishment of authenticity. As Nancy Florida argued, appearances do not conceal an inner truth, but are viewed as signs to be decoded by trained eyes, a "clue presenting itself to be read" (1995, 273). Yet even as glamour was an aesthetic central to the public practice of dandan among waria—and hence arguably that which was most open to interpretation by public audiences—it was not the only aesthetic format that their trans feminine mediations took. The practice of dandan was never a univocal style limited to glamorous display. The photographs showed that warias performed myriad styles, which ranged from the demure to the spectacular. The sheer number of photographs taken at night and in public spaces and given over to glamorous femininity nevertheless raise the question as to why this particular aesthetic played a central role in shaping the experience of public recognition.

A key shaping factor in warias' practice of dandan was, as I argued in chapter 2, the regulation of public space at the scale of the city. Tadi's photographs demonstrated how, as late as the 1980s, there continued to be differences in performances of dandan according to the time of day and location in which waria were present. This highlights the persistence of the spatial separation of forms of dandan and public gender more generally, even though warias' narratives described that such separation tapered off at the beginning of their golden age from the late 1960s onward. Indeed, perhaps the most dramatic distinction that can be observed in these photographs is between the practice of dandan at night (figures 8, 9), including the sequined gown that I introduced at the beginning of this chapter, and that which was performed during the day (figure 10). Waria's recollections of the period suggest that it was not necessarily important to practice dandan consistently in each setting in which a waria might be socially recognized. Perhaps because Tadi could not practice dandan at work, her narratives often centered on her relationship to practices of dandan explicitly undertaken for a wide public audience.

On one occasion Tadi described in detail the location in Yogyakarta where she presented herself in dandan in public, noting how the warias present stood apart from women: "In the past we had our own location. The women [sex workers] were here, and there was a ditch over there. Then, over there, were the waria. Waria were right at the back, but I was at the far end of them. I didn't want to be in the dark. I wanted to be in the light." Tadi and other warias' engagement with glamorous femininity in public spaces, albeit under certain conditions, highlights the delicate negotiation that it required. Tadi insisted that appearing in dandan in public spaces at night was a particularly important practice for her: "After meeting waria in a nearby salon, I started to practice dandan [berdandan] regularly. I started to practice dandan in public in the town square, when I was looking for men." Since the beginning of the New Order, salons have served as a crucial locus of social life and opportunity for economic advancement for warias throughout Indonesia. Tadi described how several well-known salons in the city, including the Ambassador Salon, served this function, connecting warias to a

FIGURE 9. A waria poses on a street corner in Yogyakarta at night, ca. 1984.

Source: Tadi's personal collection

FIGURE 10. A waria dressed in daytime dandan at a beach near Yogyakarta in the mid-1980s.

Source: Tadi's personal collection

wider community. These salons, and the senior leaders associated with them, provided the infrastructure through which warias organized themselves into groups that undertook a range of activities. Tadi recalled fondly the role of organized sporting competitions, both football and volleyball, that bound Yogyakarta warias together into teams, which frequently departed for competitions in other cities. Salons were also a key site where warias obtained access to the technologies of feminization through which they could cultivate expertise in makeup, hairstyling, and other forms of self-improvement. It was salons that facilitated the gendered public visibility that positioned warias alongside, yet separate from, other public forms of femininity in the Indonesian city.

The historical practices of dandan pictured in Tadi's photographs overlap with a period of significant reorganization in forms of state power during the New Order. In the early 1980s, just at the time when many of these photographs were being taken, the military and other state operatives covertly undertook what came to be referred to in the press as "mysterious killings," the targets of which were known and suspected petty criminals. One way in which the state instilled fear in citizens was through the visual forms of power it deployed, which stretched from its extensive surveillance apparatus to pictures in the pages of newspapers. James Siegel described how anxiety about "criminal types" was fed by newspapers popular among working-class people in Jakarta, in which photographs of the faces of criminals were obscured through bars over their eyes. According to Siegel, this served as a demonstration of the power of the state to erase citizenship claims. Such pictures were a "photographically imposed mask or veil," behind which was "only the face of ordinary Indonesians," an aesthetic style that Siegel interpreted as reflecting historical fears of those who claimed to be citizens but were not, a sense of something "familiar, not strange, or, rather, strange in its familiarity" (1998, 6). The public practice of dandan demanded a delicate engagement with the shadowy agents of the state and their efforts to control the limits of participation in public life, making sure that those who were "wild" (liar) were visible in their invisibility, a target for defining who was in fact a legitimate "citizen" (warga). In this respect, Tadi's photographs can be usefully contrasted with Karen Strassler's description of Indonesians' appropriation of the portrait photography used in state bureaucracy, employing the format instead for idiosyncratic purposes of family and individual memory, exceeding its role as a "fetish of state power" (Strassler 2010, 128). In contrast to the identity card—itself a visual icon that placed citizens within a gendered regime of surveillance—the practice of dandan, performed on the body and face of ordinary citizens, reflected public gender as a different kind of public sign, one that made possible claims to recognition as authentic citizens as part of a public that itself was beyond the control of the state.

Given that the practice often faced hostility from state and nonstate actors, warias' efforts to make themselves hypervisible through the performance of dandan may seem unusual. Tadi's statements on the reasons why she wanted to be visible echoed a desire commonly expressed among warias during the New Order. Tom Boellstorff (2005) described how discourses about national belonging in Indonesia have shaped deeply felt desires for recognition, even for those such as waria, gay men, and lesbian women, whose desires and embodiment might appear at first glance foreclosed by the heteronormativity of these discourses. During the New Order, the practice of dandan was similarly incorporated into discourses of national belonging. Warias came to believe that social acceptance might one day be possible if only they expended enough effort to obtain the expertise associated with a skillfully performed modern femininity, a femininity that not only showed but revealed the authenticity of their claims to citizenship.

Becoming Waria

The importance of public visibility through dandan is better understood by tracing the relationship between narratives of the self and expressions of national belonging among warias. Across all my fieldsites, warias narrated a relationship between appearances related to dandan and an inner self in ways that commonly invoked tropes that drew on visual metaphors of personhood. These often came up in spontaneous reflections on self-transformations undertaken as a source of inspiration and potential for claiming public recognition through what they called "jadi waria" [becoming waria] (Hegarty 2018, 365). One forty-year-old waria defined her selfhood as a process of becoming waria, which she narrated in terms of the externalization of visible signs, using a metaphor of an empty vessel that could be filled up over time. She described trying out different social settings and gradations of feminine gender performance before settling on becoming waria, by which she meant appearing in dandan on a consistent if not daily basis. She explained her own transition in terms of the phrase "banci kaléng," meaning a "canned" (or, as I have interpreted the term elsewhere, "empty") waria, a reference to the period during which she tentatively began to practice dandan but only within circumscribed settings, retaining a mostly masculine gender presentation on an everyday basis.[4] She conveyed to me a common narrative of the process of becoming a waria as a series of steps: "We start out as *gay ngondhek* [feminine gay], and then we become *banci kaléng*. We only become complete when we meet other waria in salons, participate in *nyébong* [spaces commonly associated with transactional sex for waria] and perform dandan." In this view, signs of "waria-ness" (*kewariaan*) are initially open only to those able to read them, gradually revealed by the adoption of knowledge and its application onto the body as a means to become visible to the public. For many warias, practicing dandan at night and during the day, in public and in private, was described as the culmination of the process of becoming waria.

This understanding of a body that becomes increasingly visible over time rests on an implicit comparison with gay men, who are understood as able to be invisible or able to conceal their sexuality. This view is not entirely straightforward, given that it relies on the assumption that there has always been a distinction between the practices that constitute identification as gay and identification as a waria. Indeed, many warias explained to me that it was only during the 1980s that a clear distinction between themselves and gay-identified men became increasingly evident. This is perhaps because the term *gay*—signifying a man who desires a person of the same gender—was itself not in wide circulation until the early 1980s (Wijaya 2019), more than a decade after the establishment of the first waria organizations in Jakarta in the late 1960s. Recall that a single term, *banci*, was used to refer to a very wide range of gender and sexual embodiment, not all of which appears to have rested on transformations made to outer appearances. Still, warias usually stressed a degree of permeability between the two subject positions while emphasizing their distinctiveness at the level of the soul, particularly at events or performances at which dandan was practiced (Boellstorff 2005, 175–77). Waria whom I spoke with commonly explained the chief difference marking them as distinct from gay men as their comfort in feminine attire across all settings, as well as the degree of skill in the adoption of knowledge and technologies of enacting a feminine appearance through dandan most of the time and in most situations.

Nevertheless, accounts of becoming waria as the culmination of a process rested on an understanding that there was also a family resemblance between identification as waria and as gay, even as they were distinct terms that indexed distinct understandings of the self. Such similarities and divergences in the gay/waria boundary eschewed a firm demarcation between sexuality and gender, suggesting a more processual understanding of personhood that renders any claim to what David Valentine called an "ontological separateness of gender and sexuality" under suspicion as a move that "transforms an analytic distinction into a naturalized, transhistorical, transcultural fact" (2007, 62). As is the case above, narrative accounts of warias often commenced with a description of a gradual revelation of character that began with being seen as ngondhek and gradually adopting dandan more of the time. That said, it is important to clarify that ngondhek is distinct from the femininity that waria accomplish through dandan, given that "it is made up of actions—gesture, language, clothing—that can be quickly set aside . . . it is not strongly linked to bodily modification" (Boellstorff

2005, 166). Warias recounted that the difference here lay in their willingness to both exercise mastery over the application of everyday practices associated with dandan and the comfort that they experienced as a result of doing so, which made it entirely distinct from *ngondhek*. Despite this degree of permeability between the two terms, warias have long stressed that the dandan gay men perform was distinct from their own, while not discounting the possibility that such performances may be the very means through which a person comes to recognize themselves as a waria.

Judith Butler provided a powerful and oft cited model for understanding gender in terms of its relationship to an audience, wherein gender naturalizes heteronormativity through the "repeated stylization of the body" (Butler 1990, 33), imagined as an alignment between inner self and the body. As Butler made clear, the seamless performative dispensations required to sustain gender as a natural property of a person come under scrutiny in contexts where gender performance—classically theorized in relation to drag performances—can also be consciously enacted and thus subverted through parody or imitation. As Esther Newton's (1979) observations of situational performances of femininity among gay men and drag queens revealed, gender performance is not necessarily univocal in the West. And in the 1960s United States, the stakes of disregarding such boundaries differed significantly along class and race lines. The full-time femininity of "low-status queens" paradoxically represented a pinnacle of "coherence and power" (Newton 1979, 30) when contrasted with white middle-class gay men, who limited their performance of femininity to private settings. This partially reflects how sexual and gender normativity was condensed through racial and class difference in the United States, helping to explain why it was that mainstream efforts to advance gay and lesbian rights in that context have predominantly rested on a formulation of sexuality (and, increasingly, gender identity) in terms of private rights and the body imagined as the property of a bounded individual. One of the effects of normative formulations of gay and lesbian rights as claims to private identity, as David Valentine described, was the gradual excising of "the excess of public sexual deviance, gender variance, and street life from the category of homosexuality and [insistence] on the gender normativity of homosexuality" (2007, 242). Distinct from the form of public symbolism in which gender nonconformity was bound up with homosexuality as a product of the individual self in the US, practices of dandan in Indonesia could (under certain conditions) refract desires for modernity that, if anything, led to an increased visibility of transgender femininity in pursuit of claims to recognition.

As previously noted, in New Order Indonesia, a capacity to style the body with the trappings of modern femininity was advanced as one strategy for social acceptance. This chiefly hinged on a relationship to the expanded visibility made possible by the mass media. Thus, the visibility of waria of various social classes does not appear to have been structured by the kinds of "trouble" that come when the "regulatory fiction" (Butler 1990, 136) of gender is disrupted in the West. As the historical accounts of public gender throughout this book suggest, the fact that there is a disjuncture between outer appearances and how people imagine themselves has not necessarily provoked a crisis of authenticity at the level of the self in this context. As demonstrated in the previous chapter, the tension between outer appearances and inner self was instead experienced in terms of navigating the relationship between self and society. As this book has shown, the public visibility of warias has been met with moments of acceptance as well as moments of rejection within Indonesian postcolonial modernity, depending on from whom they have sought recognition. This relationship to public visuality highlights the need to attend to the historical specificity of processes of defining which bodies should perform masculinity and femininity, the kinds of behaviors that those bodies are thought to index, and the spaces in which they should be visible under the conditions of postcolonial modernity. Understanding this process requires examining the distinctive technologies that yield the possibility of new modes of gendered affiliation and recognition, and in particular the kinds of technologies that are meaningful to warias themselves.

The visual technologies that constitute the practice of dandan among warias did not only incorporate feminine styles from the mass media and corresponding forms of national glamour but reflected a visual logic that drew from the powers of the state's bureaucratic practices of documentary identification. In narrative accounts of the New Order, and during my encounters in my 2014 and 2015 fieldwork, warias often struggled to obtain identity cards or other bureaucratic forms of identity issued by the state, in part due to their fraught connection to their families. In some of Tadi's photographs, a single waria was positioned alone against a wall (figure 11). In style and format, these images mirrored the portrait photographs that are commonly required for identity cards and other bureaucratic purposes in Indonesia. This use of bureaucratic-style portraits in forms of self-fashioning was not necessarily surprising; as mentioned, the identity card and its portrait photograph was a key component of New Order bureaucracy. Yet the unofficial identity card portraits presented here were not necessarily captured by a photographer for the purposes of the extensive state's surveillance apparatus. Rather, the photographer and the person photographed staged what was designed to look like a bureaucratic portrait photograph. Such images draw on the genre conventions of bureaucratic portraits even as they subvert their functionalist aesthetic by introducing a style that brings state-sanctioned femininity into dialogue with the practice of dandan as national glamour. In its photographic mediation, the practice of dandan was one way in which warias

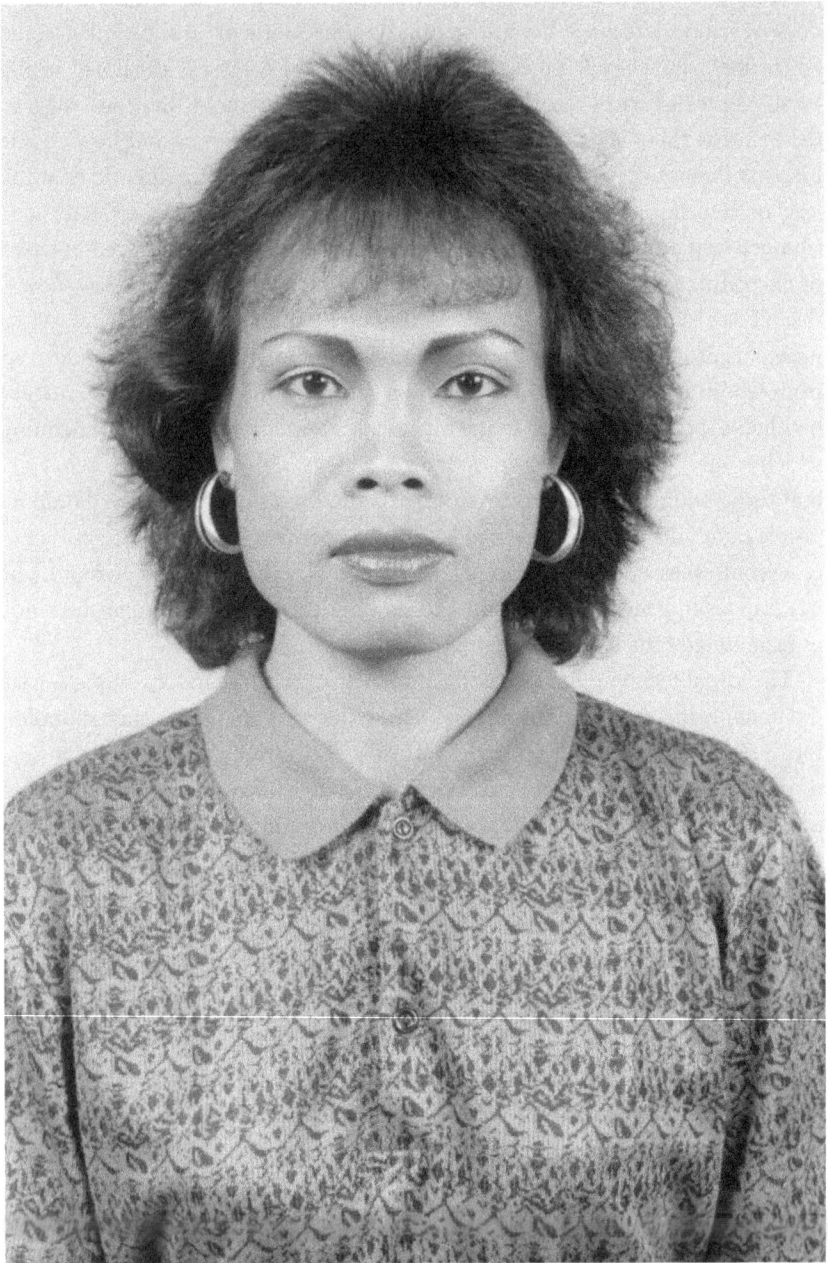

FIGURE 11. A waria poses against a plain backdrop in the style of a portrait photograph in the mid-1980s.

Source: Tadi's personal collection

seized control of the state's effort to adjudicate the boundary between the asli and the palsu, the authentic and the false. This appropriation of the aesthetics associated with the state's visual powers in these photographs makes a poignant point that for warias, the practice of dandan offered an alternative route to visual recognition by neighbors and kin that did not require the authority of the state for legibility.

Into the Lights, onto the Stage

The practice of dandan as a specific technological act was performed as part of a wider repertoire of public visibility. This understanding was reflected in Tadi's frequent use of metaphors associated with performance when expressing an early desire to practice dandan. She commonly reflected on her initial steps toward practicing dandan as a calling that was like being "on the stage" and "in the lights." On one occasion, she recalled to me, "I used to dance like I was on a stage since I was little. I used to behave like this in public settings, but my parents couldn't yet recognize why I did so." Echoing the conception of gendered visibility, encompassing dress, makeup, and narratives of selfhood that all form part of a process of becoming waria, Tadi explained that becoming aware of her woman's soul came in the form of subtle signs of femininity, which were the reflection of sexual desire for men. Like many warias, Tadi described this as a gradual process, one that was achieved through others' recognition of signs of her being a waria.

Photographs of the practice of dandan attested to warias' skillful use of technologies of feminization to transform their public gender into a form of visibility that could enable recognition. These photographs also prompt a number of questions. What kind of recognition does the practice of dandan offer to waria? What kind of audience does their performance gather, whether under the lights on a street corner or illuminated by a camera's flash? Rather than displaying or emphasizing consistency, the practice of dandan among waria highlighted the fragmented scales at which recognition was possible; certain times and places were understood as inherently more suitable than others. Some settings, waria maintained, simply facilitated recognition more readily than others. Other audiences had to be approached with caution but, given enough effort, might warm to their presence.

A desire for recognition by an audience offers further insights into how spatial governmentality shapes the meanings of the gendered body. Many photographs, whether taken on street corners or set among tropical foliage (figure 12), share parallels with Marcia Ochoa's (2014, 88) description of transnational glamour as "a way of reordering time and space around oneself for purposes of enchanting."

FIGURE 12. A waria poses amid foliage in a studio in Yogyakarta in the mid-1980s.

Source: Tadi's personal collection

Ochoa interpreted trans femininity as part of a process of ongoing transformation that was facilitated by the technologies at hand. When *transformistas* are visible on the sides of highways and streets of the Venezuelan capital, Caracas, they draw on transnational images of femininity as flexible resources that allow them to craft distinctive forms of belonging. But the space within which they are visible is not free of regulations and forms of state discipline. Like many Indonesian cities, Caracas has punitive public order regulations that justify police raids and community surveillance. As Ochoa wrote, in terms that bring to mind the municipal regulations aimed at public order that have targeted warias in Indonesia, spatial forms of regulation framed as "citizenly coexistence" in Caracas "impl[y] a social harmony that respects all citizens as long as they respect the law. But some citizens 'live together' better than others, and the law always values some existences while marginalizing others" (2008, 147). In Indonesian postcolonial modernity too, gender was a central aspect of shaping the meanings of the city that makes possible forms of both recognition and exclusion.

Following Ochoa, I interpret warias' practice of dandan as part of a mediation of transnational femininity that is entangled with forms of regulation that take place at the scale of the city. A number of Tadi's photographs demonstrated a relationship between warias' national glamour and the city as paradigmatic of an imagined modernity. Nevertheless, responses to the public performance of national glamour and this urbanized format for articulating national modernity were not uniform. If warias found that they could perform dandan in everyday life in cities, at least during their golden age, their feminine presentation also attracted increased scrutiny as a symbol of urban-centered moral decay. Just as some locations facilitated recognition more readily than others, so too did certain moments serve to point out where the limits of recognition offered by the performance of dandan might lie. Warias often recalled how they had experienced "discomfort" or outright rejection. The comfort that warias had carefully curated in their cultivation of a public could be shattered by a change as subtle as the approaching dawn, or one as violent as a pursuit by the city police.

The visibility that warias achieved must thus be interpreted within its context. Some of Tadi's photographs show the way in which warias were visible when on their way to events. One waria is pictured wearing a sheer black-mesh crop top over a dress shirt with the sleeves rolled up. A black-and-silver bow tie is attached directly to her neck. Brilliant cherry-red lipstick accentuates her mouth, and she wears eye shadow of the lightest pink and silvery hue, a diamond stud in one ear, and a dangling parrot in the other. Her fedora is decked out with a feathered plume (figure 13). Another photograph shows a waria in a tartan skirt, taking a mock curtsy beneath banana trees at night on the unused tracts of land beside railway stations where waria commonly gathered (figure 14). In yet another

FIGURE 13. A waria on her way to an event in the mid-1980s.

Source: Tadi's personal collection

FIGURE 14. A waria curtsies beneath banana trees at night, most likely near a railway station, in the mid-1980s.

Source: Tadi's personal collection

FIGURE 15.   A waria in a private home, posing on a sofa, mid-1980s.

Source: Tadi's personal collection

photo, a waria drapes herself casually on furniture in the comfort of a private home (figure 15). This reflects one way in which recognition was not imagined but spatial and embodied for warias, who had to contend with limits placed on what they should wear and where they should go at what times.

In part because of the consolidation of their position as beauty experts in the 1970s and early 1980s, warias emerged as among the very few groups of people who could successfully mount public campaigns calling for a more inclusive vision of the nation. This included campaigns to contest raids by city police on the public places where warias gathered. In particular, the drowning deaths of several warias in Jakarta in the course of police raids catalyzed an intensification of the public protest and organizing that had taken place since the beginning of the New Order (*Kompas* 1979c). With warias mounting an effective protest against police harassment, the drowning deaths received prominent treatment in the national press, evoking considerable sympathy from middle-class Jakartans, as expressed in journalistic accounts of the social life of warias published during the 1980s (Atmojo 1987).

It was in this context that Mami Myrna, the prominent leader of the Fantastic Dolls, had made it clear that warias' continuing presence on the streets reflected a lack of opportunity. Echoing claims made by warias since the late 1960s, she complained, "If warias don't have any skills, because they haven't been given any opportunities to study, how are we meant to make any money?" She continued, "We are abused by our family, abused by our neighborhood, we want to work— there aren't so many who want to understand us—so what should we do? We go to the streets!" (*Kompas* 1979c). Other warias described their fear of being sent to a rehabilitation center, where they could be subject to abuse. Myrna stressed that almost any fate would be better than a long period of confinement in one of the rehabilitation centers run by the city. Such comments illustrated how exceptional waria were in their willingness to contest mistreatment through concrete forms of organizing and mobilization, premised on a more expansive vision of what not only gender but also citizenship could be.

In chapter 2, I introduced how warias' performances of dandan emerged in dialogue with the ongoing spatial concerns within municipal governance. The efforts made by the city to regulate waria (and indeed the very development of the category) suggest how their gender performance emerged in dialogue, as Maria Valverde described in a different setting, with "creaky mechanisms of urban governance [that led] to distinct, often unpredictable outcomes, depending on a host of local factors" (2012, 195). Ali Sadikin's successor, Governor Cokropanolo (1977–1982) effectively consolidated his predecessor's view that it was his job to ensure that warias did not "disturb public order" (*Kompas* 1977, 3). Reflecting a historical pattern of resort to partial medicalization, Cokropanolo drew municipal governance into dialogue with psychiatric expertise, stating that waria had a "mental disorder" that "needed to be treated by psychological experts." Cokropanolo's vice governor, Sardjono Soeprapto (who subsequently himself became governor) noted the ongoing role for technocratic policies regarding warias. According to Soeprapto, solving what he saw as the "problem of waria"— a phrase that had been in use since the late 1960s—required expertise obtained through firsthand knowledge. "We have to know beforehand what it is that waria want. We cannot create a distinct area in the city, like the red light districts the government organized for prostitution, without researching some more what the problem is" (*Kompas* 1977, 3). Indexing a historical format for spatial governance that had long been focused on gender-nonconforming bodies in Jakarta, warias continued to operate as a crucial node in the circulation of expertise about public gender between the scale of the city and the nation.

By pushing the boundaries since the 1950s of where their presence on city streets would be tolerated, waria gradually increased the settings in which they could appear in dandan. Skillfully accomplishing iconic forms of femininity, as Tadi and other warias explained, gave them a sense of "comfort" (*nyaman*) in public by the 1980s. Other warias who had lived in Jakarta during the 1980s described to me their increased "comfort" linked to a sense that they could perform dandan at a growing number of times and in a growing number of places. In the 1980s, a time when economic transformations were leading to increasing class stratification, spatially segregated consumer-capitalist forms of femininity emerged as an ambivalent public symbol that both served as cause for celebration of the possibilities of national development while representing the threat of corruption and moral decay (Jones 2012). For warias, however, the performance of dandan served as an expansive medium that enabled increased access to public space.

Tadi's narrative accounts and the practices of dandan depicted in the photographs introduced in this chapter suggest that warias had to regulate their appearances well into the 1980s and beyond. Their orientation to an imagined public, albeit at a different historical juncture, also shaped the scope for gender nonconformity in the postauthoritarian period that followed Suharto's fall in 1998. Just as warias' prospects for recognition remain closely connected to possibilities that unfold at the scale of city, so too has the city come to play an increasingly prominent role in the disciplinary logics of gender and sexuality at the level of the nation after the New Order. Warias' historical engagement with dandan across fractured sites and publics offers an understanding of the profound fragility and power of appearances to bestow the recognition associated with state citizenship.

Indonesian Publics

Seen as more proximate to the technological moorings of Indonesian postcolonial modernity that I have outlined in this book, public gender is key to understanding historical anxieties related to authority over seeing and being seen, or what Mary Steedly described as a broad "regime of visuality" (2013, 262) shaped by histories of authoritarian rule during the New Order. Noting the interplay between the technological and historical specificity of the photographic image and dandan as an effort not only to be visible but to control the conditions of that visibility has helped to clarify how citizenship might be forged through recognition as part of a public, albeit one that ultimately remains unpredictable and unfinished. National glamour, as shown in Tadi's photographs and expressed in her narratives, reflects an understanding of citizenship that cannot be reduced to the normalizing tendencies of either state surveillance or neoliberal self-fashioning.

An ability to forge a space through making up the body for a public audience has long rested on warias' understanding that participation in mass publics could offer new opportunities to achieve acceptance. Warias' partial integration within and capacity to leverage city-level forms of governance during the New Order presented a useful work-around in the context of a state in which the boundaries of modern citizenship were resolutely heteronormative. But this conceptualization of drawing on the practice of dandan as a way to expand opportunities for public participation, a practice that was shaped by historical legacies of appearances as a vital means to contest hegemonic forms of power in Indonesia, also foreshadowed the limits of this access to citizenship. As Tadi reflected, it was not necessarily that warias were rejected, but more that they should be cautious about the kinds of dandan they practiced and how it made them visible, with particular attention paid to the intersection of gender and class norms. As Tadi explained, "There were warias who would be visible at night and during the day, but they were those who were buskers who would be visible during the day." Given that busking was seen as a form of lower-class economic participation, it marked a kind of visibility from which respectable warias sought to distance themselves. For Tadi, much of her pride emerged from her capacity to engage in practices of dandan for pleasure, rather than being reliant on gendered visibility as a means to make a living.

Economic exclusion and gender nonconformity were closely entwined among many of the warias I spoke with, including Tadi. She contrasted her capacity to make a living on her own—and particularly her freedom from the constraints of sex work, thanks to her position in the state railway—with her experiences of her early life. She described how her father, a member of the armed forces who had fought in Indonesia's revolution of independence, had struggled to provide for his family when she was growing up in the 1960s. These early experiences had clearly shaped Tadi's own sense of self and desires for recognition. Referring to one experience from her childhood, she explained, "My father would wake us up in the early morning at 3 a.m., myself and my siblings. He would tell us to get dressed, and he would bring us to the railway station. There, he would park us down in chairs in the waiting room, and we would take a place in the queue for a ticket, and we would sell our place to people who arrived later." This experience seemed to animate a desire for a form of recognition and belonging that could transcend experiences of economic exclusion, in favor of a more just opportunity for participation in public life. The practice of dandan must be considered as a form of self-expression that cannot be separated from warias' everyday sexual, gendered, and economic worlds.

Tadi's photographs, and the relationship between gender performance and selfhood that they convey, refract broader desires for national belonging and recognition. For the New Order state, public gender was a format for transforming the bodies of all citizens into participants in a national project of economic development. For this reason, the practice of dandan was not only about gender at the level of the individual but the expression of a hope for more transformative possibilities of technology to facilitate recognition. For warias, the practice of dandan was conferred with the hope that the mediations of class, gender, and nation that they undertook would be recognized by neighbors, community, and kin. Even as warias tended to approach the possibilities for integration into state citizenship on cautious terms, their participation in national publics through the practice of dandan pushed at and even expanded the boundaries of citizenship. The act of dandan appeared to invite recognition by an audience that witnessed, and in some contexts acknowledged, alternate possibilities for seeing and being seen that public gender could enable. In this guise, the practice of dandan among warias was not primarily experienced as a means of self-actualization but rather as one component of a desire for recognition that, under certain conditions, could exceed the authority of the state.

Here it is worth returning to the narratives of warias that the opportunity to be seen (*ternampak*) at all times of day and across all places was only a possibility at the dawn of their golden age in Jakarta, 1968. The history of warias contained in this book suggests that the practice of dandan on an everyday basis is not only about public gender, but shows the centrality of appearances tied to projects of self-cultivation as a citizen of the nation-state. Building on Benedict Anderson's (1996) analysis of national belonging as facilitated by print capitalism, Tadi's narratives and photographs revealed how citizenship in postcolonial

Indonesia was also shaped by limitations on what the body could do to strive to fit into the sociotechnical imaginary of the New Order. Warias' experiences of practices of dandan as a medium for recognition in public space, one premised on a process of refinement or completion of what is already there, crystallized the boundaries of class differences. Warias' deft navigation of the shifting currents of visual modes of power contribute an important historical perspective on how gender and sexuality continue to play an important role in shaping claims to recognition and the publics that they generate after Suharto (Hegarty 2022; Wijaya 2020; Paramaditha 2018). In the conclusion to this book, I turn to this more open-ended promise of the possibilities of citizenship understood in terms of the practice of dandan, and the implications of public gender as a locus for transformation after the New Order.

Conclusion

MAKING UP THE STATE

There is no easy answer as to whether warias in Indonesia successfully attained the belonging that they pursued through their partial integration into the technological aspirations of postcolonial modernity. In the end, their dream of walking through the streets of the city, holding their heads up high as respected members of society, was not a matter of fitting in or of somehow returning to a lost time when their status was recognized as part of a more authentic social role. This is because, for warias, their historical ability to not conform was the very thing that had made them visible and hence recognizable in public space since the colonial period. Warias understood the ambiguous recognition that their nonconforming status bestowed to also contain the kernel of a possibility for recognition. Warias' experience shows just how crucial a site public gender is for establishing the boundaries of citizenship and for negotiating a place from which to bring new sociotechnical imaginaries into being. The practice of dandan meant more to warias than alterations made to outer appearances. For warias, the adoption of technologies of feminization became most meaningful when they led to a recognition in the eyes of others that overcame the charge that their appearances were a veneer or the imposition of a falsehood. Expanding the times of day and locations in which the public performance of dandan was possible simply allowed warias' essential character to shine more brightly.

In becoming experts in the technologies associated with globalized norms of feminine beauty, manifest in everyday individual performances, warias emphasized the role played by the publics that encountered them. Warias commonly spoke of the desire for acceptance, usually described as a form of comfort available to them when they moved through public space, as not only a prerequisite for but as synonymous with national belonging. Warias most often described belonging in terms of an aspirational hope to be "accepted by society" (*di terima oleh masyarakat*). In using the word *masyarakat*, warias appropriated the key technical concept that was advanced by the New Order state to regulate and govern "public culture . . . understood in national terms" (Boellstorff 2005, 212). The complex negotiations that warias made with publics as a set of regulatory mechanisms, unruly responses, and creative possibilities, emerged out of Indonesian colonial and postcolonial histories in which the qualities attached to citizenship were interpreted in relation to appearances. Warias' studied attention to appearances and the public's evaluation of them show how national belonging is shaped by visual and affective experiences of recognition. Their experiences highlight the need to supplement a focus on popular media and everyday speech with the body and its spatial regulation to better understand the less rational domain of politics, that which comprises what Benedict Anderson referred to as the "separate, half-autonomous realm of human interaction . . . in which mass publics share" (1990, 162).

This book has traced the history of *waria* and *wadam* as terms that drew on the postcolonial state's deployment of the modern gender binary in a novel way. The historical emergence of waria and wadam is one example of how technological development, including the forms of knowledge that defined and in turn naturalized modern gender, addresses specific subjects in specific ways (see Haraway 1988; Strathern 1988). Ethnographic and historical attention to the relationship between technology and gender among warias demonstrates that there is no fixed, universal form of personhood in which the individual body is a natural biological entity. Attention to these histories should therefore prompt a rethinking of the conceptual deployment of a cisgender/transgender binary on theoretical terms that refer to an ontological property of a biological individual. The history of warias shows just how difficult, if not impossible, it was for the state to impose cisgender normativity as the conditions for full belonging. The state struggled to define male and female as population-level norms conceptualized at the individual level as a cluster of physiological and psychological traits that could be aligned or misaligned. That the state failed at every turn to conclusively establish a fantasy of alignment indicates the limits of addressing gender in essentialist terms. The relationship between warias and technology presented in this book makes gender more complex than claims to the universality of a cisgender/transgender binary can contend with. That the domain of the technological is such a central motif in the history of warias, moreover, contrasts with common theorization of histories of gender and sexuality beyond Euro-American contexts in relation to tradition. This book joins anthropological calls to question "the modern distinction between gender and sexuality as the truth against which local, non-Western ontologies are to be understood" (Valentine 2007, 167), which perpetuates an imaginary that limits who is able to participate in crafting knowledge and what counts as science and technology as institutions that legitimate that knowledge. This is a problem that emerges acutely when the United States and other global empires of knowledge are presented (and, if anything, increasingly consolidated) as the norm and origin of scientific and technological development. This becomes a key question as transgender is institutionalized as both a field of knowledge and political discourse in Euro-American societies. At this juncture, it is important to ask what histories are included and excluded within transgender studies and politics, and in turn how have these shaped the ontological and epistemological concepts of personhood that are taken to be normal and natural when advancing political claims to recognition. I cannot provide easy answers, but I would ask that readers start with the way that warias' participation in sociotechnical relations of gender led to conditional but very real acceptance from neighbors, community, and kin, forms of recognition in ways that challenged the fiction that the state ever really held a monopoly on recognition and authenticity.

The creation of the new term *wadam* in the late 1960s was a possibility facilitated by the changed political and economic landscape in Indonesia during the New Order led by the autocrat Suharto, which saw the expansion of technological expertise and greater access to information through the mass media. By combining the separate Indonesian words for "woman" and "man," warias inserted themselves into gender as a malleable system of semiotic classification. Warias perceptively made use of gender on terms that Donna Haraway has called "an earth-wide network of connections, including the ability partially to translate knowledges among very different—and power-differentiated—communities" (1988, 580). In particular, the practice of dandan harnessed a specific set of modern technologies in pursuit of a more expansive if unstable claim to participate in a mass public. In claiming feminine beauty as a field of expertise over which they could demonstrate their individual contribution to modern society, warias made a partial and ultimately transformative claim to participate within Indonesian public life. Warias' use of gender in this way, however, was not uncontested. The New Order state, like states in other parts of the world, drew on a range of sources of expertise to claim the authority to define "what counts as a culturally intelligible body" (Stone 1992, 167). The most common disciplinary apparatus that warias encountered was in the form of vocational training programs referred to as guidance (*pembinaan*), which naturalized a global understanding of individual personhood as a locus of economic development (Kelty 2019, 251). Even as warias negotiated cleverly with the forms of technological modernity so central to the postcolonial state, like guidance, their claims to recognition did not easily equate to acceptance as full citizens.

The governor of Jakarta, Ali Sadikin, asserted that warias could move toward integration into the public life of the city through improvements made to their appearances. Translating and debating concepts used in Western medicine and psychology—overwhelmingly derived from globalized concepts related to the term *transvestite* (rather than *homosexual*)—Indonesian doctors and psychiatrists worked with municipal experts to bestow on warias a legal but nonconforming status. Early in the 1970s, warias' and other trans women's desires for recognition were framed in relation to a global discourse of medical transsexuality as a component of the New Order as a "technological state" (Amir 2013, 161), contributing to a national discourse of progress tied to state development as a necessary corollary of national modernity. In the view of the surgeon Kusumanto Setyonegoro and Islamic scholar Buya Hamka, the application of transsexuality as a field of knowledge could relieve the suffering of warias and other trans people and facilitate their transition into the category "woman," drawing on the wonders of modern science to clarify what nature had left incomplete. Yet this did not mark the beginning of a march toward a wholesale incorporation of transsexuality into national modernity. The history of technology is far less linear, subject to diverse interruptions and discontinuities. By the late 1970s, what only appeared to be an enthusiastic adoption of medical transsexuality was revised significantly, as definitions of sex and gender as a complex combination of psychological, embodied, and genital states gave way to the idea that maleness and femaleness were innate, natural characteristics marked by chromosomal sex and roles in biological reproduction. This rearrangement in the state's definitions of sex and gender—and the rise of technological expertise trained on defining the body on individual terms—marked a shift in both the stakes and possibilities of warias' claims to belonging.

Warias' experiences of recognition in Indonesia highlight the need for a critical engagement with citizenship and related calls for inclusion, moving beyond limited political conceptualizations of identity that hold the individual as the teleological endpoint of the political as a domain of worldmaking. In making this argument, I join recent astute observations of gender and sexual politics in Indonesia. Hendri Yulius Wijaya (2019) argues that liberal understandings of recognition premised on demands for authenticity can reproduce the very discourse through which queer Indonesians are framed as incompatible with heteronormative and cisgender definitions of state citizenship and national belonging. I am inspired by his calls to move beyond a narrow concept of authenticity as an essentialized and endless grid of difference, but to view it instead as a means to generate new kinds of "Indonesian-ness," which reflects how "sexuality is constructed through a series of political negotiations" (Wijaya 2019, 149; see also Wijaya 2020). Any hope for enacting a more expansive format for a politics of gender or sexuality will have to rethink an essentialist vocabulary that privileges authenticity in terms of the bounded individual. The history of warias points to one such possibility, a dazzling engagement with sociotechnical relations and strategies in ways that cannot be captured by models of individualized gender. Warias' engagement with the possibilities offered by public participation as a route to the transformation of those very publics demands a bolder and more creative interpretation of gender, articulated as questions of class, economic participation, the governance of space, critiques of state violence, and extra-state forms of recognition by community and kin. This approach helps to move beyond a binary view of a politics of recognition as a zero-sum game of accep-tance and rejection, and toward the realization that neither the authentic nor the technological provide the ground on which figures emerge, but rather it is a continual process of negotiation and revision that weaves together past, present, and future possibilities.

Citizens of the City, Citizens of the Nation

Rather than attending to events that unfolded primarily at a national level, this book has traced the ways in which warias' experience of citizenship was an engagement that took place primarily at the scale of technological developments in the city. In the postcolonial nation, what authorities viewed as the problem of gender nonconformity was largely defined and debated by municipalities, which addressed warias as a problem to be solved along with other public nuisances. In doing so, they drew on a vocabulary of public gender that borrowed from colonial-era regulations concerned with appearances based on race that had been in place since the nineteenth century. Warias were so important because they were an object of knowledge that helped to clarify the boundaries of appear-ances, a recognizable format for determining difference on the grounds of public gender according to an infrastructure primarily concerned with racial difference. In the postcolonial state, anxieties over the mutability of racial difference were transferred onto binary gender, serving as the locus of efforts to determine the authenticity of state citizenship. Drawing on an existing regulatory apparatus that could discipline individuals on the basis of outer appearances, city authori-ties made every effort to hide gender nonconformity from view on the basis that they were protecting a seeing public. The city drew on existing regulations con-cerned directly with spatial control to pursue this end, including the provision of additional lighting and fencing and the deployment of police to undertake raids on public places. More than this, however, a concern for warias' visibility was cen-tral to establishing a definition of the twin concepts of "public order" (*ketertiban umum*) and "public morality" (*kesusilaan umum*) on the surface of the individual body in reference to public gender.

One material consequence of the recognition of warias as a legal but non-conforming status in public space was their recruitment into vocational training in beauty and sewing. Beginning in the late 1960s, city regulations developed a more sophisticated array of disciplinary mechanisms glossed as guidance. These technologies and regulations enabled participation in publics but only in a particular way, one that was focused on reformatting warias' unruly public visibility into a contribution to economic productivity. Warias commonly referred to their integration as an experience of being made more presentable, or as one waria put it, "being polished." Warias sought out such integration in relation not to the national government but in the more direct forms of participation possible through engagement with city-level officials and residents. Warias strategically drew on their recognition as a kind of public nuisance to ask for expanded forms of recognition. The perspectives of warias on the possibilities and limits provided through access to training in fields related to feminine beauty suggest an understanding of the modern self not as an inevitable process of individualization, but as one that is a process of continuous negotiation with the social. The concern for warias at the level of the municipality and the district in Indonesia highlights how a relationship between national belonging and state citizenship was not only imagined but actively cultivated in concert with the affective intensity of mass publics. In this book, I have developed a theory of citizenship that holds that the public meanings granted to bodily cultivation are central to understanding how participation in the city and the nation is governed and lived.

Attention to the gendered contours of the publics presented in this book has also helped to illuminate a concern often submerged in analyses focused on sexuality and citizenship at the level of the self: the enduring role of bodily appearance in modern forms of discipline. This is similar to an understanding that Nikolas Rose characterized as a modern form of discipline he calls "government through community," which derives its disciplinary power from "enhancing the bonds that link individuals" (1999, 136). The power of this discipline comes not from pathologizing an individual, necessarily, but in the individual's relations with others in a community that the power of discipline makes possible as a collective in which seeing and being seen is a powerful moral force. Sally Engle Merry (2001, 17) described this as a condition of discipline in contemporary cities around the world, in which "the individual offender is not treated or reformed, but a particular public is protected." This represents a "a shift to neoliberal forms of governance" and a corresponding diminishment of the "scope of collective responsibility for producing social order characteristic of governance in the modern state" (Merry 2001, 17). Collective responsibility, including the state's responsibility to care for its citizens, is shrunk to ever smaller, more privatized publics, making the possibility of recognition for those within them at once more devolved and more fragile.

One outcome of this form of governance in Indonesia was an increased emphasis on morality, through which individuals are not only responsible for their own appearances but are required to locate and expose the moral failings of their neighbors. Sharyn Davies described these forms of discipline as a sexual surveillance that arises through "webs of shame," a form of participation in public life prefigured by relationships with others, "neighbours, friends, colleagues, one's village and even the state" (2015, 33). Even as warias narrated their movement from a golden age that started in 1968 as a success that heralded expanded possibilities for participation in public life, at night and during the day, more recent events suggest that their place in municipal and national public life is far from assured. Ferdiansyah Thajib (2018, 129) described how warias in the northernmost province of Aceh displayed a "mindfulness in performing/presenting oneself to the world," which reflected the fact that "their movements within the town [were] subject to public control, enclosing them to limited timing and designated sites such as hair salons." This oscillation between visibility and invisibility also demands close attention in a context where queer organizations are increasingly addressing themselves to a counterpublic that contrasts with the wider heteronormative public endorsed by the state (Paramaditha 2018). The growing centrality of a public defined by Islamic morality after Suharto's downfall in 1998 has made it necessary for warias and many others to more delicately manage the relationship between visibility and political claims to recognition in a fragmented public sphere. Efforts to define who belongs in public and who does not has emerged as a crucial locus of political action after the New Order, as Karen Strassler observed, "a way to galvanize an Islamic public around questions of public morality and the limits of an open, democratic public sphere" (2020, 151). During fieldwork in 2014 and 2015, I observed warias pay close attention to their surroundings as they navigated public life, taking actions that for them served to seek out an affective state in which they could achieve a sense of "comfort." At the beginning of the New Order, warias became more visible as a component of Indonesian public life. Warias interpreted this visibility as a reflection of shifting opportunities for accomplishing "acceptance" and "comfort" at a moment of profound historical transformation. Rather than a fixed state that conferred universal recognition, this was a form of citizenship that was conditional on the context and that warias continued to be able to access only under limited circumstances.

This emphasis on the social dynamics of recognition parallels the experience of trans women in other parts of the world. Eric Plemons's ethnographic study of the practice of facial feminization surgery in the United States is a powerful reminder of the stakes involved in transformations made to appearances. Plemons described the experience of recognition for his interlocutors as always in emergence, or in what he called a "dynamic process of exchange," one that sheds light on the fact that "being seen as a woman on the street may constitute an interpersonal enactment that is very meaningful, but it is also one that is refused at the level of the state" (2017, 91). The everyday ways in which warias negotiate seeing and being seen similarly demonstrate the need for historical and ethnographic theories that grapple with citizenship as the product of an uneasy and dynamic effort, one that can place considerable pressure on those for whom social and legal recognition can diverge. The 1980s was a moment of heightened anxiety about public space and the limits of the New Order state's vision of economic development. The photographs of practices of dandan taken during this period reflect the need to interpret public gender not at the level of the individual self, but as a crystallization and expression of desires for movement across boundaries of economy, nation, sexuality, and publics. The aesthetic form of practices of dandan usefully draws attention to the careful negotiations of warias as they move through public space on an everyday level. Throughout postcolonial history in Indonesia, the regulation of conformity and nonconformity at the level of the city—reflected in the centrality of attention to outer appearances—has shaped the boundaries of participation in a national public. As readers of this book will recognize, a concept of the public at the scale of the city is deeply ingrained in the historical construction of the meanings of public gender, setting the stage for possibilities of belonging and dangers of rejection within it.

In Indonesia after Suharto, regulations governing participation in public life at the scale of the city continue to shape the boundaries of national belonging, creating tremors that resonate at the center of political life. Although efforts at democratic reform (*reformasi*) under way since Suharto's downfall in 1998 have been uneven, the administrative levels of the city, the district, and the region have if anything increased their lawmaking powers across several domains. The form of decentralization known as regional autonomy has been an enduring theme in Indonesian politics and in related struggles that could enable the expression of a diverse "[character] of regional feeling" (Legge 1961, 1) while holding together a unified state. The period after 1998 saw a surge in the number of municipalities, districts, regions, and provinces, as well as the number of democratically elected bodies to represent them. Of the thousands of laws passed by municipalities, many pertain to public order and from the outset focused attention on questions of public morality (Butt 2010). Regional authorities, including city governments, have established dozens of regulations concerned with gender and sexuality, including many that prohibit same-sex sexuality and gender-nonconforming behavior (Katjasungkana and Wieringa 2016). In the late 2010s, a large number of municipalities passed a number of regulations related to "the protection of the family" (*ketahanan keluarga*), effectively imposing, under threat of fines and forms of rehabilitation, the heteronormative form of the nuclear family and the biological conception of reproduction on which it is predicated. Such laws, introduced at the level of the municipality and the district, have in turn worked as a platform for the rapid growth in political mobilization in support of the criminalization of homosexuality at the national level, serving as a demonstration of their popular support. Although at a remove from the context of municipal law within which they emerged, these municipal legal regulations share a concern for public order and public morality, both commonly invoked to justify punitive measures that criminalize homosexuality in terms of its visibility to mass mediated publics.[1] The clearest state regulation of non-heteronormative gender and sexuality introduced after the New Order at the national level, the 2008 Pornography Law, does not limit regulation to the practices or materials related to pornography itself. The first article of the law states its remit as "performances in public that contain obscenity or sexual exploitation that violates the moral norms in society" (cited in Lindsay 2010, 42). As Jennifer Lindsay wrote, "The criminal law thus defines pornography in terms of its effect on the perceiver/s, not in terms of objective or absolute identifiable acts, things or works" (2010, 173; see also Bellows 2011). The historical relationship between publics imagined at the scale of the nation and the municipality has opened new opportunities to be seen, but also for that visibility to become a target of surveillance and punishment.

Throughout 2016, the Indonesian news media reported widely that the LGBT political movement was a foreign—and specifically Euro-American—threat to the nation. Although this was by no means the first or only moral panic related to gender and sexuality that has transformed Indonesian society, the speed and collective force of attention given to LGBT politics were intense. The efforts of gender and sexual minorities to claim greater recognition were met with the counterclaim, made much more vociferously, that non-heteronormative forms of intimacy and embodiment should be rejected (*ditolak*) from the fabric of the nation (see Boellstorff 2016). These events served as the backdrop to those that took place in September 2019, when the Indonesian parliament announced that it would pass a long-awaited revision to the Criminal Code—including regulations that would criminalize all forms of "indecent behavior" (*perbuatan cabul*).[2] The announcement of the introduction of this legislation to parliament and its likely passage into law was followed by some of the largest street protests that had taken place since 1998. Hundreds of thousands of protesters, including warias, gathered to contest this exclusionary vision of a national public. Visible among the marchers' signs were slogans invoking solidarity with transnational claims to LGBT, transgender, and feminist rights. The draft code was not passed at this time, although plans to reintroduce it have been announced and again postponed several times, with no clear path forward. As these transformations in Indonesia after the New Order have shown, democracy and the appeals to a unified public that accompanied it have not provided warias with the opportunities for recognition that they have long sought. If anything, they reflect the continued centrality of the body as a locus of competing claims to speak for and about the public, and gender as a hopeful horizon for articulating collective visions of social justice.

Transpuan

The historical efforts of warias to orient themselves toward a public within which they could achieve acceptance show how citizenship is not assured but better understood as a constant negotiation. At a public meeting with municipal officials in 1968, Indonesian warias, made up in the accoutrements of a modern femininity only recently available to Indonesians of any gender, announced that they would no longer be described officially in public as *bancis*, with that term's connotation of ambiguity and public sexuality, but rather with the modern term *wadam*. This was a powerful claim that not only addressed but shaped the meanings of a modern public that was still in formation at that time. In the wake of these warias' meeting with the Jakarta governor, Ali Sadikin, and thanks in part to this new term and presentable new public appearance, warias created the first organizations to promote their rights. These organizations—and their integration into the scale of the municipality—offered warias a platform from which they could protest their mistreatment at the hands of the police and neighbors.

In drawing this book to a close, I point to the historical legacy of efforts to forge new practices and new terms that draw on gender as a technology that facilitates global connection to expand the forms of participation possible in public life. Since the mid-2010s, some Indonesian activists have drawn on and integrated the terms *trans* and *transgender*—the very analytical and theoretical concepts that I deployed in this book—to advance new claims to recognition. One effect of these claims has been the creation of the new term *transpuan*, which sits in a distinctive relationship to *waria*.[3] In the late 2010s, *transpuan* began to circulate on both national online news websites and social media as one term used to refer both to warias and a wider array of trans feminine populations. *Transpuan* was coined by activists in Jakarta, and popularized by progressive media outlets and nongovernmental organizations in the capital city. As a term that combines the first syllable of the English word "transgender" and the last syllable of one Indonesian word for "woman" (*perempuan*), the formulation recalls the process of creating the term *wadam* as a presentable, modern alternative. Indeed, echoing the shift from *banci* to *wadam* that took place in 1968, some groups of mostly Jakarta-based transgender activists, their allies, and the progressive media asserted that *transpuan* was a more presentable replacement for the term *waria*. In some accounts on social media, *waria* was described as having an unequivocally offensive and even hurtful meaning when used in reference to trans women. But the use of the terms *waria* and *transpuan* in Indonesia, and their relationship, is contested. Some older warias described the adoption of *transpuan* to me in generational terms, an assessment that aligns with my own observations of social media and conversations with transpuan. In response to claims that *transpuan* was a more progressive term that should replace *waria*, these warias claimed that the latter was a term that already had broad public appeal and had achieved widespread recognition in Indonesian society. In different community forums and social media, I also observed senior trans women who questioned whether replacing terms had political efficacy; regardless of the term used, they said, in some public settings trans women were never going to be accepted anyway. *Transpuan* is also a term that is distinct from *waria* in several respects, but none so important as the two words that it combines. As noted earlier in this book, *waria* combines Indonesian words for woman and man. Tom Boellstorff (2007, 92) observed that, at the time that he conducted his research, the combination of woman and man reflected a shared understanding among many waria that even as they might be socially legible as women, they understood themselves in some respects to be men. By contrast, *transpuan* has no reference to men or maleness. As such, it opens the possibility for a definition of trans femininity that falls within the broader orbit of identification as women.

This places the term *transpuan* in a compelling conversation with the women's movement and feminist activists, a conversation that has emerged since the end of the New Order. In part, *transpuan* is made possible by a semantic shift away from the use of *wanita*, the other Indonesian word for woman used by the organs of the New Order state. As a result, *wanita* brings to mind patriarchal forms of state power and the subordination of women (Suryakusuma 1996). By contrast, more widespread use of the alternate Indonesian word for woman, *perempuan*, grew out of the struggles of women's activists in the wake of the gendered violence that took place during the New Order and immediately after Suharto's fall from power, culminating in the establishment of the National Commission for Women, Komnas Perempuan (Anggraeni 2014). The universal promise of citizenship tied to *perempuan* was claimed as a vehicle not only by transpuan but by other marginalized feminine figures too. Describing activist attempts to grapple with the sexual violence toward Chinese Indonesian women in 1998, Karen Strassler (2020, 78) described *perempuan* as "a category that could transcend racial, ethnic, and religious differences." Similarly, *transpuan* brings warias and other trans feminine populations into the orbit of a specific, national understanding of woman, *perempuan*, a word that articulates a hopeful dream of the universal possibility of rights and recognition through citizenship.

Tracing the history of *transpuan* is complicated by the fact that it has been defined cumulatively and iteratively on social media platforms like Twitter and Instagram. The production of knowledge about *transpuan* is thus both decentralized and subject to the dynamic, if anonymous and fleeting, character of social media exchanges. The transformed media technologies through which *transpuan* emerged make it difficult to establish precisely what organizations and individuals authorized the term and why some activists have framed it as more presentable than *waria*. The first published Indonesian-language account by a transpuan activist that I have found is an edited collection of stories titled *Acceptance: Stories of Acceptance of Transpuan by Their Parents* (Halim 2019). Stephanie Kevin Halim, who is trained as a psychologist, offered a definition of "trans" in her foreword to the book:

> Trans is an umbrella terminology for describing people whose gender identity is not the same as the gender identity given to them at birth. Trans individuals refer to themselves using one or more variants of terminology, including (and not limited to) transgender, transsexual, gender queer, gender fluid, non-binary, gender variant, cross dresser, genderless, agenda, nongender, third gender, two-spirit, bi-gender, trans laki-laki [trans man], trans puan [trans woman], trans masculine, trans feminine, and so on. (Halim 2019, 1)

The hurt caused by being "rejected by family, rejected by society, and rejected by the nation" (Halim 2019, 25) animates a desire for acceptance by a public that is experienced as proximate. Halim's emphasis here recalls moments when belonging for warias seemed within reach during the New Order. Recall that Ali Sadikin pleaded with residents of the city to see warias "as human beings, with rights as citizens of the city, and rights as citizens of the nation" (Atmojo 1987, 18). Both formulations call for empathy from a public who is immediately present, encouraging citizens to imagine the deep hurt that exclusion from public life must cause.

In a rhetorical stance that linked transpuans' struggle for acceptance directly to national belonging, Halim also pointed to Indonesia's effort to achieve independence from Dutch colonial rule. Folding transpuan into the revolutionary origins of the Indonesian nation, Halim opened her book with reference to her hopeful anticipation of transgender rights in Indonesia, drawing a comparison to Indonesian independence from the Dutch in 1947. She wrote, "It has been seventy-four years since Indonesia declared independence, but until now in 2019, I rarely hear stories about parents accepting their trans children" (2019, 1). The relationship between national belonging and transpuan also helps to explain to prominence in the title of the book of the word "acceptance" (*penerimaan*), which Halim tied closely to the family, a paradigmatic form of modern recognition in the history of the modern Indonesian nation (Siegel 2006, 158). Considering this early and likely first published Indonesian account written by a transpuan, it is notable that the concept of acceptance emerged at the outset as part of a critical vocabulary for making a claim to rights and recognition. Despite its relationship to a global transgender imaginary, then, *transpuan* appears to be imagined as a term that is also national in scale, reflecting one way in which gender continues to shape the boundaries of participation in public life as well as to agitate for an expansion of it. Nevertheless, the dream of establishing a unified viewing public who will admit the presence of warias and transpuan on unconditional terms remains as yet unrealized.

This emphasis on acceptance as pivotal to national belonging and the parallel that Halim drew between trans rights and a national Indonesian revolution of independence also bring to mind the formation of the name given to Indonesia itself as a term of identification and its entanglement with science and technology. The term *Indonesia* was first developed in the fields of ethnology and geography in Europe in the mid-nineteenth century to describe inhabitants and geographical features of the archipelago (van der Kroef 1951). It is a combination word, drawing together the word *India* and the suffix *-nesia*, derived from the Greek *nēsos* (island), and emerging as part of a classificatory matrix for insular subdivisions among ethnologists and geographers, including those of Polynesia and Melanesia. Throughout the colonial period, distributed through networks of scholarly and popular knowledge, *Indonesia* served as a fashionable replacement for other terms previously used by scientists, including the "Malay Archipelago" (Wallace 1872). The popularity of the term was precipitated through its use and distribution by Indonesian nationalists engaged in anticolonial struggle from the early twentieth century onward. They quickly appended *Indonesia* to the names of their organizations, including the first nationalist organization, Perhimpunan Indonesia (Ingleson 1975). The Dutch colonial government was so concerned about the revolutionary potential invoked by *Indonesia* that it attempted to ban the word's use in official documentation (van der Kroef 1951). The colonial state's efforts to control the use of *Indonesia* and the multiplication of *Indonesians* was futile.

Emerging as an arcane reference to a geographical area and drawing on racialized scientific divisions that attempted to categorize and classify human difference into graspable units for analysis, *Indonesia* gave birth to a form of consciousness and means to contest political exclusion. This is a characteristic it shares with the terms *transpuan* and *waria*, both of which have a fractured relationship to global forms of scientific and technological knowledge about sex, gender, and sexuality. In noting this parallel, I draw attention to the conceptual possibilities that emerge by attending to citizenship and attendant claims to recognition not within a teleological framework of technological determinism, but as a capacity to draw together, translate, and create new and more inclusive visions for participation in public life. These struggles demonstrate that Indonesia, along with warias' place in it and the opportunities to obtain citizenship that result from the collective struggle to see and be seen, remains a work in progress that continues to be made and unmade in new ways.

Notes

INTRODUCTION

1. The terms *wadam* and *waria* are similar inasmuch as they both draw on different words to index a combination of masculinity and femininity within a single body, and I located no significant difference in how the terms were used among those who identified as such. *Wadam*'s clever appropriation of the names of Adam and Eve gives that term a quirky religious emphasis compared to *waria*'s combination of the secular words for male and female. Indonesia's minister of religion announced the replacement of *wadam* with the new term *waria* in 1978. The decision was made after reported protests by Islamic groups from East Java over the incorporation of the name Adam, a symbol of the unity of humanity in the Quran, to refer to forms of gender nonconformity and same-sex sexuality that had historically chafed with pious organizations and individuals. The combination of these specific words is interesting, given the origin myth of Eve's creation from Adam's own body being a prominent example of the one-sex model of sex and gender that prevailed until the late eighteenth century (Herdt 1996). Thomas Laqueur (1990) traced the movement from a one-sex model used in Greek antiquity—a masculine body and mind inscribed on an incomplete female body—to a two-sex model as part of a shift in understanding male and female as ontological rather than sociological categories.

2. In both its contemporary and historical use, *banci* indexes more wide-ranging forms of gender and sexual variance than *waria*, as reflected in the common meaning of the term as an expression of "ambiguity" (Oetomo 2000, 48). As I encountered the term during fieldwork in 2014–15, both gay men and warias commonly used *banci* to refer to one another and themselves in circumscribed social settings generally not oriented toward a public audience. When used by non-warias or at heated moments between warias, the term held a derogatory meaning, and public use of the term was generally avoided. Warias explained that the creation of *wadam* as a new, more presentable and respectable term in the late 1960s was driven by an understanding that *banci* was an offensive and even hurtful term of address.

3. Although the historical focus of this book means that it does not directly address the impact of the HIV epidemic or engage with the political claims of transgender rights, both are being drawn on by warias to lay claim to forms of recognition. A particularly powerful source of knowledge in the everyday lifeworlds of warias belonging to the urban poor since the mid-2000s has been their identification as "key populations" at risk of contracting HIV and AIDS. The HIV epidemic has shaped the ways in which warias narrate themselves as transgender under certain conditions (Hegarty 2017b) and led to new claims to political recognition (Mallay et al. 2021).

4. Anthropologists have demonstrated how it is not so much that Southeast Asian cultures are free from cosmologies grounded in dualism, but rather that explanatory assumptions based on the constitution and relations of dominant Euro-American dualisms of male/female and mind/body at the individual level can lead to significant misunderstandings (Helliwell 2000; Errington 1990). It is precisely the superficial similarities between dualisms in diverse cultures that have served as justification for many of the universal assumptions underpinning Euro-American theoretical accounts of sex and gender, including at the level of nature/culture (see Ortner 1972). This book is not concerned

with overcoming or resolving binary gender but rather follows the approach taken by Michael Lambek in his cross-cultural interpretation of the mind/body problem, to understand how such dualisms offer ways to explore how "different cultures do not map directly onto one another, but leave problems of translation . . . discrepancies [that] open up new avenues for investigation" (1998, 105).

5. The history of femininity in colonial and postcolonial Indonesia constitutes an entire field of discussion and debate, with significant attention paid to historicizing the gender ideology of the New Order. *Fantasizing the Feminine in Indonesia*, edited by Laurie Sears (1996), and *Indonesian Women in Focus*, edited by Elspeth Locher-Scholten and Anke Niehof (1992), are two influential examples of edited volumes that attend to gender as central to social transformation in Indonesia (see also Brenner 1998). This book contributes to this rich legacy of historical and ethnographic scholarship about Indonesian femininity by challenging the assumptions of Euro-American theoretical frameworks that interpret gender difference at the level of the individual as an essential and authentic part of the self.

6. An understanding of bodies along a cisgender/transgender binary has historical parallels with the reconsolidation of binary gender in conservative psychological and medical theories in the United States in the middle of the twentieth century. Jules Gill-Peterson (2018) has traced the historical emergence of this meaning of gender via experimentation and clinical practice on intersex children in the 1940s and 1950s at Johns Hopkins University, which revealed binary sex as far too simplistic an explanatory concept in endocrinology. A psychological and social concept of gender emerged at precisely the point that binary sex was in crisis in the United States, playing a part in undoing "the idea that humans were naturally bisexual or sexually indeterminate" and "though children were born exceptionally plastic, that plasticity needed to grow in a developmental direction, *either* male or female, *to prevent social stigma*" (Gill-Peterson 2018, 119, emphasis in original).

7. This account generally pertains to cities during the New Order, particularly the regulations governing the roles of Indonesian municipalities adopted in 1974, which effectively consolidated existing colonial-era laws that emphasized decentralization (Malo and Nas 1991). Another key aspect of municipal governance was the central role of the military, with mayors and governors sourced from military commands. Following the end of the New Order in 1998, Indonesian cities and their administration have shifted somewhat through a revitalized process of decentralization in which the central government has granted cities and regions greater autonomy over their own affairs (Butt 2010).

1. BANCI, BEFORE WARIA

1. The status conferred by belonging to one of these three legally defined categories was fundamental to social life in the Dutch East Indies, given that those belonging to them were placed within separate and unequal legislative and administrative systems (Fasseur 1994). I refer to these categories as racial because of the fact that they were rooted in an understanding of white superiority, in which European status was hierarchically superior, although this does not mean they were always defined in relation to race. Historians have pointed out that definitions of race in the Dutch East Indies were for the most part not premised on an essential biological and psychological origin, and in that sense are perhaps better understood as a form of racialized status organized under a notion of the superiority of Europeanness. European status was not necessarily limited to white people but could also be achieved by the ruling elite of indigenous populations and others, such as the Japanese, who were recognized as such in 1899 (Luttikhuis 2013, 545).

2. In Java, where modernist Islamic reformers have expressed staunch opposition to the common presence of gender nonconformity in ritual practices and myth since the

nineteenth century, trans performers nevertheless remained a popular expression of the possibility of holding together distinct elements in a single body or figure well into the twentieth century (Peacock 1978). In the popular lower-class theater genre known as *ludruk*, the combination of masculinity and femininity in a single body was celebrated as late as the 1960s as a symbol of the processes of modernization (Peacock 1968). Opposition to trans performers did not derive from the doctrinal condemnation of homosexuality and gender nonconformity alone, but rather from what James Peacock (1978, 129) described as the "outrageous creativity" of figures able to draw together two or more elements in a single figure as a demonstration of cosmic unity, including that of high (*halus*) and low (*kasar*) status. At stake was not only the public performance of practices that came to be interpreted as gender, into which other symbolic forms were incorporated, but the power to grant recognition to the effects of such combinations.

3. Tom Boellstorff (2007, 85–86) interpreted how *banci* and other terms took shape within a colonial cartographic approach to difference, in which indigenous people were imagined as relating to one another only at the scale of the local (see also Boellstorff 2002).

4. Dekker and van de Pol (1989, 50), in their account of what they called "female cross-dressers," referred to *kwee* as derived from "an old Dutch word for a hermaphroditic cow that cannot have young . . . in fact, the only original Dutch word with the same meaning as hermaphrodite." The inclusion of *kwee* as one translation for banci in Batavia suggests a parallel with popular Dutch definitions of male homosexuality at the time. From the eighteenth century onward, Dutch medical and legal accounts had begun to define "sodomites" more closely through recourse to physical evidence of feminine gender presentation (Boon 1989). The Dutch army in particular may have been one important site through which sexual knowledge and terms spread throughout the Dutch East Indies (Hekma 1991). The prevailing focus on historical forms of gender crossing as symptoms of same-sex sexuality in the historical record means that trans experience has largely been elided.

5. There is a historical overlap between a concerted interest in banci in the late nineteenth and early twentieth centuries and developments in the broader field of sexology in Europe and the United States. Although their views varied, prominent sexologists drew on accounts of colonized people to define male homosexuality as evident in their physical gender expression (see Bauer 2006). Siobhan Somerville (1994, 249) illustrated how the development of scientific theories of homosexuality based on "somatic differences" by nineteenth-century sexologists, including those of British sexologist Havelock Ellis, were closely informed by scientific racism. Somerville outlined how the historical "invention" of the homosexual body and the reformulation of race as essentialized forms of difference in the United States relied on a shared concern that linked them to a no less essentialist definition but one that stressed inner state.

6. Although Hirschfeld interpreted same-sex behavior as implicitly related to gender expression (Valentine 2007), his definition of transvestite allowed for an account of gender crossing as a complex phenomenon unable to be reduced to homosexuality (Hirschfeld [1910] 2006).

7. I have not located a written version of the lecture or the press reports of it that Hirschfeld refers to. After arriving in the Dutch East Indies in 1927, van Wulfften Palthe was an eclectic figure who was active in the emerging field of psychoanalysis and a participant in lively debates at the end of the colonial period as to the "nature of the native mind" (Pols 2018, 190). In one essay, he interpreted Indonesian independence within a Freudian psychoanalytic framework, offering an exculpatory theory that ignored the brutal economic exploitation of colonialism and promoted a fantasy that Dutch and Indonesians had previously lived within a "harmonious colonial family" (Pols 2011, 161).

8. Frances Gouda (1997) interpreted the powerful use of gendered metaphors at the end of Dutch colonial rule, ascribing masculinity to the Dutch and femininity to Indonesians.

It would be interesting to investigate whether *banci*, a term referring to a more general state of gendered ambiguity, was a metaphor deployed by the Dutch or among Indonesians during the period of anticolonial struggle or in the newly independent nation.

9. This article, appearing in the Sino-Malay newspaper *Soemanget*, refers to widespread concern expressed about the public visibility of banci in Batavia in the late 1920s.

10. This article was part of a special issue published during the early New Order as part of a municipal-level response to a perceived crisis of gender nonconformity in public space in Jakarta. The magazine articles included firsthand reports that prioritized the voices of those the journalists identified as banci.

11. The journalist paid close attention to the race (*bangsa*) of each person, with the classification of homosexuality emerging through a racialized concept of public gender. Dutch men were described as "active homosexuals," and banci were "passive homosexuals." The journalist also distinguished the race of the man discovered in an embrace with the banci described in the article as not a "native" (*pribumi*), but as a "Chinese youth" (*pemuda Tionghoa*), noting just how easily the Chinese student had been deceived. The ambiguous position of Chinese Indonesians in the new nation, though distinct, echoed that of banci, providing a parallel set of legal and symbolic resources. In chapter 3, I describe how the possibilities for changing legal gender that accompanied the emergence of medical transsexuality in Indonesia in the mid-1970s drew on regulations that only applied to Chinese Indonesians. The shared histories of the fragility of Chinese Indonesians and warias' claims to citizenship in Indonesia make up a thread that demands further exploration.

12. The "dress circular" of March 1905, which abandoned attempts to regulate dress according to ethnicity, was issued in the context of the introduction of the Ethical Policy, a set of liberal reforms introduced in the Netherlands in response to popular outcry over the exploitative conditions of Dutch colonial rule in the Indies. Arnout van der Meer (2020, 119–20), however, described how the 1905 circular removing restrictions on dress came about largely due to efforts by Chinese residents to claim respect and equality in the colonial state following the decision to grant European status to the Japanese.

13. This manual, reproducing legal regulations in Dutch and Malay, was produced for native teachers in legal science training schools. The discussion of disguise—and reference to gender crossing on parallel lines to race—is roughly the same as that discussed in reference to the "law of disguise" reproduced in the periodical *Soenda Berita* in 1904 (cited in Siegel 1997, 86). This concern for fraud was in part provoked by a conservative turn in the colonial state's management of the indigenous population, which resulted in intensifying surveillance and modernization of the police in the colony in the early twentieth century (Shiraishi 2003; Bloembergen 2007).

14. Arnout van der Meer (2020, 143) described the fierce contestations over what was appropriate clothing for women among Indonesian nationalist groups during the 1920s and 1930s, with a gradual consensus on "traditional attire as Indonesian women's national dress," cementing women's association with domesticity and motherhood (see also Suryakusuma 1996).

2. JAKARTA, 1968

1. Jakarta has the administrative status of a province (*daerah tingkat I*), the Special Capital Region of Jakarta, or Daerah Khusus Ibukota Jakarta. Although this means that Jakarta is managed by a single governor and council (who are in some ways similar to a mayor and city council), the province is further divided into the municipalities of North, South, East, West, and Central Jakarta (Nas and Grijns 2000, 18). These cities have a mayor but no elected city council, a form of governance that favors business and elite interests

(Kusno 2014). Abidin Kusno described how Jakarta's role as the capital, and the correspondingly overt role played by the central government in governing the city, has made Jakarta a "city with restricted citizen participation" (2014, 20). Warias offer a perspective on the centrality of public gender in engaging with this restricted form of participation in the Indonesian city.

2. Following the 1965 coup, Suharto was sworn in as acting president in 1967 (for a detailed account see Anderson and McVey 1971). Suharto was elected president the following year. Saskia Wieringa (2002, 338) has deconstructed the centrality of a gendered moral panic to the founding myth of the New Order regime, in particular the establishment of patriarchal control over women through propaganda that circulated spurious accounts of women belonging to the Indonesian Communist Party having committed sexual violence against generals murdered in 1965.

3. Although the origins of this legal apparatus were in Dutch colonial law, a legal charge akin to public indecency was gradually incorporated into debates and the eventual criminalization of pornography in 2006, which stressed the effects of images on a seeing public rather than being limited to a concern for the pornographic image as material object (Lindsay 2010).

4. Like wadam, female sex workers were also addressed through a technocratic yet moralistic new term in Sadikin's Jakarta: "woman without morals" (*wanita tuna susila*, abbreviated to WTS) (Sedyaningsih-Mamahit 1999; Murray 1991). Unlike the case with warias, however, the bureaucratic abbreviation WTS seems to have created neither an opportunity to exert greater control over presentation nor the basis for asserting citizenship rights. The other group that was consistently framed as a risk to public order on parallel terms to warias, and was thus linked to ambiguous threats tied to the dangers of unrestricted public gender and sexuality, were homeless people (*gelandangan*) (see Suparlan 1974). Each of these populations was organized into an overarching framework of social deviance in relation to the governmental category "People with Social Welfare Problems" (*Penyandang masalah kesejahteraan sosial*), abbreviated to PMKS.

5. From 1983 to 1985, urban militias and uniformed police officers eliminated thousands of petty criminals and associated individuals from the urban underclasses in what were known as the "mysterious killings," murdering them and leaving their bodies in public places for all to witness (Siegel 1998; van der Kroef 1985). Neither the perpetrators of the violence nor the government figures that orchestrated it have ever been brought to justice. Warias, perhaps through their ambiguous integration into the public visuality of the New Order owing to their relationship to the municipal government, appeared to escape this fate.

6. Warias' use of the particular turn of phrase *zaman emas* brings to mind a powerful trope in both Indonesian political cultures and classical Javanese thought famously described by Benedict Anderson as a concentration of power, a period "of cosmic order and social well-being, in which each person plays out his appointed role, hierarchies are maintained, and harmony prevails" (1990, 242).

7. Born in 1908, Hamka (an acronym for Haji Abdul Malik Karim Amrul) was an influential and conservative, if idiosyncratic, Indonesian Islamic scholar (Howell 2010; Aljunied 2018). Hamka mentioned firsthand accounts of bancis to illustrate the doctrinal condemnation of homosexuality in Islam. Describing bancis as "no different from homosexuals in Europe," he interpreted the presence of gender nonconformity in Jakarta as a reflection of forms of immorality that had originated in the West (1981, 275). The version of the *Tafsir* I cite was published in 1981 by Yayasan Latmojong in Surabaya but appears to be a reprint of the original version, published in 1967.

8. This impact of racial status as European on the Indonesian municipality is reflected in the fact that areas initially classified as cities—and hence bestowed with political and economic clout—were areas with large European populations. European citizens were nevertheless required to recognize and adapt to the presence of the indigenous population.

9. Warias' claims appeared to demand recognition of the fact that, although municipalities are able to enforce forms of public order, the authority to prosecute or punish individuals under the criminal code can only be made by the national police. Warias' encounters with the state are usually through what I have called municipal or city police, known as the Satuan Polisi Pramong Praja (Satpol PP), who are responsible for enforcing separate regional regulations and who report to mayors or governors (on the colonial origins of the development of the format of municipal police forces see Lev 1985; Bloembergen 2007). Although such raids most definitely have taken a disciplinary format, and are described by warias in everyday life as "being arrested" (*di tangkap*), throughout the New Order they increasingly entailed a form of detention for purposes of rehabilitation within an emerging format of social welfare.

3. THE PERFECT WOMAN

1. My choice of the phrase "sex reassignment surgery" here is both a translation of the commonly used Indonesian phrase *operasi penggantian kelamin* and conveys a critical component of the translation and interpretation of transsexuality among Indonesian experts. I hope that preserving this use helps to sustain a trenchant historical critique of the state's appropriation of transsexuality as a medical discourse embedded in legacies or racism and colonialism (see especially Stryker 2013). While the tendency of the Indonesian state was to silence the voices of warias and other trans people in the historical archive, I hope that the more ethnographic analytical stance toward warias' lives in other chapters allows this book to both enable and to engage with "trans people as active participants in the construction and contestation of medical discourse . . . rather than as passive objects of knowledge" (Gill-Peterson 2018, 16; see also Latham 2019; Strahan 2020).

2. In 1966, Johns Hopkins University Hospital founded a Gender Identity Clinic to provide sex reassignment surgery, which was followed by other centers, including at Stanford University and the University of California, Los Angeles (Meyerowitz 2002). The rise of a medical and scientific establishment saw the establishment of patient groups who identified as transsexuals and who contested the grounds on which they were treated as patients (Stone 1992). These complex shifts can be understood, broadly, as reflecting a reorganization of concepts of the modern self in the United States across the same period that was tied to values of self-expression and self-transformation (Meyerowitz 2002).

3. Afsaneh Najmabadi (2014) described a similar process in the history of determining the differences between transsexuality and same-sex sexuality in Iran, reflecting how nations outside of the West engaged with medical and scientific technologies to establish distinctive modern paradigms for defining sex, gender, and sexuality.

4. During the New Order, a national identity card (known as the *kartu tanda penduduk*, abbreviated to KTP) possessed by individual citizens supplemented a document known as the "family card," and the more relational form of gendered citizenship it implied (Strassler 2010, 135). Prior to the 1960s, bureaucratic documentation like the family card does not appear to have explicitly listed a person's sex on individual terms. This is not to say that gender was not an important marker of personhood tied to citizenship, but rather that it rested on assumptions about appearances and social roles that were left relatively undefined.

5. A psychologist at the University of Surabaya trained in Germany, Tjiptono Darmadji referred to the presence of "tribal groups" who "still [had] specific rituals in which

wadam [had] roles that classif[ied] them as women" (1969, 3). Similarly, Karsono (1973, 89) framed banci in terms of existing practices related to individuals found throughout the archipelago.

6. The violence of this and other encounters with medicine, remembered bitterly by elderly waria to whom I spoke, reflects the normalizing and pathologizing logic of a medical discourse of transsexuality underpinned by a disavowal of trans people's own self-knowledge. Poor Indonesian trans women experienced a parallel regime to that of the United States, where a model of medicine that "disavows its own racial knowledge and racial violence" rests on "the presumption of special access to black people's bodies for experimental research that was frequently nontherapeutic, practiced without consent, painful, and destructive" (Gill-Peterson 2018, 27; see also Snorton 2017).

7. In addition to playing an important role in modernizing psychiatric training in Indonesia, Setyonegoro had traveled to the University of California, San Francisco, as part of an exchange program with the University of Indonesia (Pols 2006, 366). This training may have influenced his ongoing engagement with transsexuality; in addition to providing expert commentary, Setyonegoro played a prominent role in developing guidelines for the diagnosis of transsexuality that were adopted for use in 1978 (Indonesian Department of Health 1978).

8. The Christian concept of the soul, with its emphasis on a deep interiority, reflects a historically specific form of personhood and genealogy of the modern self (see Taylor 1989). It is but one instance of configurations of personhood premised on inner and outer parts (Lambek 1998). Clifford Geertz (1976, 232) clarified how the most usual dualism signifying this in Javanese personhood differs from the meanings associated with body and soul; *batin* "consists in the fuzzy, shifting flow of subjective feeling in all its phenomenological immediacy," and *lahir* refers "to that part of human life which, in our culture, strict behaviorists limit themselves to studying—external actions, movements, postures, speech." Rather than a "separate seat of encapsulated spirituality detachable from the body" (232) there is an integrated, interpenetrating relationship between the interior life of an individual and bodily cultivation (see also Errington 1989, 75).

9. Jules Gill-Peterson (2018) has traced the history of a concept of psychologized gender back to the experimentation and clinical practice on intersex children in the 1940s and 1950s at Johns Hopkins University, which revealed binary sex as far too simplistic an explanatory concept in endocrinology. A psychological and social concept of gender emerged at precisely the point that binary sex was in crisis in the United States, playing a part in undoing previous notions of sex as naturally bisexual yet nevertheless replacing it with a notion of developmental growth as either male or female.

10. Where they do attend to the topic, ethnographic accounts have found that those who identify as waria usually downplay or dismiss outright the need to transform their genital morphology to better align their appearances with their gender (Boellstorff 2007, 94–95; Davies 2010, 142). This is not to posit a sharp difference in forms of personhood between different times and places; for example, Eric Plemons's (2017) account of facial feminization surgery among trans women suggests that transformations to outer appearances are more central to the recognition of gender on social terms than has sometimes been admitted.

11. Ratnam developed a significant regional reputation in Southeast Asia for sex reassignment surgeries for trans men and women, which he performed approximately four hundred times (S. S. Ratnam, interview by Soh Eng Khim, October 3, 1997, audio recording, Medical Services in Singapore Oral History, National Archives of Singapore).

12. I pieced together this history from dozens of articles reporting on Vivian's case in the *Kompas* newspaper and the reputable national weekly magazine *Tempo*. I am grateful to Holy Rafika for his assistance in locating these articles.

13. The film appears to have served a didactic purpose, with time reserved for medical professionals to explain the latest scientific expertise to the film's audience (Murtagh 2013). The film echoes popular accounts of transsexuality in the United States, in which medical authority was used to convey the legitimacy of transsexuality, as Joanne Meyerowitz (2002, 66) wrote, "cloaking it in the language of science and removing it from the realm of sex." In one scene, a psychiatrist speaks directly to the camera to clarify that there are four types of wadam: "transsexuals," "transvestites," "wadam," and "*banci kaléng*." Although the doctor defines the last term as "men who wear women's clothes for profit"—and as firmly set apart from the first three—during fieldwork I found that waria often used the expression *banci kaléng* in everyday narratives of the self to refer to the first stages at which waria start to make their "woman's soul" visible through the application of makeup and wearing women's clothing (Hegarty 2018, 359).

14. This ruling has served as a precedent for Indonesians wishing to change their gender and name as it is listed on their identity documents, although doing so involves a legal and bureaucratic process that is complicated and difficult to complete.

15. The Iranian and Indonesian contexts developed a divergent set of debates on the topic. Whereas in Iran transsexuality gradually came to be recognized as an acceptable procedure according to a combination of Islamic and scientific reasoning (Najmabadi 2014), in Indonesia the limited medical and legal guidelines governing the "operation to perfect the genitals" and "changing sex" appear to have been restricted to intersex people.

16. There was significant semantic slippage as Indonesian psychiatrists, doctors, and journalists communicated just how and in what ways gender would be transformed, moving between the terms for "changing" (*penggantian*), "transforming" (*perubahan*), "perfecting" (*penyempurnaan*), and "refining" (*penghalusan*) a person's gender. With respect to the latter two, Indonesian doctors had likely incorporated John Money's concept of "genital unfinishedness," according to which, with help from surgery, intersex individuals (usually children) would be able to reach a "finished" or "completed" developmental status (Reis 2009, 145). Yet the introduction of the term "refinement" also brings to mind conceptions of personhood expressed in everyday life in Indonesia, including trans women's description of the effects of the practice of dandan, highlighting how universal scientific and medical knowledge addresses its subjects within specific cultural and historical contexts.

17. How Netty Irawati came to the attention of medical staff as a candidate for Indonesia's first state-sanctioned surgery and hormonal treatment for transsexuality is troubling, and her surgery appears to have been on some level coerced. Netty appears to have been recruited as an experimental patient following her detention for psychiatric treatment for "hanging around in public" (a euphemism for soliciting sex with men in public), where she encountered the surgeon who led the operation, Professor Hanifa Wiknyosastro (*Tempo* 1975b).

18. The use of *khunsa* here further highlights the integration of Islam into the technological emphasis of the New Order state. The newly established Indonesian Council of Ulema, of which Buya Hamka was chair, issued a fatwa related to "sex change operations" in 1980. Not legally binding but holding a degree of moral authority, the fatwa asserts that surgeries that would "change" the sex of transsexuals are not permitted, whereas surgeries for intersex people (explicitly clarified as *khunsa*) should be permitted (Indonesian Council of Ulema 1980).

19. The decree identified six hospitals where gender reassignment surgery would be undertaken and the medical specialists required to perform it (*Kompas* 1979d; Indonesian Department of Health 1979). Saskia Wieringa (2015) has written an illuminating ethnographic account of Indonesian medical approaches to intersex children after the New Order.

4. BEAUTY EXPERTS

1. I refer to national publics to highlight the way that the boundaries between private citizenship and collective experience are not stable but shaped by an array of affective intensities that thwart efforts to instate authority over cultural order, or what William Mazzarella called those "performative dispensations" where "the performative is not just a matter of adhering to social scripts or adequately playing roles . . . [but] involves a constant multisensory activation of gesture, bodily comportment, and aesthetic potentialities within and against such scripted expectations" (2013, 42). Following Lauren Berlant, I locate warias' participation in citizenship not as individualized expressions of sex/gender/sexuality but within national publics that offer the possibility to "establish an archive for a different history, one that claimed the most intimate stories of subordinated people as information about everyone's citizenship" (1997, 221).

2. The form that youth culture took was diverse and did not always take an explicitly political guise, although the 1970s saw the rise of student groups who organized mass protests to oppose the regime. This period was followed by a significant crackdown on the political organizing on campus that had marked the first significant challenge to the Suharto regime (Aspinall 2005, 118).

3. This description of personhood is commonly theorized in relation to *malu*, a key concept in studies of the emotions in Indonesia which has several analogues, such as *isin* in Java and *lek* in Bali. Although usually translated as either "shame" or "embarrassment," these terms are imprecise, implying "a distance between actor and role, and so between self and social persona, which is misleading" (Keeler 1983, 161). Johan Lindquist described how, for migrant female sex workers, *malu* is a productive emotion when it enables them to engage in activities they otherwise see as immoral, and thus is an emotional state that "describes the failures to live up to the ideals of the nation" (2009, 14). This is the case for gay men and increasingly for warias, whose appearances and claims to recognition, made to a national public, have been met with affectively charged and even violent forms of rejection (Boellstorff 2004).

4. Nancy Florida, in her study of a text composed in the nineteenth century, described a similar understanding in *semu*, a classical Javanese concept that refers to a science of reading outer signs open to refined or skilled persons able to read glimpsed, perceptible signs of the inside, thus developing an understanding of a partly concealed truth. Florida noted that this epistemology shaped by a "science of semu" (276) was reflected in the term *pasemon*—also the word for face—was which was "a kind of epistemologically constructed 'mask' which reveals insofar as it appears to conceal" (276). In this respect, the relationship between concealment and revelation described here has greater parallels with projects related to the modern self than has otherwise been acknowledged. In the early twentieth-century United States, the increasing use of cosmetics among women was part of widening participation in consumer culture that gestured to a move away from a "physiognomic paradigm" (Peiss 1996, 320) that emphasized the face as a reflection of the inner self. The availability and popularity of makeup heralded a move toward selfhood conceived as a performance, one that had ambiguous consequences for women: on the one hand, women were expected to wear makeup in public, while women who wore cosmetics that were either excessive or undertaken in the wrong context were held under suspicion of insincerity, fraudulence, or sexual impropriety. Although dandan is shaped by regional histories of personhood, its invocation of a subtle interplay between concealment and revelation produced new possibilities when it encountered a concept of modern gender with a more recent and global history.

5. This included the presence of internationally recognized groups of trans women performers, including the famous French troupe Le Carrousel, which performed at venues in

Jakarta several times in 1973. The fragmentary relationship between the category *waria* and transnational forms of knowledge related to transgender femininity—established through knowledge about medical transsexuality that started to circulate in the decade prior—continued through the appearance of such groups in Jakarta. Waria and possibly other categories for gender nonconformity played an important yet underexamined role in the application and distribution of the gendered body as a regional form of development in Asia and a key node in the biopolitical distribution of citizenship in the second half of the twentieth century.

6. Given that there are few written accounts of the Fantastic Dolls and other performance groups based in Jakarta, the account in this section is based on oral history interviews and ethnographic research I conducted in 2015 with trans women who had a relationship to the Fantastic Dolls, particularly Chenny Han, Meifei, and Nancy Iskandar. Chenny Han is a well-known beautician who was formerly a member of the Fantastic Dolls during the 1970s. The Fantastic Dolls was an important staging for Indonesia's small number of trans women celebrities, most notably Dorce Gamalama, who was one of Indonesian television's best-known figures during the 1980s and 1990s (Murtagh 2017). I also draw on Kemala Atmojo's (1987) journalistic account of warias in Jakarta in the 1980s. Although membership changed frequently, the Fantastic Dolls continued to perform up until the mid-2000s, outlasting the New Order state.

7. The Bambang Brothers group, which appeared in the film made about Rubianti's life (Murtagh 2013, 40), was founded in the late 1960s by Mami Myrna, who was later the head of Himpunan Wadam Jakarta, or "Hiwad," a short-lived waria organization in Jakarta (Boellstorff 2007).

8. Meifei, whom I interviewed in Jakarta in May 2015, was one of several warias who reflected on warias' emergence as beauty experts not only on national terms but in relation to a broader project of regional development that rested on comparisons with neighboring Southeast Asian nations. Meifei recalled that the inspiration for the name of their group came from a performance group called the Paper Dolls from the Philippines, which had visited Jakarta in the mid-1970s. "Paper Dolls" was a common expression used in the Philippines to refer to trans feminine performance, derived from one well-known performance group in Manila established in the 1980s (Garcia 2009, 204). Meifei, in addition to several other warias, spoke of frequently traveling from Indonesia to Singapore from the late 1960s onward, where they met other trans women from throughout the region.

9. Indonesian writers and warias themselves engaged in a process of sorting that reflected an alternative genealogy of the modern self. One account in the *Mingguan Djaja* special issue listed a taxonomic table that defined banci as either "permanent transvestites" who "[wore] women's clothes at day and at night" and "partial transvestites" whose "glances, voice, gait and movement [were] different from those of regular men" (*Mingguan Djaja* 1968c, 4). This was in some respects a process of sorting out categories from "a tangled thicket of varied conditions of sex, gender, and sexuality" (Meyerowitz 2002, 7) similar to that which proceeded in the United States.

10. The consistency of this performance with those of previous decades is also suggested by other sources that use the same tagline for performances (Atmojo 1987; *Kompas* 1982).

11. In 2014–15, warias in Yogyakarta arrested in raids under suspicion of undertaking sex work were forcibly required to participate in gendered vocational training programs along with other marginalized groups whose presence was framed as a disruption of public order (see Hegarty 2016). These programs, which are described by the city as "rehabilitation," have inherited many of the logics of New Order guidance programs—situating the self as both a locus of transformation and a potential barrier to smooth social interactions (for one ethnographic account of these forms of rehabilitation, and their impact on people with severe mental illnesses, see Nanwani 2018). Such programs, which rely on

a connection between economic progress and the cultivation of appearances, remain an important component of the Indonesian state's efforts to address undesirable forms of difference in the body of the nation.

5. NATIONAL GLAMOUR

1. The public visibility of warias and practices of dandan in Indonesia appear to have reduced significantly from the 1990s onward. The reduction in warias' visibility in cities throughout Indonesia since this time has been widely noted among warias as an effect of the privatization of and growing surveillance over public space in Indonesian cities. Most warias have attributed this to several factors, chief among them the increasing hostility they faced in public space, including from state security forces (see, e.g., Thajib 2018). The shrinking of spaces for warias to be present in in the city after the New Order has moved apace with the introduction of various new regional and municipal regulations and restrictions governing public morality and public order (Butt 2010).

2. Anthropologists of Indonesia writing about the 1980s observed the New Order state's blend of cultural ritual and concern for security as part of an anxious effort to assert a monopoly on recognition of distinctions in the body of the nation (Keeler 1988; Pemberton 1994; Siegel 1998). Patterns of violence that underpinned the act of seeing—integrated into the texture of everyday meanings of the state in the life of its citizens—were the crucial means through which the state sought to maintain control, albeit via a visual format of power that generated a "haunting trace of difference" (Pemberton 1994, 318) that could never be entirely erased.

3. Tadi explained that she was arrested several times throughout the 1970s and 1980s during routine police raids. A number of times, her arrest resulted in her being driven to the outskirts of the city, still made up in dandan, and being forced to walk the several hours back to town.

4. Tadi's use of the term *banci* to suggest her own temporal movement toward identification as waria—a change from a less permanent feminine appearance to a more permanent one enabled through technologies of feminization—indicates a significant overlap between understandings of personhood in relation to the self and the narrativization of broader forms of historical change.

CONCLUSION

1. The 2008 pornography law is a well-known example, but public morality is a widespread justification for limits placed on democratic expression in Indonesia, contained in many different regulations by different government bodies. For example, the national broadcasting commission has released regulations that ban television or internet images that include "male femininity" (*kebancibancian*) and the "promotion of LGBT" (*mengampanyekan LGBT*) as a way to protect public morality. In Indonesia, it seems as though almost all efforts to regulate gender and sexuality invoke the "public," taken to refer to collectives made up of spectators who are simultaneously imagined at the scale of the village, the city, the nation, and the internet.

2. Although the considerations and impetus for the changes have shifted across time, the justification given for revising the Criminal Code has largely been framed as the need to bring it into line with the nation's character. As one justice minister expressed in 2005, a revised code offered an opportunity to "bring [the law] more in line with Indonesian culture and religion" (Blackwood 2007, 300). In 2016, a constitutional court case brought by the Family Love Alliance to criminalize same-sex (and indeed, a vast range of non-heteronormative) sexual practices was defeated (Yulius 2019). Draft revisions to the penal

code debated since the late 2010s also included provisions for criminalizing a wide range of sexual behavior under the category "indecent acts" (*cabul*) (Butt 2019). Gender nonconformity has not been the subject of criminalization in these draft revisions, perhaps because matters pertaining to public decency (under which warias have long been subject to punitive regulations) were regulated at the district level (Pausacker 2020). As of mid-2022, the state of the draft bill of the Criminal Code and of the codes governing gender and sexuality within it remain unclear.

3. During fieldwork, I observed those who identified as warias draw on the category "transgender" in regard to local and national concerns to forge distinctive claims to recognition (Hegarty 2017b; 2017a). In particular, the forms of knowledge and articulation of rights to testing and treatment for HIV—and since 2020, the COVID-19 pandemic—have provided one context where warias have been shaped by a global framework of transgender rights (e.g., Mallay et al. 2021). This process has accelerated since the time that the research took place, yet it has also shown how *trans* has served as a useful vehicle for claiming national belonging through a language that brings together technological modernity and human rights in the same frame. Although I focus on warias and that term's relationship to trans, a concurrent discourse of trans in relation to female-bodied and transgender masculine individuals is under way in Indonesia (Blackwood 2010, 179–201). The adoption and use of "trans man" appears to predate the development of the term *transpuan*, and the term *priawan* (combining male and female in a similar logic of combination to *waria*) was used during the New Order. Both the diminished visibility granted to transgender men and their engagement with the logic of combination that I describe make the forms of public and political participation shaped by trans masculinity an important focus for further research.

References

Abeyasekere, Susan. 1990. *Jakarta: A History*. Singapore: Oxford University Press.

Aizura, Aren Z. 2018. *Mobile Subjects: Transnational Imaginaries of Gender Reassignment*. Durham, NC: Duke University Press.

Alexeyeff, Kalissa, and Niko Besnier. 2014. "Gender on the Edge: Identities, Politics, Transformations." In *Gender on the Edge: Transgender, Gay, and Other Pacific Islanders*, edited by Niko Besnier and Kalissa Alexeyeff, 1–30. Honolulu: University of Hawai'i Press.

Aljunied, Syed Muhd Khairudin. 2018. *Hamka and Islam: Cosmopolitan Reform in the Malay World*. Ithaca, NY: Cornell University Press.

Amir, Sulfikar. 2013. *The Technological State in Indonesia: The Co-constitution of High Technology and Authoritarian Politics*. New York: Routledge.

Anderson, Benedict R. O'G. 1990. *Language and Power: Exploring Political Cultures in Indonesia*. Ithaca, NY: Cornell University Press.

——. 1996. *Imagined Communities: Reflections on the Origin and Spread of Nationalism*. 7th ed. London: Verso.

Anderson, Benedict R. O'G., and Ruth T. McVey. 1971. *A Preliminary Analysis of the October 1, 1965, Coup in Indonesia*. Ithaca, NY: Southeast Asia Program, Cornell University.

Anggraeni, Dewi. 2014. *Tragedi Mei 1998 dan lahirnya Komnas Perempuan* [The Tragedy of May 1998 and the birth of the National Commission on Violence Against Women]. Jakarta: Penerbit Buku Kompas.

Aspinall, Edward. 2005. *Opposing Suharto: Compromise, Resistance, and Regime Change in Indonesia*. Stanford, CA: Stanford University Press.

Atmojo, Kemala. 1987. *Kami Bukan Lelaki* [We are not men]. Jakarta: PT Pustaka Utama Grafiti.

Aultman, B. 2014. "Cisgender." *TSQ: Transgender Studies Quarterly* 1 (1–2): 61–62.

Barendregt, Bart. 2011. "Tropical Spa Cultures, Eco-Chic, and the Complexities of New Asianism." In *Cleanliness and Culture*, edited by Kees van Dijk and Jean Gelman Taylor, 159–92. Leiden: KITLV Press.

Barker, Joshua. 2001. "State of Fear: Controlling the Criminal Contagion in Suharto's New Order." In *Violence and the State in Suharto's Indonesia*, edited by Benedict R. O'G Anderson, 20–53. Ithaca, NY: Cornell University Press.

——. 2005. "Engineers and Political Dreams: Indonesia in the Satellite Age." *Current Anthropology* 46 (5): 703–27.

——. 2015. "Guerilla Engineers: The Internet and the Politics of Freedom in Indonesia." In *Dreamscapes of Modernity: Sociotechnical Imaginaries and the Fabrication of Power*, edited by Sang-Hyun Kim and Sheila Jasanoff, 199–218. Chicago: University of Chicago Press.

Bartky, Sandra Lee. 1990. *Femininity and Domination: Studies in the Phenomenology of Oppression*. New York: Routledge.

Bauer, J. Edgar. 2006. "Magnus Hirschfeld: Panhumanism and the Sexual Cultures of Asia." *Intersections: Gender, History and Culture in the Asian Context*, no. 14 (November). http://intersections.anu.edu.au/issue14/bauer.html#n102.

——. 2017. *The Hirschfeld Archives: Violence, Death, and Modern Queer Culture.* Philadelphia: Temple University Press.

Beauchamp, Toby. 2019. *Going Stealth: Transgender Politics and U.S. Surveillance Practices.* Durham, NC: Duke University Press.

Bellows, Laura. 2011. "The Aroused Public in Search of the Pornographic in Indonesia." *Ethnos* 76 (2): 209–32.

Berlant, Lauren. 1997. *The Queen of America Goes to Washington City: Essays on Sex and Citizenship.* Durham, NC: Duke University Press.

Besnier, Niko. 2002. "Transgenderism, Locality, and the Miss Galaxy Beauty Pageant in Tonga." *American Ethnologist* 29 (3): 534–66.

Blackwood, Evelyn. 2005a. "Gender Transgression in Colonial and Postcolonial Indonesia." *Journal of Asian Studies* 64 (4): 849–79.

——. 2005b. "Transnational Sexualities in One Place: Indonesian Readings." *Gender and Society* 19 (2): 221–42.

——. 2007. "Regulation of Sexuality in Indonesian Discourse: Normative Gender, Criminal Law and Shifting Strategies of Control." *Culture, Health & Sexuality* 9 (3): 293–307.

——. 2010. *Falling into the Lesbi World: Desire and Difference in Indonesia.* Honolulu: University of Hawai'i Press.

Bleys, Rudi C. 1996. *The Geography of Perversion: Male-to-Male Sexual Behaviour outside the West and the Ethnographic Imagination, 1750–1918.* New York: NYU Press.

Bloembergen, Marieke. 2007. "The Dirty Work of Empire: Modern Policing and Public Order in Surabaya, 1911–1919." *Indonesia,* no. 83: 119–50.

——. 2011. "Being Clean Is Being Strong: Policing Cleanliness and Gay Vices in the Netherlands Indies in the 1930s." In *Cleanliness and Culture,* edited by Kees van Dijk and Jean Gelman Taylor, 117–45. Leiden: KITLV Press.

Boellstorff, Tom. 2002. "Ethnolocality." *Asia Pacific Journal of Anthropology* 3 (1) (May): 24–48.

——. 2004. "The Emergence of Political Homophobia in Indonesia: Masculinity and National Belonging." *Ethnos* 69 (4): 465–86.

——. 2005. *The Gay Archipelago: Sexuality and Nation in Indonesia.* Princeton, NJ: Princeton University Press.

——. 2007. *A Coincidence of Desires: Anthropology, Queer Studies, Indonesia.* Durham, NC: Duke University Press.

——. 2016. "Against State Straightism: Five Principles for Including LGBT Indonesians." *E-International Relations,* March 21. http://www.e-ir.info/2016/03/21/against-state-straightism-five-principles-for-including-lgbt-indonesians/.

Boellstorff, Tom, Mauro Cabral, Micha Cárdenas, Trystan Cotten, Eric A. Stanley, Kalaniopua Young, and Aren Z. Aizura. 2014. "Decolonizing Transgender: A Roundtable Discussion." *TSQ: Transgender Studies Quarterly* 1 (3): 419–39.

Boomgaard, Peter. 2012. "Male-Male Sex, Bestiality and Incest in the Early-Modern Indonesian Archipelago: Perceptions and Penalties." In *Sexual Diversity in Asia, c. 600–1950,* edited by Raquel A. G. Reyes and William G. Clarence-Smith, 141–60. London: Routledge.

Boon, L. J. 1989. "Those Damned Sodomites: Public Images of Sodomy in the Eighteenth Century Netherlands." *Journal of Homosexuality* 16 (1–2): 237–48.

Bourchier, David. 1990. "Crime, Law and State in Indonesia." In *State and Civil Society in Indonesia,* edited by Arief Budiman, 177–212. Monash Papers on Southeast Asia. Clayton, Australia: Centre of Southeast Asian Studies, Monash University.

Brenner, Suzanne. 1998. *The Domestication of Desire: Women, Wealth, and Modernity in Java*. Princeton, NJ: Princeton University Press.

——. 1999. "On the Public Intimacy of the New Order: Images of Women in the Popular Indonesian Print Media." *Indonesia*, no. 67 (April): 13–37.

Budiman, Arief. 1969a. "Ali Sadikin: One-Man Revolt." *Quadrant* 13 (5): 75.

——. 1969b. "'Wanita-Adam'—Sebuah Persoalan." *Kompas*, January 16.

Butler, Judith. 1990. *Gender Trouble: Feminism and the Subversion of Identity*. New York: Routledge.

Butt, Simon. 2010. "Regional Autonomy and Legal Disorder: The Proliferation of Local Laws in Indonesia." *Singapore Journal of Legal Studies*, July: 1–21.

——. 2019. "The Constitutional Court and Minority Rights: Analysing the Recent Homosexual Sex and Indigenous Belief Cases." In *Contentious Belonging: The Place of Minorities in Indonesia*, edited by Greg Fealy and Ronit Ricci, 55–74. Singapore: ISEAS—Yusof Ishak Institute.

Cannell, Fenella. 1999. *Power and Intimacy in the Christian Philippines*. New York: Cambridge University Press.

Chao, Sophie. 2022. *In the Shadow of the Palms: More-Than-Human Becomings in West Papua*. Durham, NC: Duke University Press.

City of East Jakarta. 1972. "Laporan Bulanan Walikota Jakarta Timur" [Monthly report of the East Jakarta mayor], January 1972, 21–22.

Coppel, Charles A. 1983. *Indonesian Chinese in Crisis*. Kuala Lumpur: Oxford University Press.

Darmadji, Tjiptono. 1969. "Masalah wadam dan pemetjahannya" [The problem of wadam and its prevention]. *Kompas*, January 16.

Davies, Sharyn Graham. 2007. *Challenging Gender Norms: Five Genders among Bugis in Indonesia*. Belmont, UK: Thomson Wadsworth.

——. 2010. *Gender Diversity in Indonesia: Sexuality, Islam and Queer Selves*. London: Routledge.

——. 2015. "Surveilling Sexuality in Indonesia." In *Sex and Sexualities in Contemporary Indonesia: Sexual Politics, Health, Diversity, and Representations*, edited by Linda Rae Bennett and Sharyn Graham Davies, 29–51. London: Routledge.

Dekker, Rudolf M., and Lotte C. van de Pol. 1989. *The Tradition of Female Cross-Dressing in Early Modern Europe*. London: Macmillan.

Dwyer, Leslie K. 2002. "Spectacular Sexuality: Nationalism, Development and the Politics of Family Planning in Indonesia." In *Gender Ironies of Nationalism: Sexing the Nation*, edited by Tamar Mayer, 25–62. London: Routledge.

Errington, Shelly. 1989. *Meaning and Power in a Southeast Asian Realm*. Princeton, NJ: Princeton University Press.

——. 1990. "Recasting Sex, Gender and Power: A Regional Theoretical Overview." In *Power and Difference: Gender in Island Southeast Asia*, edited by Jane Monnig Atkinson and Shelly Errington, 1–58. Stanford, CA: Stanford University Press.

Fasseur, C. 1994. "Cornerstone and Stumbling Block: Racial Classification and the Late Colonial State in Indonesia." In *The Late Colonial State in Indonesia: Political and Economic Foundations of the Netherlands Indies, 1880–1942*, edited by R. B. Cribb, 31–56. Leiden: KITLV Press.

Feith, Herbert. 1962. *The Decline of Constitutional Democracy in Indonesia*. Ithaca, NY: Cornell University Press.

Florida, Nancy K. 1995. *Writing the Past, Inscribing the Future: History as Prophecy in Colonial Java*. Durham, NC: Duke University Press.

Foucault, Michel. 1978. *The History of Sexuality, Vol. 1: An Introduction.* Translated by Robert Hurley. New York: Pantheon Books.

Garcia, J. Neil C. 2009. *Philippine Gay Culture: Binabae to Bakla, Silahis to MSM.* Hong Kong: Hong Kong University Press.

Geertz, Clifford. 1976. *The Religion of Java.* Chicago: University of Chicago Press.

Geertz, Hildred. 1963. *Indonesian Cultures and Communities.* New Haven, CT: Human Relations Area Studies.

Ghoshal, Neela. 2020. "Transgender, Third Gender, No Gender: Part II." *Human Rights Watch* (blog), September 8. https://www.hrw.org/news/2020/09/08/transgender-third-gender-no-gender-part-ii.

Gill-Peterson, Jules. 2018. *Histories of the Transgender Child.* Minneapolis: University of Minnesota Press.

Goss, Andrew. 2011. *The Floracrats: State-Sponsored Science and the Failure of the Enlightenment in Indonesia.* Madison: University of Wisconsin Press.

Gouda, Frances. 1997. "Languages of Gender and Neurosis in the Indonesian Struggle for Independence, 1945–1949." *Indonesia* 64 (October): 45.

Gundle, Stephen. 2008. *Glamour: A History.* Oxford: Oxford University Press.

Hacking, Ian. 1999. "Making Up People." In *The Science Studies Reader*, edited by Mario Biagioli, 161–71. New York: Routledge.

Halim, Kevin. 2019. *Penerimaan: Kumpulan Cerita Penerimaan Orang Tua Dengan Anak Trans Puan* [Acceptance: A collection of stories of acceptance by parents of their transpuan children]. Jakarta: Gaya Warna Lentera Indonesia (GWL-INA).

Hamka, Buya. (1975) 1981. *Tafsir Al-Azhar Juzu' XIX* [The Al-Azhar Tafsir number 19]. 2nd ed. Surabaya, Indonesia: Yayasan Latimojong.

Hannah, Willard. 1968. "Pak Dikin's Djakarta." *American Universities Fieldstaff Reports: Southeast Asia Series* 17 (1): 7.

Haraway, Donna. 1988. "Situated Knowledges: The Science Question in Feminism and the Privilege of Partial Perspective." *Feminist Studies* 14 (3): 575–99.

——. 1991. "'Gender' for a Marxist Dictionary: The Sexual Politics of a Word." In *Simians, Cyborgs, and Women: The Reinvention of Nature*, 127–48. New York: Routledge.

Hasse, W. F., and W. Boekhoudt. 1905. *Boekoe Penoentoen Akan Dipakai Oleh Priaji2 Dalam Pemeriksaan "Voorloopig Onder Zoek"* [A Guidebook to be used in the civil servants' examination). Batavia.

Hatley, Barbara. 1971. "Wayang and Ludruk: Polarities in Java." *Drama Review: TDR* 15 (2): 88–101.

Hegarty, Benjamin. 2016. "Seeking a 'Zone of Safety.'" *New Mandala* (blog), April 18. https://www.newmandala.org/seeking-a-zone-of-safety/.

——. 2017a. "The Value of Transgender: Waria Affective Labor for Transnational Media Markets in Indonesia." *TSQ: Transgender Studies Quarterly* 4 (1): 78–95.

——. 2017b. "'When I Was Transgender': Visibility, Subjectivity, and Queer Aging in Indonesia." *Medicine Anthropology Theory* 4 (2): 70–80.

——. 2018. "Under the Lights, onto the Stage." *TSQ: Transgender Studies Quarterly* 5 (3): 355–77.

——. 2019. "The Perfect Woman: Transgender Femininity and National Modernity in New Order Indonesia, 1968–1978." *Journal of the History of Sexuality* 28 (1): 44–65.

——. 2021. "Governing Nonconformity: Gender Presentation, Public Space, and the City in New Order Indonesia." *Journal of Asian Studies* 80 (4): 955–74.

———. 2022. "Sex, Crime and Entertainment: Images of LGBT in the Indonesian News Media." *Indonesia and the Malay World* 50 (146): 33–51.

Hekma, Gert. 1991. "Homosexual Behavior in the Nineteenth-Century Dutch Army." *Journal of the History of Sexuality* 2 (2): 266–88.

———. 1996. "A Female Soul in a Male Body: Sexual Inversion as Gender Inversion in Nineteenth-Century Sexology." In *Third Sex, Third Gender: Beyond Sexual Dimorphism in Culture and History*, edited by Gilbert H. Herdt, 213–39. Princeton, NJ: Zone Books.

Helliwell, Christine. 2000. "'It's Only a Penis': Rape, Feminism, and Difference." *Signs* 25 (3): 789–816.

Herdt, Gilbert H. 1996. "Introduction: Third Sexes and Third Genders." In *Third Sex, Third Gender: Beyond Sexual Dimorphism in Culture and History*, edited by Gilbert H. Herdt, 21–84. Princeton, NJ: Zone Books.

Heryanto, Ariel. 1988. "The Development of 'Development.'" Translated by Nancy Lutz. *Indonesia*, no. 46: 1–24.

Hirschfeld, Magnus. 1935. *Women East and West: Impressions of a Sex Expert*. London: W. Heinemann.

———. (1910) 2006. "Selections from 'Transvestites, the Erotic Drive to Cross Dress'" In *The Transgender Studies Reader*, edited by Stephen Whittle and Susan Stryker, 28–39. New York: Routledge.

Hoesterey, James Bourk. 2016. *Rebranding Islam: Piety, Prosperity, and a Self-Help Guru*. Stanford, CA: Stanford University Press.

Howell, Julia Day. 2010. "Indonesia's Salafist Sufis." *Modern Asian Studies* 44 (5): 1029–51.

Hull, Terence H., and Valerie Hull. 2005. "From Family Planning to Reproductive Health Care: A Brief History." In *People, Population, and Policy in Indonesia*, 1–69. Jakarta: Equinox.

Indonesian Council of Ulema. 1980. "Operasi perubahan/penyempurnaan kelamin" [Operations to change or perfect sex]. *Fatwa* no. 6.

Indonesian Department of Health. 1978. "Seminar operasi penggantian kelamin" [A seminar on sex change operations]. *Majalah Kesehatan* 67: 11–13, 67–68.

———. 1979. "Keputusan menteri kesehatan Republik Indonesia tentang penunjukan rumah sakit dan tim ahli sebagai tempat dan pelaksana operasi penggantian kelamin" [Decree of the minister for health regarding the implementation of sex change operations]. No. 253/Men.Kes/SK/VI/1979.

Indonesian Department of Social Welfare. 2008. *Pedoman umum pelayanan sosial waria* [A general guide for providing social support to warias]. Jakarta: Directorate General for Services and Social Welfare, Division of Services and Rehabilitation of Social Deviance.

Ingleson, John. 1975. *Perhimpunan Indonesia and the Indonesian Nationalist Movement, 1923–1928*. Monash Papers on Southeast Asia. Clayton, Australia: Centre of Southeast Asian Studies, Monash University.

Jackson, Peter. 2003. "Performative Genders, Perverse Desires: A Bio-history of Thailand's Same-Sex and Transgender Cultures." *Intersections: Gender, History and Culture in the Asian Context*, no. 9 (August). http://intersections.anu.edu.au/issue9/jackson.html.

Jakarta Special Region. 1969. "Kegiatan Komisi 'A' Gotong Royong Dewan Perwakilan Rakyat Daerah Provinsi Daerah Khusus Ibukota Jakarta" [The agenda for Commission 'A' Gotong Royong, the Jakarta Provincial House of Representatives], 11–12. April 19.

——. 1972. "Peraturan Daerah Daerah Khusus Ibukota Jakarta tentang ketertiban umum dalam wilayah Daerah Khusus Ibukota Jakarta No. 3" [Regional regulation of the Special Capital Region of Jakarta on public order number 3], December 9.

Jones, Carla. 2010. "Better Women: The Cultural Politics of Gendered Expertise in Indonesia." *American Anthropologist* 112 (2): 270–82.

——. 2012. "Women in the Middle: Femininity, Virtue, and Excess in Indonesian Discourses of Middle Classness." In *The Global Middle Classes: Theorizing through Ethnography*, edited by Rachel Heiman, Carla Freeman, and Mark Liechty, 145–68. Santa Fe: SAR.

Karsono. 1973. "Sedikit Tentang Hal Banci." *Majalah Kesehatan* 37 (6): 89–90.

Katjasungkana, Nursyahbani, and Saskia E. Wieringa. 2016. *Creeping Criminalisation.* Edited by Grace Poore. New York: Outright Action International.

Keeler, Ward. 1983. "Shame and Stage Fright in Java." *Ethos* 11 (3): 152–65.

——. 1988. "Sharp Rays: Javanese Responses to a Solar Eclipse." *Indonesia*, no. 46: 91–101.

Kelty, Christopher M. 2019. *The Participant: A Century of Participation in Four Stories.* Chicago: University of Chicago Press.

Kessler, Suzanne J. 1998. *Lessons from the Intersexed.* New Brunswick, NJ: Rutgers University Press.

Kim, Sang-Hyun, and Sheila Jasanoff. 2015. "Future Imperfect: Science, Technology, and the Imaginations of Modernity." In *Dreamscapes of Modernity: Sociotechnical Imaginaries and the Fabrication of Power*, edited by Sang-Hyun Kim and Sheila Jasanoff, 1–33. Chicago: University of Chicago Press.

Kompas. 1968a. "Di Djakarta terdapat 15,000 bantji" [In Jakarta there are 15,000 banci]. August 5, p. 2.

——. 1969a. "Razzia wadam" [Raids on wadam]. January 17, p. 3.

——. 1969b. "Menjelajah nusantara: Queen of wadam" [Exploring the archipelago: Queen of wadam]. January 17, p. 2.

——. 1972. "Bambang Brothers, pelawak dan penari striptease 'wadam'" [Bambang Brothers, comedians and striptease dancers]. February 8, p. 5.

——. 1973a. "Para wadam ibukota memprotest polisi" [The wadam of the capital protest the police]. February 28, p. 3.

——. 1973b. "Pengadilan mengabulkan permohonan Iwan Rubianto berganti status wanita" [Court grants Iwan Rubianto's request to change status to woman]. November 15, pp. 1, 8.

——. 1973c. "Biaya operasinya dua juta rupiah" [The cost of the operation was two million rupiah]. September 21, p. 5.

——. 1973d. "'Sex kejiwaan' Iwan memang wanita" [The "mental sex" of Iwan is in fact that of a woman]. October 10.

——. 1973e. "Buya Hamka mengenai kasus ganti kelamin & pertunangan" [Buya Hamka regarding cases of sex change and its process]. September 22, p. 1.

——. 1973f. "Dr. Herman: Persoalan Vivian jangan dibuat berlarut-larut" [Dr Herman: Don't drag out the case of Vivian]. September 29, p. 1.

——. 1975a. "RSTM akan lakukan operasi perubahan kelamin pertama di Indonesia" [Tjipto Mangkusumo Hospital to undertake the first sex change operation in Indonesia]. May 24, p. 3.

——. 1975b. "Berkenalan dengan Benny Runtuwene yang menjadi Netti Irawaty [*sic*]" [Introducing Benny Runtuwene who has become Netty Irawaty]. August 15, p. 1.

——. 1977. "Bagaimana mengatasi masalah wadam menurut Tjokro" [How to overcome the problem of wadam according to [Governor] Tjokro]. November 26, p. 3.

——. 1979a. "Jakarta kita dan suatu malam di jalan Krakatau" [Our Jakarta and one night on Krakatau Street]. November 4, p. 2.

——. 1979b. "Jakarta kita dan sekali peristiwa di Taman Lawang" [An incident in Lawang Park]. July 1, p. 2.

——. 1979c. "Mereka berkabung: Berilah kami kesempatan hidup yang layak" [Those who mourn: Give us a chance to live a decent life]. October 30, pp. 1, 13.

——. 1979d. "Enam RS ditunjuk untuk pelaksanaan operasi ganti kelamin" [Six specific hospitals to implement sex change surgery]. July 27, p. 12.

——. 1982. "Sasana karya waria dan germo disambut antusias pembangunanya" [The development of a training center for warias and pimps is enthusiastically welcomed]. May 15, p. 3.

——. 1990. "Mencoba mengikis pandangan negatif masyarakat" [Trying to shift society's negative view]. November 18, p. 5.

Kusno, Abidin. 2014. *After the New Order: Space, Politics and Jakarta*. Honolulu: University of Hawai'i Press.

Lambek, Michael. 1998. "Body and Mind in Mind, Body and Mind in Body: Some Anthropological Interventions in a Long Conversation." In *Bodies and Persons: Comparative Perspectives from Africa and Melanesia*, edited by Michael Lambek and Andrew Strathern, 103–23. Cambridge: Cambridge University Press.

Laqueur, Thomas. 1990. *Making Sex: Body and Gender from the Greeks to Freud*. Cambridge, MA: Harvard University Press.

Latham, J. R. 2019. "Axiomatic: Constituting 'Transexuality' and Trans Sexualities in Medicine." *Sexualities* 22 (1–2): 13–30.

Leeuwen, Lizzy van. 2011. *Lost in Mall: An Ethnography of Middle-Class Jakarta in the 1990s*. Leiden: KITLV Press.

Legge, J. D. 1961. *Central Authority and Regional Autonomy in Indonesia: A Study in Local Administration, 1950–1960*. Ithaca, NY: Cornell University Press.

Lev, Daniel S. 1985. "Colonial Law and the Genesis of the Indonesian State." *Indonesia*, no. 40: 57–74.

Li, Tania. 2007. *The Will to Improve: Governmentality, Development, and the Practice of Politics*. Durham, NC: Duke University Press.

Lim, T. H. 1974. "Hoge raad Nederland tentang perobahan pencatatan sipil" [The High Council of the Netherlands on changes in civil registration]. *Kompas*, March 14, p. 4.

Lindquist, Johan. 2009. *The Anxieties of Mobility: Migration and Tourism in the Indonesian Borderlands*. Honolulu: University of Hawai'i Press.

Lindsay, Jennifer. 2010. "Media and Morality: Pornography Post Suharto." In *Politics and the Media in Twenty-First Century Indonesia: Decade of Democracy*, edited by Krishna Sen and David Hill, 172–95. London: Routledge.

Ling, Tan Tjiauw. 1968. "Beberapa segi daripada laporan preminier research bantji." *Djiwa* 1 (2): 45–54.

Locher-Scholten, Elsbeth, and Anke Niehof, eds. 1992. *Indonesian Women in Focus: Past and Present Notions*. Leiden: KITLV Press.

Long, Nicholas. 2007. "How to Win a Beauty Contest in Tanjung Pinang." *Review of Indonesian and Malaysian* 41 (1): 91–117.

Luttikhuis, Bart. 2013. "Beyond Race: Constructions of 'Europeanness' in Late-Colonial Legal Practice in the Dutch East Indies." *European Review of History / Revue Européenne d'histoire* 20 (4): 539–58.

Mallay, Rully, Benjamin Hegarty, Sandeep Nanwani, and Ignatius Praptoraharjo. 2021. "One Transgender Community's Experience of the COVID-19 Pandemic: A Report from Indonesia." *TSQ: Transgender Studies Quarterly* 8 (3): 386–93.

Malo, Manasse, and Peter J. M. Nas. 1991. "Local Autonomy: Urban Management in Indonesia." *Sojourn: Journal of Social Issues in Southeast Asia* 6 (2): 175–202.

——. 1997. "Queen City of the East and Symbol of the Nation: The Administration and Management of Jakarta." In *The Dynamics of Metropolitan Management in Southeast Asia*, edited by Jürgen Rüland, 99–132. Singapore: Institute of Southeast Asian Studies.

Manshur, M. I. Aly, and Noer Iskandar Al-Barsany. 1981. *Waria dan pengubahan kelamin, ditinjau dari hukum Islam* [Waria and sex change from the perspective of Islam]. Yogyakarta: Nur Cahaya.

Masdani, A. 1968. "Pemeriksaan psikologik pada bantji" [A psychological examination of banci]. *Djiwa* 2 (April): 55–60.

Mayer, L. Th. 1942. *Practisch Maleisch-Hollandsch en Hollandsch-Maleisch handwoordenboek: Benevens een kort begrip der Maleische woordvorming en spraakleer* [Practical Malay-Dutch and Dutch-Malay Dictionary: In addition to a short understanding of Malay word formation and speech]. Gravenhage, Netherlands: Boekhandel en Drukkerij V/h G. C. T. van Dorp.

Mazzarella, William. 2013. *Censorium: Cinema and the Open Edge of Mass Publicity.* Durham, NC: Duke University Press.

Merry, Sally Engle. 2001. "Spatial Governmentality and the New Urban Social Order: Controlling Gender Violence through Law." *American Anthropologist* 103 (1): 16–29.

Meyerowitz, Joanne J. 2002. *How Sex Changed: A History of Transsexuality in the United States.* Cambridge, MA: Harvard University Press.

Mingguan Djaja. 1968a. "Charles d'Eon: Pria jang hidup sebagai wanita" [Charles d'Éon: A man who lived as a woman]. November 23, pp. 14–15, 29.

——. 1968b. "Korban2 lesbianisme" [The victims of lesbianism]. November 30, pp. 14–15.

——. 1968c. "Masalah (béntjong) di Ibukota: Kekuatan do'a dalam usaha menjingkirkan kebéntjongan" [The problem of béncong in Jakarta: The power of prayer in trying to get rid of banci-ness]. November 2, pp. 3–4, 12.

——. 1968d. "Rumah tangga béntjong dan penghuninja" [A house of béncong and its inhabitants]. October 26, p. 36.

——. 1968e. "Tjerita seorang bantji jang berpendidikan universiter" [The story of a university-educated banci]. October 19, p. 4.

Moon, Suzanne. 2007. *Technology and Ethical Idealism: A History of Development in the Netherlands East Indies.* Leiden: CNWS.

——. 2015. "Building from the Outside In: Sociotechnical Imaginaries and Civil Society in New Order Indonesia." In *Dreamscapes of Modernity: Sociotechnical Imaginaries and the Fabrication of Power*, edited by Sang-Hyun Kim and Sheila Jasanoff, 179–218. Chicago: University of Chicago Press.

Mrázek, Rudolf. 2002. *Engineers of Happy Land: Technology and Nationalism in a Colony.* Princeton, NJ: Princeton University Press.

——. 2010. *A Certain Age: Colonial Jakarta through the Memories of Its Intellectuals.* Durham, NC: Duke University Press.

Murray, Alison J. 1991. *No Money No Honey: A Study of Street Traders and Prostitutes in Jakarta*. Singapore: Oxford University Press.

Murtagh, Ben. 2013. *Genders and Sexualities in Indonesian Cinema: Constructing Gay, Lesbi and Waria Identities on Screen*. London: Routledge.

——. 2017. "Double Identities in Dorce's Comedies." *Bijdragen Tot de Taal-, Land- En Volkenkunde*. 173 (2–3): 181–207.

Najmabadi, Afsaneh. 2014. *Professing Selves: Transsexuality and Same-Sex Desire in Contemporary Iran*. Durham, NC: Duke University Press.

Nanwani, Sandeep. 2018. "Containing Madness: Care for the Homeless with Major Mental Illness in Yogyakarta, Indonesia." Master's thesis, Harvard University.

Nas, Peter J. M. 1990. "The Origin and Development of the Urban Municipality in Indonesia." *Sojourn: Journal of Social Issues in Southeast Asia* 5 (1): 86–112.

Nas, Peter J. M., and Kees Grijns. 2000. "Jakarta-Batavia: A Sample of Current Socio-historical Research." In *Jakarta-Batavia: Socio-cultural Essays*, edited by Kees Grijns and Peter J. M. Nas, 1–24. Leiden: KITLV Press.

Nas, Peter J. M., and Manesse Malo. 2000. "View from the Top: Accounts of the Mayors and Governors of Jakarta." In *Jakarta-Batavia: Socio-cultural Essays*, edited by Kees Grijns and Peter J. M. Nas. 229–44. Leiden: KITLV Press.

Nasution, Adnan Buyung. 1978. "Kasus Vivian beberapa permasalahan hukum" [A number of legal problems in the case of Vivian]. *Hukum Dan Pembangunan*, no. 2 (March): 621–32.

Newton, Esther. 1979. *Mother Camp: Female Impersonators in America*. Chicago: University of Chicago Press.

Niehof, Anke, and Firman Lubis. 2003. *Two Is Enough: Family Planning in Indonesia under the New Order 1968–1998*. Leiden: KITLV Press.

Nordholt, Henk Schulte. 1997. *Outward Appearances: Dressing State and Society in Indonesia*. Leiden: KITLV Press.

Ochoa, Marcia. 2008. "Perverse Citizenship: Divas, Marginality, and Participation in 'Loca-lization.'" *Women's Studies Quarterly* 36 (3–4): 146–69.

——. 2014. *Queen for a Day: Transformistas, Beauty Queens, and the Performance of Femininity in Venezuela*. Durham, NC: Duke University Press.

Oetomo, Dédé. 2000. "Masculinity in Indonesia." In *Framing the Sexual Subject: The Politics of Gender, Sexuality, and Power*, edited by Richard Guy Parker, Regina Maria Barbosa, and Peter Aggleton, 46–59. Berkeley: University of California Press.

Ortner, Sherry B. 1972. "Is Female to Male as Nature Is to Culture?" *Feminist Studies* 1 (2): 5–31.

Paramaditha, Intan. 2018. "Q! Film Festival as Cultural Activism: Strategic Cinephilia and the Expansion of a Queer Counterpublic." *Visual Anthropology* 31 (1–2): 74–92.

Pausacker, Helen. 2015. "Indonesian Beauty Queens." In *Sex and Sexualities in Contemporary Indonesia: Sexual Politics, Health, Diversity, and Representations*, edited by Linda Rae Bennett and Sharyn Graham Davies, 273–92. Milton Park, Abingdon, Oxon: Routledge.

——. 2020. "Homosexuality and the Law in Indonesia." In *Crime and Punishment in Indonesia*, edited by Tim Lindsey and Helen Pausacker, 430–62. London: Routledge.

Peacock, James L. 1968. *Rites of Modernization: Symbolic and Social Aspects of Indonesian Proletarian Drama*. Chicago: University of Chicago Press.

——. 1978. *Muslim Puritans: Reformist Psychology in Southeast Asian Islam*. Berkeley: University of California Press.

Peiss, Kathy. 1996. "Making Up, Making Over: Cosmetics, Consumer Culture and Women's Identity." In *The Sex of Things: Gender and Consumption in Historical Perspective*, edited by Victoria DeGrazia, 311–36. Berkeley: University of California Press.

Peletz, Michael G. 2009. *Gender Pluralism: Southeast Asia since Early Modern Times*. New York: Routledge.

Pemberton, John. 1994. *On the Subject of "Java."* Ithaca, NY: Cornell University Press.

Plemons, Eric. 2017. *The Look of a Woman: Facial Feminization Surgery and the Therapeutics of Trans- Medicine*. Durham, NC: Duke University Press.

Pols, Hans. 2006. "The Development of Psychiatry in Indonesia: From Colonial to Modern Times." *International Review of Psychiatry* 18 (4): 363–70.

——. 2007. "The Nature of the Native Mind: Contested Views of Dutch Colonial Psychiatrists in the Former Dutch East Indies." In *Psychiatry and Empire*, edited by Sloan Mahone and Megan Vaughan, 172–96. Houndmills, UK: Palgrave Macmillan.

——. 2011. "The Totem Vanishes, the Hordes Revolt: A Psychoanalytic Interpretation of the Indonesian Struggle for Independence." In *Unconscious Dominions: Psychoanalysis, Colonial Trauma, and Global Sovereignties*, edited by Warwick Anderson, Deborah Jenson, and Richard C. Keller, 141–65. Durham, NC: Duke University Press.

——. 2018. *Nurturing Indonesia: Medicine and Decolonisation in the Dutch East Indies*. Cambridge: Cambridge University Press.

Reis, Elizabeth. 2009. *Bodies in Doubt: An American History of Intersex*. Baltimore: Johns Hopkins University Press.

Roem, Mohamad. 1977. *Bunga rampai dari sejarah: Wajah-wajah pemimpin dan orang terkemuka Indonesia* [Anthology of history: The faces of Indonesia's leaders and prominent figures]. Vol. 2 of 3 vols. Jakarta: Bulan Bintang.

Roosmalen, Pauline K. M. van. 2015. "Netherlands Indies Town Planning: An Agent of Modernization (1905–1957)." In *Cars, Conduits, and Kampongs*, 87–119. Leiden: Brill.

Rose, Nikolas S. 1999. *Powers of Freedom: Reframing Political Thought*. Cambridge: Cambridge University Press.

Rudnyckyj, Daromir. 2010. *Spiritual Economies: Islam, Globalization, and the Afterlife of Development*. Ithaca, NY: Cornell University Press.

Sadikin, Ali. 1992. *Bang Ali: Demi Jakarta (1966–1977)* [Uncle Ali: For Jakarta (1966–1977)]. Jakarta: Pustaka Sinar Harapan.

Saraswati, L. Ayu. 2013. *Seeing Beauty, Sensing Race in Transnational Indonesia*. Honolulu: University of Hawai'i Press.

Scott, James C. 1998. *Seeing Like a State: How Certain Schemes to Improve the Human Condition Have Failed*. New Haven, CT: Yale University Press.

Sears, Clare. 2015. *Arresting Dress: Cross-Dressing, Law, and Fascination in Nineteenth-Century San Francisco*. Durham, NC: Duke University Press.

Sears, Laurie J., ed. 1996. *Fantasizing the Feminine in Indonesia*. Durham, NC: Duke University Press.

Sedyaningsih-Mamahit, Endang R. 1999. *Perempuan-perempuan Kramat Tunggak* [The women of Kramat Tunggak]. Jakarta: Pustaka Sinar Harapan bekerjasama dengan the Ford Foundation.

Selecta. 1968. "Bantji2 kini di tangan Bang Ali" [Banci are now handled by Bang Ali]. September 9, p. 19.

Sen, Krishna. 1994. *Indonesian Cinema: Framing the New Order*. London: Zed.

Sen, Krishna, and David T. Hill. 2006. *Media, Culture and Politics in Indonesia*. Jakarta: Equinox.

Shiraishi, Saya. 1997. *Young Heroes: The Indonesian Family in Politics*. Ithaca, NY: Cornell University Press.

Shiraishi, Takashi. 2003. "A New Regime of Order: The Origin of Modern Surveillance Politics in Indonesia." In *Southeast Asia over Three Generations: Essays Presented to Benedict R. O'G. Anderson*, edited by James T. Siegel and Audrey R. Kahin, 47–74. Ithaca, NY: Cornell University Press.

Siasat. 1951. "Beberapa Tjatatan Tentang: Orang-orang bantji" [A few notes about: bancis]. Vol. 216. May 20, p. 13.

Siegel, James T. 1997. *Fetish, Recognition, Revolution*. Princeton, NJ: Princeton University Press.

——. 1998. *A New Criminal Type in Jakarta: Counter-Revolution Today*. Durham, NC: Duke University Press.

——. 2006. *Naming the Witch*. Stanford, CA: Stanford University Press.

Simone, AbdouMaliq. 2014. *Jakarta, Drawing the City Near*. Minneapolis: University of Minnesota Press.

Simpson, Bradley R. 2008. *Economists with Guns: Authoritarian Development and U.S.-Indonesian Relations, 1960–1968*. Stanford, CA: Stanford University Press.

Snorton, C. Riley. 2017. *Black on Both Sides: A Racial History of Trans Identity*. Minneapolis: University of Minnesota Press.

Soemanget. 1932. "Suara podjok: Si bantji dimoesoehin" [Voice from the corner: The despicable banci]. July 30, pp. 2–3.

Soerohadipoerno, R. S. 1938. *Boekoe tipoean* [The book of fraud]. Batavia: Elektronische Drukerij Fortuna.

Somerville, Siobhan. 1994. "Scientific Racism and the Emergence of the Homosexual Body." *Journal of the History of Sexuality* 5 (2): 243–66.

Steedly, Mary Margaret. 1993. *Hanging without a Rope: Narrative Experience in Colonial and Postcolonial Karoland*. Princeton, NJ: Princeton University Press.

——. 2013. "Transparency and Apparition: Media Ghosts of Post–New Order Indonesia." In *Images That Move*, edited by Patricia Spyer and Mary Margaret Steedly, 257–94. Santa Fe, NM: SAR.

Stoler, Ann Laura. 1992. "Sexual Affronts and Racial Frontiers: European Identities and the Cultural Politics of Exclusion in Colonial Southeast Asia." *Comparative Studies in Society and History* 34 (3): 514–51.

——. 1995. *Race and the Education of Desire: Foucault's History of Sexuality and the Colonial Order of Things*. Durham, NC: Duke University Press.

Stone, Sandy. 1992. "The Empire Strikes Back: A Posttranssexual Manifesto." *Camera Obscura* 10 (2 (29)): 150–76.

Strahan, Dylan. 2020. "What Are Your Gender Goals? Starting Hormones as a Trans Young Person in 2010s Victoria." Honors diss., University of Melbourne.

Strassler, Karen. 2009. "The Face of Money: Currency, Crisis, and Remediation in Post-Suharto Indonesia." *Cultural Anthropology* 24 (1): 68–103.

——. 2010. *Refracted Visions: Popular Photography and National Modernity in Java*. Durham, NC: Duke University Press.

——. 2020. *Demanding Images: Democracy, Mediation, and the Image-Event in Indonesia*. Durham, NC: Duke University Press.

Strathern, Marilyn. 1988. *The Gender of the Gift: Problems with Women and Problems with Society in Melanesia*. Berkeley: University of California Press.

———. 1993. "Making Incomplete." In *Carved Flesh / Cast Selves: Gendered Symbols and Social Practices*, edited by Vigdis Broch-Due, Ingrid Rudie, and Tone Bleie, 41–52. Oxford: Berg.

———. 1996. "Cutting the Network." *Journal of the Royal Anthropological Institute* 2 (3): 517–35.

Stratz, Carl Heinrich. 1898. *De vrouwen op Java: Eene gynaecologische studie* [The women of Java: A gynecological study]. Amsterdam: Scheltema & Holkema.

Stryker, Susan. 2013. "Kaming Mga Talyada (We Who Are Sexy): The Transsexual Whiteness of Christine Jorgensen in the (Post)Colonial Philippines." In *The Transgender Studies Reader 2*, edited by Susan Stryker and Aren Z. Aizura, 543–52. London: Routledge.

———. 2017. *Transgender History: The Roots of Today's Revolution*. 2nd ed. Boulder, CO: Seal.

Suharto. 1968. "Speech on the Occasion of the Djakarta Fair 1968." Jakarta, June 15.

Suparlan, Parsudi. 1974. "The Gelandangan of Jakarta: Politics among the Poorest People in the Capital of Indonesia." *Indonesia*, no. 18: 41–52.

Suryakusuma, Julia. 1996. "The State and Sexuality in New Order Indonesia." In *Fantasizing the Feminine in Indonesia*, edited by Laurie J. Sears, 92–119. Durham, NC: Duke University Press.

———. 2011. *State Ibuism: The Social Construction of Womanhood in New Order Indonesia*. Depok, Indonesia: Komunitas Bambu.

Sysling, Fenneke. 2015. "Faces from the Netherlands Indies." *Revue d'Histoire des Sciences Humaines* 27 (September): 89–107.

Taylor, Charles. 1989. *Sources of the Self: The Making of the Modern Identity*. Cambridge, MA: Harvard University Press.

Taylor, Jean Gelman. 1997. "Costume and Gender in Colonial Java, 1800–1940." In *Outward Appearances: Dressing State and Society in Indonesia*, edited by Henk Schulte Nordholt, 86–112. Leiden: KITLV Press.

Tempo. 1973a. "Aturan bongkar pasang kelamin" [The rules of reconstructing sex]. September 29, pp. 14–15.

———. 1973b. "Vivian memancing hukum" [Vivian fishes the law]. October 13, p. 36.

———. 1973c. "Sah perempuan" [A legitimate woman]. December 1, p. 15.

———. 1975a. "Operasi penghalusan" [Refinement surgery]. July 5, p. 38.

———. 1975b. "Kelamin itu sudah berobah" [My sex has been changed]. June 21, pp. 40–41.

Thajib, Ferdiansyah. 2018. "The Making and Breaking of Indonesian Muslim Queer Safe Spaces." *Borderlands* 17 (1): 1–24.

Towle, Evan B., and Lynn M. Morgan. 2002. "Romancing the Transgender Native: Rethinking the Use of the 'Third Gender' Concept." *GLQ: Gay and Lesbian Quarterly* 8 (4): 469–97.

Tsing, Anna Lowenhaupt. 1993. *In the Realm of the Diamond Queen: Marginality in an Out-of-the-Way Place*. Princeton, NJ: Princeton University Press.

Valentine, David. 2007. *Imagining Transgender: An Ethnography of a Category*. Durham, NC: Duke University Press.

Valverde, Mariana. 2011. "Seeing Like a City: The Dialectic of Modern and Premodern Ways of Seeing in Urban Governance." *Law & Society Review* 45 (2): 277–312.

———. 2012. *Everyday Law on the Street: City Governance in an Age of Diversity*. Chicago: University of Chicago Press.

van der Kroef, Justus M. 1951. "The Term Indonesia: Its Origin and Usage." *Journal of the American Oriental Society* 71 (3): 166–71.

———. 1985. "'Petrus': Patterns of Prophylactic Murder in Indonesia." *Asian Survey* 25 (7): 745–59.

van der Meer, Arnout. 2020. *Performing Power: Cultural Hegemony, Identity, and Resistance in Colonial Indonesia*. Ithaca, NY: Cornell University Press.

van Dijk, Kees. 1997. "Sarongs, Jubbahs, and Trousers." In *Outward Appearances: Dressing State and Society in Indonesia*, edited by Henk Schulte Nordholt, 45–67. Leiden: KITLV Press.

Varia. 1970. "Porno, nafsu berahi, nsb" [Porno, lust, nsb]. May 6, p. 25.

Wahrman, Dror. 2004. *The Making of the Modern Self: Identity and Culture in Eighteenth-Century England*. New Haven, CT: Yale University Press.

Wallace, Alfred Russel. 1872. *The Malay Archipelago, the Land of the Orang-Utan and the Bird of Paradise: A Narrative of Travel, with Studies of Man and Nature*. 4th ed. London: Macmillan.

Weston, Kath. 1993. "Lesbian/Gay Studies in the House of Anthropology." *Annual Review of Anthropology* 22 (January): 339–67.

Wieringa, Saskia. 2002. *Sexual Politics in Indonesia*. Houndmills, UK: Palgrave Macmillan.

———. 2015. "Discursive Contestations Concerning Intersex in Indonesia." In *Sex and Sexualities in Contemporary Indonesia: Sexual Politics, Health, Diversity, and Representations*, edited by Linda Rae Bennett and Sharyn Graham Davies, 169–82. London: Routledge.

Wijaya, Hendri Yulius. 2019. "Localising Queer Identities: Queer Activisms and National Belonging in Indonesia." In *Contentious Belonging: The Place of Minorities in Indonesia*, edited by Greg Fealy and Ronit Ricci, 133–52. Singapore: ISEAS.

———. 2020. *Intimate Assemblages: The Politics of Queer Identities and Sexualities in Indonesia*. London: Palgrave Macmillan.

Index

Amir, Sulfikar, 68
Anderson, Benedict, 130, 133, 151n6
appearance
  and contestation of colonialism, 35–36
  and fraud, 36–37
  and performance of Indonesian
    authenticity, 37–41
  and public gender, 47–48
  and race, 26, 35–36
  and recognition, 36, 37, 138–39
  See also clothing; dandan (making up)
asli, 38
  gendered relationship between *palsu* and, 9
  and imitation in relation to gender for
    warias, 98
  mapped onto technologies of gender and
    sexual classification, 39
  See also authenticity
aspal, 39
Association of Wadam of Jakarta, 62
authenticity
  and Fantastic Dolls performances, 102
  performance of Indonesian, 37–41
  of racial appearances, 10
  recognition and, 27, 40–41, 135–36
  of warias, 39–40
  and warias as beauty experts, 95–99
  of warias' claims to citizenship, 109–16
  See also *asli*

Bambang, Myrna, 59, 99–100, 101, 127
Bambang Brothers, 99, 156n7
banci
  categorization of, 156n9
  emergence of term, 149n3, 149n8
  Hamka on, 151n7
  modern femininity of, 35, 37–38
  and performance of Indonesian
    authenticity, 37–41
  public gender of, 32–37
  scientific definitions of, 73
  shifting meanings and effects of
    term, 25–26
  shift to *wadam* from, 26, 141, 147n2

and struggles over classification of gender,
  26–27
as transvestites, 5, 27
use of term, 26, 117, 147n2
See also wadam; waria(s)
banci kaléng, 116, 154n13
Banci Research Project, 48, 71–72
Barker, Joshua, 50
Bartky, Sandra Lee, 91
Batavia. *See* Jakarta
beauty experts, warias as, 85–90, 132–33
  and authenticity and imitation, 95–99
  and Fantastic Dolls, 99–102
  and gendered publics, 90–95
  and public order, 102–4
beauty pageants, 18–19, 85, 86–87, 91, 94, 97,
  102, 103–4
belonging
  and *asli*, 38, 98
  and citizenship, 137
  and public gender, 59–62, 67, 133
  and race in the Dutch East Indies, 148n1
  and recognition, 133
  of warias, 132–33
  See also national belonging
Benjamin, Harry, 69, 74
Berlant, Lauren, 102, 155n1
bissu, 25
Blackwood, Evelyn, 48
Bleys, Rudi, 28
Bloembergen, Marieke, 29–30
Boekhoudt, W., 36
Boellstorff, Tom
  on *asli* and belonging, 38, 98
  on *banci*, 149n3
  on definition of warias, 77
  on gender and citizenship, 100
  on internal state and external presentation of
    warias, 20
  on Malay language, 28
  on recognition and national belonging, 115
  on *waria*, 142
  on warias as beauty experts, 91
  on wedding salon work, 90

Jakarta (*continued*)
  increased visibility of gender nonconformity
    in, 43
  military modernization in, 86
  official recognition for warias in, 12–16
  regulation of wadam in, 47–50
  under Sadikin, 51–56
Jakarta Fair, 18–19, 56–57, 86, 95–97
jiwa, 74
jiwa perempuan, 2, 20, 32, 72–78, 81
Jones, Carla, 35, 66

Karsono, 75–76, 152n5
Kelty, Christopher, 20, 45, 104
kesusilaan umum, 12, 44, 136–37. *See also*
    public morality
ketertiban umum, 12, 44, 49, 136–37. *See also*
    public order
khunsa, 80, 83, 154n18
Kinsey, Alfred, 73
Kusno, Abidin, 150n1

Lambek, Michael, 147n4
Laqueur, Thomas, 147n1
Le Carrousel, 155n5
LGBT rights after the New Order, 23, 140–41
Lim, T. H., 79
Lindquist, Johan, 155n3
Lindsay, Jennifer, 140
Ling, Tjiauw, 71–72
Long, Nicholas, 91
ludruk, 148n2
Luttikhuis, Bart, 27

Malay language, 28
Malo, Manesse, 14
malu, 25, 155n3
marriage law, 77
Masdani, Johanna, 71, 72
masyarakat, 20, 89–90, 108, 133
Mazzarella, William, 155n1
Meifei, 99, 156n8
"mental sex," 76, 79
Merry, Sally Engle, 137
Meyerowitz, Joanne, 75, 154n13
military modernization, 86
Money, John, 69, 154n16
Moon, Suzanne, 17, 20, 89–90
"mysterious killings," 50, 114, 151n5

Najmabadi, Afsaneh, 75, 76, 152n3
Nas, Peter, 14
Nasution, Adnan Buyung, 79

national belonging, 130
  acceptance and, 132–33, 144
  citizenship and, 137
  narratives of self and expressions of, 116
  public gender and, 67, 90
  and public participation, 139
  recognition and, 116, 132–33
  technologies of bodily transformation and
    defining, 35
  trans and claiming, 148n3
  transpuan and, 143–44
  of warias under Sadikin, 67
  See also belonging
national glamour, 109, 111–12, 119, 121, 123, 129
New Look fashion, 34, 35
New Order
  anxieties about authenticity in, 39
  development in, 7
  gender and governmentality in, 66
  gender during, 3–4, 46–47
  governance in, 50–51
  incorporation of Euro-American popular
    culture in, 86
  integration of gender nonconformity in, 47
  and Jakarta Fair, 56–57
  and recognition of warias, 16
  state-imposed restrictions on women's
    fertility in, 93
  technological gender in, 68–72
  visual format of power during, 107–8
  See also Suharto
Newton, Esther, 55, 118
ngondhek, 117–18

Ochoa, Marcia, 92, 111, 121–23
Ortner, Sherry, 9

palsu, 9, 38, 39, 98
Paper Dolls, 156n8
Paradise Hall, 95, 96
pasemon, 155n4
Peacock, James, 25, 96, 148n2
Pemberton, John, 107
pembinaan, 20, 45, 49–51, 52, 57, 58–59, 85–86,
    89, 103–4, 134–35, 137
perempuan, 142–43
personhood
  appearance and authenticity and, 111
  cisgender, as marker of civilizational status, 29
  and cisgender/transgender binary, 9–10, 133
  dandan and, 93
  demarcation between sexuality and gender
    and understanding of, 117

www.ingramcontent.com/pod-product-compliance
Lightning Source LLC
Chambersburg PA
CBHW030841270326
41928CB00007B/1163